Modelling Text As Process

Shift of process types by text

Modelling Text As Process

A Dynamic Approach to
EFL Classroom Discourse

Xueyan Yang

continuum

Continuum International Publishing Group
The Tower Building   80 Maiden Lane
11 York Road   Suite 704
London SE1 7NX   New York, NY 10038

British Library Cataloguing-in-Publication Data
A catalogue record for this book is available from the British Library.

ISBN   978-1-4411-7878-7 (paperback)

Library of Congress Cataloging-in-Publication Data
A catalog record for this book is available from the Library of Congress.

Typeset by Newgen Imaging Systems Pvt Ltd, Chennai, India
Printed and bound in Great Britain by the MPG Books Group

Contents

Acknowledgements

My heartfelt gratitude goes first and foremost to Professor Zhuanglin Hu who supervised my PhD dissertation, which amounts to an early version of this manuscript. Without his warm encouragement, patient guidance, inspiring suggestions and insightful comments, the study presented here would not have gone this far. I am also grateful to Professor Hu for opening my eyes to Systemic Functional Linguistics over 20 years ago, and for keeping me informed about the expanding scope and dimensions of linguistics through the years by his books, articles and our personal communication. To me, he is both anchor and rudder, grounding me solidly and guiding me gently but firmly. Without him I could not have reached the present stage of my professional life.

My special thanks go to Runqing Liu and Yi'an Wu at Beijing Foreign Studies University. It is Professor Liu who (to quote him) 'converted' me from literature to linguistics in 1983 through his graduate course called Schools of Linguistics, and who has ever since been a major source of inspiration for my research work. Professor Wu's advice on the design of my research project, and her encouragement to keep working on EFL classroom discourse, have made the project not so overwhelming a task as it could have seemed.

I am also indebted to Delu Zhang at Tongji University, whose view on text structure as multi-stratal inspired me to venture further into the issue, and who patiently listened to my view before giving me detailed suggestions; to James Martin at the University of Sydney, whose lectures as well as discussions with me during his stay in Beijing in 2005 enabled me to understand better his genre theory and register theory; and to Christian Matthiessen at Hong Kong Polytechnic University, who kindly spared me some time for discussions on 'logogenesis' and on the Subject Person system while visiting Tsinghua University in 2005. My deep appreciation goes to Xuanwei Peng at Beijing Normal University, for the detailed and insightful discussions on both functional linguistics and linguistic philosophy.

My sincere thanks go to the ten anonymous teachers and their students who kindly agreed to have their classes recorded, thus providing me with authentic data for my research. I would also like to acknowledge the financial support I won from the Chinese Education Ministry through the Excellent Young Teachers Program (EYTP), which made data collection much easier; the technical support I received from Dr Min Wen, who was always there when I got into difficulties with the computer; and the moral support I enjoyed from my friends both at home and overseas, particularly Ching Chih Liu at the University of Hong Kong, Xiaoping Yao at Beijing Foreign Studies University, Xing Lu at DePaul University, Shisheng Liu and Wenfang Fan at Tsinghua University, Jingxian Mao at CCTV, Guisen Tian and Hong Jiang at Beijing Normal University, and Zhen Ren at Capital Normal University. Without the various kinds of support that I received, my project would not have been completed so smoothly and so enjoyably.

I also wish to thank my former colleagues and graduate students at China Foreign Affairs University – in particular Shaoren Wang, Ying Xu, Liqiu Guo, Xiaowen Deng and Yuanyuan Yang – for their encouragement and help of all kinds during the entire period of my research project. I am especially grateful to Shouyi Fan, the chair of the English Department, for having reduced my workload whenever possible so as to allow me more time on my project.

I owe the deepest debt to my husband, Renhe Zhang, and my son, Yinan Zhang, for their patience and consideration throughout the period when I was occupied in writing this book. They never begrudged the simple meals and lost weekends. Without their loving care, unfailing support, and absolute confidence in me, I could not have completed this project – or even started it. I am particularly grateful to my son for his self-management throughout his high school years, which not only enabled me to concentrate on my project, but also won him an offer from the University of Hong Kong along with a full scholarship.

Finally, I would like to express my sincere thanks to the anonymous reviewer of my book proposal for the invaluable suggestions that helped me so much in improving this manuscript, particularly its organization and its reader-friendliness.

Xueyan Yang
Professor of English and Linguistics
Beijing

Preface

I take the greatest pleasure and pride in prefacing Dr Xueyan Yang's *Modelling Text As Process: A Dynamic Approach to EFL Classroom Discourse*. The image of the writer, and her abundant outpouring of witty remarks in this book, have long been rooted in my memory, and I am sure will remain fresh and green all my life.

As early as in 1985, when Xueyan was writing her MA thesis at Beijing Foreign Studies University, she approached me for advice. I was even then forcibly struck by her meticulous analysis of a piece of drama, at a time when the art of discourse analysis was still in its infancy on Chinese campuses. It has also been a great enjoyment to read her other articles since then.

At the turn of the century when I was a guest professor at Beijing Normal University, Xueyan expressed her desire to do her doctoral work under my supervision. She started her work in 2003, and she lived up to my expectations. By 2007, she had finished all her work and gained her doctoral degree.

Xueyan owes her success to a variety of factors. Apart from her good command of English and hard work, she is conscientious, intelligent and an original thinker. She is also able to work independently and hold fast to her viewpoints.

Xueyan has worked as a teacher of English at tertiary level for 27 years. Being dedicated to her work, passionate and caring, she has been greatly admired by her students. In a recent teaching evaluation given by students taking her graduate course in systemic functional linguistics, she earned an impressive score of 99.68/100. I think she is a teacher who knows her students, and is loved by them. This has helped her with the collection of data and the interpretation of interpersonal meanings.

Xueyan has been even more highly recognized for her research work. As mentioned above, she ranks among the pioneers of discourse analysis in China. She has already published in refereed journals about 20 articles, which are all characterized by critical and original thinking, to say nothing of detailed analysis. During the four years of her doctoral studies, she not only published eight articles, the responses to which helped her greatly in developing her work and meeting the challenges facing her; but she also attended four conferences on systemic functional linguistics or discourse analysis, both at home and abroad. She was also sufficiently advanced to discuss SFL issues with Professor James Martin and Professor Christian Matthiessen when they visited China.

There are several features of the book which will draw our attention. First, it focuses on modelling text as process rather than as product, a principle adhered to by SF linguists; secondly, the notion of 'register' (i.e. the sub-potential that engenders texts) is reinterpreted as two distinct but symbiotically interacting subsystems, one being synoptic and the other dynamic, but both being multi-stratal and multi-metafunctional; thirdly, the highly valued model TEXT TYPE is proposed, which is both grammar-based and oriented towards the process of language use; fourthly, a number of revisions or extensions have been made of such systems as Mood, Subject Person and Textual Theme, while several new systems such as Participant Type, Elliptical Clause and Repetition have been established; fifthly, it offers a new approach to discourse analysis that takes grammatical choices not as constituents forming a clause structure but as semantic features linking successive clauses into an unfolding text, and this approach has already proved feasible and effective in the analysis of spoken discourse in EFL classrooms; sixthly, it offers a data-informed dynamic system network that is applicable (or in M. A. K. Halliday's latest term, 'appliable') – either as a whole or in part – in the analysis of the process of EFL classroom discourse; and finally, the ten class hours' EFL classroom discourse used as data, plus more than ten hours a day the writer had often spent on her research, weekdays and weekends alike, will fully support the credibility and value of this book.

The book also offers a multi-stratal description of the features of EFL classroom discourse in the Chinese context, which brings important facts about EFL teaching and learning before the eyes of EFL teachers, educators and researchers. Thus, it will no doubt make a tremendous contribution to the study of EFL teaching.

Finally, Xueyan's book is well-organized, clearly presented, and easily accessed. It will no doubt attract the attention of systemic-functional linguists, discourse theorists and analysts, and applied linguists. It will also be appreciated by teachers, educators, researchers and students involved in EFL or ESL, as well as those in areas such as education or inter-cultural communication.

I offer my best wishes on the publication of this book, and my warmest congratulations to Dr Xueyan Yang as its author. Although this might mark the beginning of her academic career in its real sense, what begins well fruits well!

Zhuanglin Hu
Professor of English and Linguistics
Peking University

List of Tables

List of Figures

Chapter 1

Introduction: Setting the Scene

The study presented in this book is intended as an effort to model text as process within the framework of Systemic Functional Linguistics (SFL). It offers a model of text as process called TEXT TYPE, and then demonstrates the model in an actual analysis of EFL classroom discourse in the Chinese context, which in turn leads to the establishment of a dynamic system network applicable to future analyses of the process of EFL classroom discourse. This chapter introduces (1) the rationale behind the study, and (2) both the objectives of the study and the approach adopted.

1.1 Rationale

The rationale behind the study can be specified by answering three questions: (1) Why SFL? (2) Why text as process? (3) Why EFL classroom discourse?

1.1.1 Why SFL?

The present study is concerned with the applicability of SFL in discourse analysis due to an initial concern with discourse analysis itself. SFL is chosen because it is considered as a theory of discourse as well as a general theory of language. This can be seen by briefly tracing the development of Discourse Analysis (DA).

A turn to discourse

Although the study of language use, i.e. discourse or text, can be traced back to classical rhetoric over 2,000 years ago (van Dijk 1985a), it did not enter the realm of modern linguistics until the mid-1960s. In the first half of the twentieth century, linguists generally adopted Saussure's (1960) view that the legitimate object of linguistic investigation should be *langue* rather than *parole*. They followed a structuralist approach, viewing language as a system of relations. Consequently, they regarded it as their task to segment a language into units, to define the relations among such units, and to discover the rules that underlie those relations. The structuralist methods did lead to many achievements in phonology, and some in morphology, but fewer in lexicology, and even fewer in syntax – as these linguistic levels actually form an order of increasing connection with language use. As sentence grammar was found incapable of explaining many a linguistic phenomenon, the linguists decided to turn to discourse (Beaugrande 1996).

However, this turn to discourse did not occur in linguistics alone. It was soon also found in a number of such language-related disciplines as poetics, semiotics, linguistic philosophy, psychology, sociology and anthropology; and later in the 1980s, in less language-related disciplines such as artificial intelligence, cognitive science, information processing, and so on (van Dijk 1985, 1990; Hu 1994; Xu 1995; Beaugrande 1997; Miao 2005). The renewal of interest in discourse not only led to the emergence of a new branch of linguistics called Discourse Analysis; but it also enabled discourse to become an object of study, and DA a method of study, in a wide range of other disciplines in humanities and social sciences.

In fact, due to such a widespread turn to discourse (also referred to as a 'discursive turn') in the latter half of the twentieth century (Parker 1999; Sarangi and Coulthard 2000; Harré 2001; Weatherall 2002), DA has come to be described as multi-disciplinary or interdisciplinary (van Dijk 1997, 1999; Schiffrin 1994; Wood and Kroger 2000), with the more linguistically oriented label 'discourse analysis' often replaced by the more general label 'discourse studies' or 'discourse research' (see Renkema 1993; van Dijk 1997; Jaworski and Coupland 1999). The term discourse itself has come to be used as the general term for language use. As Brown and Yule (1983: 1) state, 'the analysis of discourse is, necessarily, the analysis of language in use.' Fasold (1990: 65) further says, 'the study of discourse is the study of any aspect of language use.'

A turn to other disciplines

Among so many different approaches to DA, the linguistically-based approaches did not seem to be very successful at first. For example, Text Grammar (e.g. van Dijk 1972), developed in response to the original call by Harris (1952) for a linguistic discourse analysis, was conducted in conformity with Chomsky's transformational-generative grammar, aiming at a set of rules that would generate units called 'textemes'; but it soon proved to be a method 'largely speculative, imprecise, and partly misguided' (van Dijk 2004).

On the other hand, approaches based on other disciplines thrived, such as those discussed in Schiffrin's (1994) book entitled *Approaches to Discourse*. (1) Speech Act Theory based on philosophy (Austin 1962; Searle 1969), focusing on actions performed by means of sentences; (2) Interactional Sociolinguistics based on anthropology (Gumperz 1982) and sociology (Goffman 1974), focusing on interpretation of both linguistic and social meanings created during face-to-face encounters; (3) Ethnography of Communication based on anthropology (Hymes 1972), focusing on language and communication as cultural behaviours; (4) Pragmatics based again on philosophy (Grice 1975), focusing on inferential routes to a speaker's communicative intentions; (5) Conversation Analysis based on sociology, focusing on sequential structures in conversation such as adjacency pairs (Schegloff and Sacks 1973) and turn-taking (Sacks et al. 1974), whereby social members construct social order; and (6) Variation Analysis based on sociolinguistics (Labov 1972; Labov and Waletsky 1967), focusing on social as well as linguistic constraints on patterns of variation at syntactic, semantic and text levels.

Thus it became obvious to the linguists that the tool of linguistics alone was inadequate in the study of discourse, and that they must turn to other disciplines following their turn to discourse.

Two tendencies

Along with the linguists' turn to other disciplines, there have appeared two tendencies. One can be called **disconnection** from linguistics. Take the socially oriented approach called Critical Discourse Analysis (CDA) for example (for details, see Toolan 2002). Very much concerned with social and political problems in the real world, CDA focuses on the relation of public discourse with power, especially the hidden power of ideology. As Fairclough (1989: 23) puts it, 'linguistic phenomena *are* social phenomena of a special sort, and social phenomena *are* (in part) linguistic phenomena' (original emphasis). Van Dijk (2004) even describes CDA as 'a movement of – theoretically very different – scholars who focus on social issues and not primarily on academic paradigms.'

The other trend can be called **integration** of linguistics with other disciplines. One example is Text Linguistics, which mediates between linguistics and cognitive science, taking into account both linguistic qualities of texts and the producer/receiver of the text, along with the context of situation wherein the text and participants are situated (Beaugrande 2002). However, Text Linguistics only provides 'broad outlines' to be 'filled in by the concerted integration of researchers sharing a commitment to the study of language use as a crucial human activity' (Beaugrande and Dressler 1981/2002). In other words, it is not intended to develop from a theory of text into a theory of language in general. Nor is Variation Analysis, which combines linguistics with sociology.

The view held here is that, from a linguist's point of view, **integration** is necessary, not just 'because of multi-faceted nature of discourse' (van Dijk 2004), or because 'discourse is too rich and diversified' so that it has to be described 'in linguistic, cognitive and social terms' (Beaugrande 1996); but because the studies of discourse will enhance the study of language in general. In other words, this circle of development in the study of discourse can be closed by returning to the very discipline where much of the study had started in the first place, i.e. linguistics – by integrating an understanding of language use into an understanding of the nature of language, and by integrating theories of discourse into a general theory of language (cf. Schiffrin 1994). In this way, not only will a linguistic theory be strengthened, but the strengthened linguistic theory in turn will be more readily applicable to DA. It is exactly in this regard that SFL is considered as a distinctive linguistic theory.

The distinctiveness of SFL

SFL views the linguistic system as meaning potential, i.e. a resource for making meaning in context. The theory, as Halliday (1999: 6) explains, is derived from 'two founding traditions of the study of language in context.' One is American, represented by Sapir and Whorf, which views language as a form of reflection or something to think with; the other is British, represented by Malinowski and Firth, which views language as a form of action or something to act with. That is to say, SFL is concerned with the **cognitive** and **social** as well as the **linguistic** context of discourse. And to incorporate these three kinds of context into SFL, Halliday defines the context of situation in terms of three variables, i.e. the field, tenor and mode of discourse; and he classifies meaning into three corresponding metafunctions: ideational, interpersonal and textual (Halliday 1973, 1978, 1985b). Moreover, he views all lexicogrammatical systems as organized around the three metafunctions (Halliday 1985/1994, 2004), hence his Functional Grammar (capitalized to refer exclusively to the grammar established by Halliday; same hereinafter). In so doing, Halliday has built up a semantic stratum as an interface between context and lexicogrammar, thus offering a model that accounts for actual language use both multi-functionally and multi-stratally.

As Halliday (1985a) makes very clear, SFL is a theory open to influences from outside, and ready to evolve and function in context. The theory has met with criticism in the course of its evolution, especially regarding the relationship between semantics and syntax (Butler 1985; Fawcett 1987), the metafunctions (Fawcett 1999), and the cognitive dimension of meaning (Fawcett 1980; Peng 2002, 2005). But efforts have also been constantly made to further explicate and strengthen the SFL framework (e.g. Halliday 1996, 2004, 2007; Halliday and Matthiessen 1999; see also Yang 2006). Indeed, the theory has been evolving in context, integrating theories of language use into a general theory of language and self-improving all along. And it has been functioning in context, being widely applied in the analysis of various types of discourse: literary, educational, social, legal, clinical, and so on (see Christie and Martin 1997; Ghadessy 1999; Martin and Veel 1998; O'Halloran 2004; Unsworth 2000). This is why Halliday calls his theory an 'appliable' linguistics (2007: 189), and also why SFL is chosen in this study as the very theory to be applied in discourse analysis.

1.1.2 Why text as process?

Before moving on to answer this question, it is necessary to clarify two terms: 'text' and 'discourse'. Actually, various attempts have been made to distinguish them. Wood and Kroger (2000) identify three trends: (1) they are used interchangeably; (2) text is used for written forms and discourse for spoken forms; (3) text is associated with *langue* and discourse with *parole*. In this book, however, none of these trends applies. Here, both terms are used to refer to language use, written or spoken, while text has a narrower sense than discourse. That is, discourse refers to language use itself, which **may be** approached from any perspective – sociological, psychological, educational, as well as linguistic; while text refers to language use that **is being** approached from the linguistic perspective as an instantiation of the linguistic system. Thus **EFL classroom discourse** is the type of language use this book is concerned with; when analysed linguistically it is referred to as **text**.

To come back to the question, the present study is particularly concerned with text as process because the process of language use has been well described in many other discourse theories but is yet to be dealt with fully and explicitly in SFL.

Other approaches to the process of language use

Other discourse theories examine language use also in terms of linguistic choices, but they generally do not interpret such choices from the linguistic perspective. Van Dijk (1997) portrays the area of DA as a triangle of discourse–cognition–society. That is, DA is generally conducted from three perspectives: (1) discourse itself, (2) discourse communication as cognition, and (3) discourse as social practice.

From the discourse perspective, the process of language use is seen as 'a reasonably self-contained purposeful interaction' between language users (Hoey 2001: 11), which in turn is described in terms of patterns of discourse organization, global or local (Hoey 1986; Östman and Virtanen 2001; Schiffrin et al. 2001; Scott and Thompson 2001). From the cognitive perspective (see Semino and Culpeper 2002; Virtanen 2004), discourse is seen as a dynamic process of language communication among human beings with cognitive as well as linguistic capacity, which in turn is described in terms of memory representation of discourse, knowledge and beliefs necessary for processing discourse, and so on. From a social perspective, discourse is seen as a process of social interaction during which members of a society use language to complete various tasks in their social life (Schiffrin et al. 2001), which in turn is described through various models of institutional discourse (Drew and Heritage 1992), professional discourse (Gunnarsson et al. 1997), or situated discourse (Gu 1996, 1997, 1999). Gu (1999), for example, defines discourse as 'a joint purposeful social process' along three dimensions: goal development, talk exchange development, and interpersonal management. While acknowledging a theoretical link with Halliday's three metafunctions, Gu (ibid.: 173) claims that whereas Halliday focuses on **language rather than language use**, his tripartite model 'restores the actual user to its dominating role, reducing language to a subordinate position.'

The SFL approach to the process of language use

SFL views the linguistic system as meaning potential and the actual use of language as a unit of meaning, i.e. an instance of the linguistic system (hence the term 'text'). But the question that faces systemicists is how to model a unit of meaning not only as a finished product but also as an ongoing process, so that SFL can serve as an adequate model in discourse analysis – that is, in the analysis of **language use rather than language**.

So far, when SFL is applied in discourse analysis, it is mainly the Functional Grammar along with the context theory that is being applied. Halliday defines a functional grammar as a grammar 'pushed in the direction of semantics' (1994: xix) and constructed 'for purposes of text analysis' (ibid.: xv). Such a grammar does provide discourse analysts with a model that both describes and explains how and why a text means what it does; this is why it is widely applied. But being a **grammar**, it inevitably takes the clause or group, rather than the text, as the unit of analysis. Therefore, it is more at home explaining syntactic features in a text as a finished product, than meaning flows in a text as an ongoing process. This is presumably why Gu (1999: 173) says that 'Halliday skips the actual use of language . . . takes the actual use as given, and explores its impact on language'; and also why SFL, in spite of being 'more suitable for discourse analysis than any other theories' (Huang 2001: 2), is only considered as a source of discourse theories (van Dijk 1985a), and not as an approach to discourse *per se* (e.g. Schiffrin 1994).

In other words, a clause-based approach to the process of language use has its problems, which Halliday is not unaware of. As early as in the 1980s he had admitted that 'the major problem perhaps is that of interpreting the text as process' (1985a: 10). Later he said again 'the problem for text analysis is that it is much harder to represent a process than it is to represent a product' (1994: xxii). To solve the problem, he only offered a 'general principle', i.e. to explain phases of a text 'in terms of the theoretical concepts developed in lexicogrammar', particularly the concept of logico-semantic relations (2002b: Ch.13). More recently, he explicitly raised the question 'How can we model text as an ongoing process of meaning?' (2004: 524), and suggested looking into (1) the system of COHESION, and (2) logogenetic patterns, for solution. As for the former, its text-based elaboration can be found in Martin's work (1992; Martin and Rose, 2003) which – 'pursued within the framework of critical linguistics' (1992: 2) – provides a comprehensive set of discourse analyses focusing on meanings that construct social activity. As for the latter, Halliday (2004: 529–32) describes them in terms of phases of dominant/minor thematic motifs, favoured process type(s), favoured selections in mood and attitudinal lexis, and so on, that can be found in a text, without attempting to model such patterns in systemic terms. Thus **how** to model text as process within the SFL framework remains an intriguing question. This is why an attempt is made in this study to further explore the question.

1.1.3 Why EFL classroom discourse?

In this study, EFL classroom discourse is chosen as the object of analysis. For one thing, in an exploration into a theoretical question, which is how to model text as process in this case, it is practical to start with one particular type of discourse rather than with mixed types. For another, EFL classroom discourse itself is also an important concern here. For those engaged in EFL teaching (like the present author), it is quite clear how much the actual EFL classroom process – which is realized through discourse and largely controlled by the teacher – can affect the result of EFL learning. It is believed that the analysis of EFL classroom discourse will provide insights into the nature of EFL classroom process, which in turn will suggest implications for the improvement of EFL teaching and hence EFL learning. However, not many systematic analyses of EFL classroom discourse have been made. What is more, while the analysis of language classroom discourse is by no means new in Western countries, it has not received attention in China.

The situation in Western countries

In Western countries, since the early 1970s when DA was just beginning to take shape, discourse analysts have been addressing issues in education in general (Adger 2001) and language teaching in particular (McCarthy 1991; McCarthy and Carter 1994; Riggenbach 1999; Olshtain and Celce-Murcia 2001). While most work in education is meant to illuminate the nature of classroom interaction so as to find out how and where teaching and learning succeed or fail, work in language teaching is particularly concerned with how to create classroom environments that promote language learning.

In fact, such a discourse perspective on classroom teaching and learning is also inspired by socially oriented (vs. psychologically oriented) theories of second language acquisition (Firth and Wagner 1997), which stress patterns of classroom interaction that facilitate language acquisition. As Allwright defines it, classroom interaction is 'live person-to-person encounters' upon which input, practice opportunities and receptivity all have to rely (Allwright 1984; Allwright and Bailey 1991). So the analysis of language classroom discourse mainly focuses on such related issues as (1) the amount of student speech, as an indicator of practice opportunities (e.g. Foster 1998); (2) teacher talk, as input and with an impact on the students' comprehension of other input (see Chaudron 1988: Ch. 3; Ellis 1994: Ch. 13); (3) teachers' questions, since some question types encourage thinking and output while others do not (see Yang 2007a); (4) negotiation of meaning, defined in terms of such discoursal adjustments as comprehension check, request for repetition, request for confirmation, etc. (Long 1983), which have been shown (by Pica et al. 1987, 1989; Pica 1988) to be able to generate both comprehensible input (see Krashen 1981, 1985) and comprehensible output (Swain 1985), which in turn are facilitative to language acquisition. Negotiation in EFL classroom discourse is also studied (e.g. Boulima 1999).

While studies on these issues are revealing about the possible effects of classroom interaction on language acquisition, a more rigorous and comprehensive analysis of language classroom discourse is needed in order to describe the various aspects of the classroom environment – including the role relationship between the teacher and students, the content of their talk, the organization of the discourse, and so on – which all have an impact on the result of learning.

The situation in China

In China, according to a survey made by Yang (2003), studies on EFL teaching and learning largely focus on teaching methodology, the teaching of language areas and skills, and learner factors or strategies. Very few studies have been made on classroom interaction, and no attempt of a systematic kind has been made to analyse EFL classroom discourse. Moreover, such a lack of research into EFL classroom discourse is in sharp contrast with an urgent need for this kind of research in China. The need arises from (1) the environment of English teaching and learning in China, and (2) the current state of Chinese EFL teachers.

First, in China, English is taught and learnt in a 'foreign language' rather than 'second language' environment. The learners have few opportunities to use the target language in their daily life. For the learners to have input as well as output, the EFL classroom is a very important site, if not the most important site (as in those under-developed parts of the country). In other words, classroom interaction is an even more important factor in foreign language learning than in second language learning. For this reason, it is especially necessary to reveal the nature of EFL classroom interaction, and to help the EFL teachers to improve their management of classroom interaction.

Second, in a populous country like China and in an age of globalization, qualified EFL teachers are in great demand. But investigations indicate that the majority of EFL teachers in China have not acquired the necessary qualifications, such as a degree in education or in applied linguistics; nor have they received sufficient pre-service or in-service training (Gao et al. 2000; Dai 2001; Xia 2002; Zhou 2005). Besides, these EFL teachers are all Chinese, and thus EFL learners themselves (though at a more advanced level): they may not always find it easy to express themselves while conducting a class in English. To train these teachers, one of the most important things to inform them is the nature of EFL classroom interaction and its role in EFL learning, together with the possible kinds of discourse behaviours they could engage in to facilitate learning in the classroom – as well as how such behaviours can be appropriately realized in lexicogrammatical terms in English.

So, the present study is also intended as an effort to promote EFL classroom discourse analysis, which is a highly needed but less developed area of study, especially in China.

1.2 Objectives and approach

The present study has two objectives, with one playing a guiding role and the other playing a supporting role.

The guiding objective is the development of a model of text as process within the SFL framework, which hopefully will help make Functional Grammar equally applicable in the analysis of dynamic meaning flows of an unfolding text just as in the analysis of synoptic grammatical features of a finished text, thus enhancing the applicability of SFL in discourse analysis (see Part I of this book). This objective is achieved through the following steps:

1. exploring the SFL philosophy of language, so as to locate the concept of text as defined in the philosophical framework of SFL, as well as to contextualize the present effort to model text as process (see Chapter 2);
2. reviewing major models pertaining to the description of text as process within the SFL school, so as to bring out their inadequacies as well as their insights into the issue (see Chapter 3);
3. developing a model of text as process based on the philosophical framework of SFL, and by drawing on insights offered both by the reviewed models and by new developments in SFL, so as to make Functional Grammar equally applicable in the analysis of text as process (see Chapter 4);
4. applying the newly proposed model to an actual analysis of EFL classroom discourse, so as to demonstrate the model and its feasibility (see Part II).

The supporting objective is the establishment of a dynamic system network applicable to the analysis of EFL classroom discourse, which hopefully will help to promote systematic analysis of this type of discourse. This objective is achieved as a result of applying the newly proposed model to the analysis of EFL classroom discourse. It is called 'supporting' in the sense that the system network set up here mainly serves as evidence for the feasibility of the new model. Nevertheless, it is also meant to serve as an analytic model that can be applied in future analyses of the process of EFL classroom discourse.

The validity of the established system network of EFL classroom discourse is ensured through the design of the application, briefly stated as follows (for details see Chapter 5):

1. the data used in the analysis is authentic and considerably large, including 10 texts transcribed from audio-recordings of 10 class-hours' EFL classroom discourse, involving 10 teachers from 8 universities in Beijing;
2. the analysis of every text follows the same 7 rigorous steps;
3. every text is coded move by move before it is interpreted;
4. the analysis is essentially qualitative (to ensure a clear demonstration of the new model) but is complemented by quantitative analysis where necessary.

For the sake of clarity, presentation of the analysis of EFL classroom discourse is organized around the three metafunctions: interpersonal, ideational and textual (see Chapters 6, 7 and 8); while co-articulations across metafunctions are pointed out wherever they occur. In order to make the established system network of EFL classroom discourse easily accessible to future analysts, each system in the network is summarized in the form of a table, which can serve as a handy checklist. As a further illustration of how the network can be used, a whole text (i.e. Text 5) is analysed in detail in the third section of each of the three chapters, with its coding sheets being provided in the appendices. Discussions about the features of EFL classroom teaching and learning in the Chinese context can be found in these chapters as well. It is hoped that the network will be applied – either as a whole or in part – in future studies of the classroom environment, the process of classroom interaction, or the discourse strategies of teachers and students.

Part I

Modelling Text As Process

Chapter 2

Exploration of the SFL Philosophy

This chapter explores the philosophical framework of SFL, with a view to locating the concept of text as it is defined in the SFL philosophy of language, and hence contextualizing the present study – both the modelling of text as process, and the application of the model proposed here to EFL classroom discourse.

It is clear to many that text is viewed in SFL as an instance of the linguistic system. This implies that the nature of text is largely dependent upon the nature of the system, or rather, upon how language as a whole is viewed in SFL. In many of his articles published in the latter half of the twentieth century, Halliday had clearly defined the basic concepts in the SFL theory, including system and text, semantics and grammar, context of situation, metafunction, instantiation, etc. But it was only around the turn of the century that he seemed to be explicitly building up, based upon the previously defined theoretical constructs, the so-called 'architecture of language' (Halliday 2004, 2007), i.e. the framework of the SFL philosophy of language.

This chapter is organized around the SFL architecture of language, deriving the nature of text from the nature of language as defined in the architecture, particularly from the three dimensions of the architecture – metafunction, stratification and instantiation. The chapter ends with implications for a model of text as process within the SFL framework.

2.1 Language as a semiotic system

According to Halliday (1978, 1985b, 2007), language is a semiotic system. But it is 'not in the sense of a system of signs, but a systematic resource for meaning – what I have often called a meaning potential' (Halliday 1985a: 7). In other words, unlike Saussure (1960), who is interested in individual signs whose meanings are defined in terms of their syntagmatic and paradigmatic relations within the linguistic system, Halliday is interested in a sign system, that is, the entire linguistic system as meaning potential from which meaning choices can be made. In this sense, a semiotic system is a system of meaning, and meaning is choice. Such a unique semiotic view on language has three consequences.

One consequence is an extension of the object of linguistic study from the linguistic system proper into its context, since meanings of the entire system can hardly be defined in terms of relations within the system alone. In fact, Halliday leads linguistic study into the realm of culture. He takes culture as the higher-order semiotic system, and language – along with painting, sculpture, music, and so on – as a lower-order semiotic system constituting culture. In this sense, culture is the context for language and defines meanings expressed by the linguistic system, while the linguistic system serves as a mode of making meaning. Furthermore, since culture is 'synonymous with' the social system (Halliday 1985b: 4), the linguistic system can be said to be a mode of making social meaning, hence 'social semiotic' (Halliday 1978).

Another consequence is an emphasis on paradigmatic rather than syntagmatic relations, since the meaning potential of the overall system of a language can hardly be represented as an inventory of structures. In SFL, language is modelled paradigmatically – as a system network – irrespective of where in the syntagm the meanings happen to be located. While 'system' is in the sense of a set of options from which a choice can be made, 'network' is in the sense of interlocking systems that are either associated because simultaneous choices must be made, or different in delicacy so that entry into one system depends on entry into another. Moreover, the paradigmatic complexity allows the meaning potential of a language to expand more or less indefinitely. As Halliday (2007: 8) says, 'the power of a language resides in its organization as a huge network of interrelated choices.'

Still another consequence is a stress on both the system and text, since potential implies choice and choice implies a potential lying behind. While the system is meaning potential, text represents meaning choice – as 'a product of a continuous process of choices in meaning that we represent as multiple paths or passes through the networks that constitute the linguistic system' (Halliday 1985b: 11). Therefore Halliday says:

> In fact, we usually use the term 'system' to cover both system and process: both the potential and the instances that occur; thus a semiotic system is a meaning potential together with its instantiation in acts of meaning. (Halliday 1996: 4)

Again, unlike Saussure (1960), who believes linguistics is a theory of *langue* rather than *parole*, Halliday follows Hjelmslev (1961) in encompassing both. He takes text as an instrument, asking what it reveals about the system of the language in which it is engendered. As he states, 'the way into understanding about language lies in the study of text' (1985b: 5). He further explains his position:

> It is of little use having an elegant theory of the system if it cannot account for how the system engenders text; equally, it adds little to expatiate on a text if one cannot relate it to the system that lies behind it, since anyone understanding the text does so only because they know the system. (Halliday, 1994: xxii)

Thus in SFL, language is both system and text. The system is meaning potential, represented as a system network; while text is its instantiation, constituted of actual meaning choices from the potential. In this sense, text is an act of meaning – and of course an act of social meaning, since the system it instantiates is social semiotic.

2.2 Dimension 1: metafunction

As to what kinds of social meaning language may serve to express, Halliday answers the question through the concept of metafunction, which in effect yields one of the three semiotic dimensions in the architecture of language.

Halliday's answer is much influenced by (1) 'two founding traditions of the study of language in context' (Halliday 1999: 6), i.e., the view of Malinowski and Firth on language as a form of action and the view of Sapir and Whorf on language as a form of reflection; (2) the results of his own explorations of the functions of children's protolanguage (Halliday 1973, 1975). Halliday argues that language evolved in all cultures to express, simultaneously, three general kinds of meaning, that is, to perform three generalized functions – referred to as metafunctions. They are the ideational (both experiential and logical), interpersonal, and textual meanings/functions, which are briefly summarized as follows (for details see Halliday 1978, 1985b, 1998, 2004, 2007; Halliday and Matthiessen 1999).

First, language expresses **experiential** meaning, representing various phenomena in the real world as they are apprehended in the human mind, including creatures and objects, events and actions, states and qualities, and so on. Language in its experiential function is a mode of reflecting, i.e. a way of interpreting the world, which construes human experience – construe in the sense of 'construct in the mind' (Halliday 1999: 7). This is why the experiential function of language is taken as part of the **ideational** function.

Associated with the experiential function is the **logical** function of language. That is, language also expresses fundamental logical relations such as 'and', 'or' and 'if'. This function serves to construe our interpretation of the connection between one quantum of experience and another; and that is how the logical joins the experiential in becoming part of the **ideational** function.

Second, language expresses **interpersonal** meaning, representing various aspects of our participation as speakers in the speech situation, including the speech roles we adopt and assign to others, as well as our wishes, feelings, attitudes and judgements. Language in its interpersonal function is a mode of doing, i.e. a way of interacting with other people, which enacts personal and social relationships.

Third, language expresses **textual** meaning, creating texture – that is, organizing ideational and interpersonal meanings into a text that coheres both within itself and with the context of situation. Language in its textual function enables the other two functions to operate and hence enables a text to do its job in its context.

Since language is viewed as a semiotic system that expresses social meaning through systemic choices actually made, the above three types of meaning/ function as classified by Halliday are actually all oriented towards the actual use of language in social context: the ideational function is the 'content function', the interpersonal the 'participatory function', and the textual the 'enabling function' (see Halliday 1978: 112). In other words, the three metafunctions are all oriented towards, as well as interwoven in, the text. And text, in this sense, is not merely an act of social meaning but, more precisely, a multi-functional act.

Furthermore, the three metafunctions are viewed, in SFL, as components of the **semantic system** – in the sense of the semiotic system of a human language, represented as a network of systems; and as such they form 'the basis of the organization of the entire linguistic system' (Halliday 1978: 47). In other words, the entire linguistic system (network) is organized around the three metafunctions; therefore the system is often referred to as a 'semantic' or 'functional' system (with the two terms being interchangeable in SFL). Or more precisely, it can be called a **multi-functional** system. And text, being an instance of a multi-functional system, cannot but be a multi-functional act – with all systemic choices in a text being organized, just as in the system, around the three metafunctions.

2.3 Dimension 2: stratification

Another dimension in the architecture of language is stratification. Apart from being organized into a multi-functional system, language is also a stratified system. That is, the linguistic system is organized into several strata.

According to Halliday (1975), in an infant's protolanguage, as well as in human language at the beginning of its evolution, meaning is expressed directly by sound. In other words, the language has only two strata. In Hjelmslev's (1961) terminology, they are the 'content' plane and 'expression' plane. By using concepts in adult language, they are semantics (meaning) and phonology (sounding). The problem with such a bi-stratal system is that it is a limited inventory of signs, with limited sounds expressing pre-existing meanings.

Later, however, as language develops in an individual and evolves in the human species, along with a need to expand the meaning potential, grammar (wording) 'emerges through deconstructing the original sign and reconstructing with the content plane split into two distinct strata, semantics and lexicogrammar'[1] (Halliday 1996: 6), thus turning the language system into a tri-stratal one. But the real significance of the stratification of the content plane into semantics and grammar is that it allows meaning to be further organized into wording as it is being expressed in sounding.

According to Halliday (1995, 1996, 2004), it is grammar that enables the meaning potential of a language to expand more or less indefinitely. He explains it by drawing on Lemke's (1993, 1995) view that the social practices constituting eco-social systems (i.e. human communities) are at once **material** and **semiotic**, with a constant interplay between the two. Halliday takes language as a semiotic system interfacing with the material environment – semantics interfacing with social processes going on in the real world, and phonology with articulatory processes taking place in the human body. Grammar, on the other hand, being a stratum between semantics and phonology, does not directly interface with either of the phenomenal realms in the material environment of language. It is, therefore, an entirely abstract semiotic construct that enables 'an indefinite amount of "play" between the two' (Halliday 1996: 6). In this way, grammar is able to 'turn a closed, meaning-bearing system into an open, meaning-creating one' (Halliday 2007: 14). This is why SFL is in fact a linguistic theory based on grammar – a grammar oriented towards semantics, i.e. a functional grammar.

Thus the linguistic system, as a powerful meaning potential, has three strata: semantics, grammar and phonology.[2] One of its outer interfaces, i.e. the processes of speech production, is excluded from the system proper though it is the object of phonetics. But the other outer interface, i.e. the processes of human existence, can hardly be excluded; since it constitutes the cultural context in which language makes meaning, and since culture is viewed in SFL as the higher-order semiotic system that defines meaning made by language – in terms of the three metafunctions. Figure 2.1 is an illustration of the stratification of the linguistic system intersecting with the three metafunctions.

As for the stratal relationship, Halliday defines it as one of **realization**: culture is realized in semantics, semantics is realized in grammar, and grammar is realized in phonology. However, realization is not a one-way relationship. It does not mean that culture exists first and determines language, nor that meanings can exist without wordings. Language also creates reality in a culture, and meanings have no ready-made categories in the real world other than those

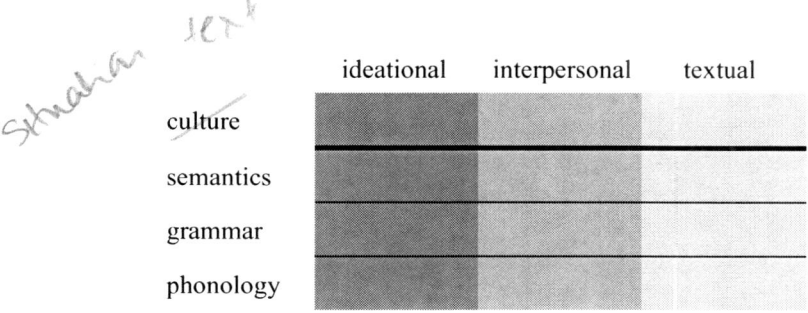

FIGURE 2.1 Stratification intersecting with metafunction

encoded in a grammar. As Halliday (1999: 15) puts it, 'this is a relationship that can be traversed, or activated, in either direction.'

This view on language as a multi-stratal system suggests that text, which instantiates the system, must also be multi-stratal. In other words, text is not only a process of making meaning choices by going through the networks that constitute the linguistic system, but also a process of making meaning choices that activate choices in wording that in turn activate choices in sounding. The difference between system and text in terms of stratification only lies in the context: the context for system is culture, whereas the context for text is situation (see 2.4 for more on this).

2.4 Dimension 3: instantiation

The third dimension in the architecture of language is instantiation, which links observable acts of meaning going on around us all the time, with the meaning potential lying behind all such acts. In other words, it is the dimension of instantiation that links text with the linguistic system. And in this sense, text and system are not different things but the same phenomenon seen from different standpoints of the observer, analogous to weather and climate in the physical world (Halliday 1996, 1999, 2004).

It is held in SFL that, while the linguistic system is instantiated in text, culture is instantiated in situation; and while culture is realized in the linguistic system, situation is realized in text. See Figure 2.2 for an illustration of instantiation intersecting with realization (adapted from Figure 1, Halliday 1999: 8).

The context of situation, according to Halliday (1978: 142), is 'an instance of the meanings that make up the social system', hence a semiotic construct rather than the material environment of a text. It is defined as a semiotic structure organized into three variables: (1) the field of discourse, i.e. the nature of the social activity in which the text has some role to play (e.g. teaching and learning); (2) the tenor of discourse, i.e. the kind of role relationship between

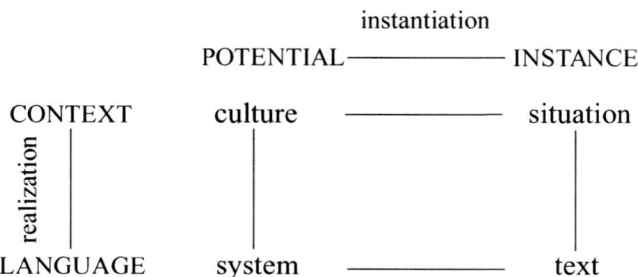

FIGURE 2.2 Instantiation intersecting with realization

participants in the creation of a text (e.g. teacher vs. student, questioner vs. answerer); (3) the mode of discourse, i.e. the particular role assigned to the text by the participants in this activity, including the medium and genre allotted to the text (e.g. spoken classroom dialogue). (For details, see Halliday 1978, 1985b.) It is the field, tenor and mode of discourse (FTM) that together specify the semiotic properties of a situation type for a text to realize.

However, FTM cannot directly determine the semantic choices constituting a text. To establish continuity between a text and its situational context, Halliday sets up a systematic relationship between the situational variables and the semantic components – relating field with ideational meaning, tenor with interpersonal meaning, and mode with textual meaning. In this way, FTM are able to specify a particular range of meaning potential from which actual meaning choices can be made in producing a text in a given situation type. And this particular range of meaning potential is what Halliday means by 'register', defined as follows:

> It can be defined as a configuration of meanings that are typically associated with a particular situational configuration of field, mode, and tenor. But since it is a configuration of meanings, a register must also, of course, include the expressions, the lexicogrammatical and phonological features, that typically accompany or REALIZE these meanings. (Halliday 1985b: 38–9)

That is to say, a register is (1) composed of meaning patterns, hence semantic in nature; (2) both the realization of a situation type, and being realized in grammar and conveyed by sound. This further suggests that a register is also organized multi-functionally and multi-stratally, just like the text as well as the system.

The significance of the notion of register is that it allows the dimension of instantiation to appear in the form of a cline, instead of being binary as it sounds like. It is a cline, with the overall system and text at the two ends and with register in between them. The overall system is the entire meaning potential of a language, i.e. the semantic system; register is the subpotential, i.e. a semantic variety accessible in a given situation type; and text is a specific act of meaning, i.e. a product of semantic selection in the context of situation. Seen along the dimension of instantiation, text is in fact an instance of register, which in turn is an instance of the overall system; and the three of them are equally multi-functional and multi-stratal. See Figure 2.3 for an illustration.

2.5 Implications

All in all, language is viewed in Halliday's SFL theory as a semiotic system functional in context, and it is described as a three-dimensional architecture in which the system and register and text are inseparable. This philosophical

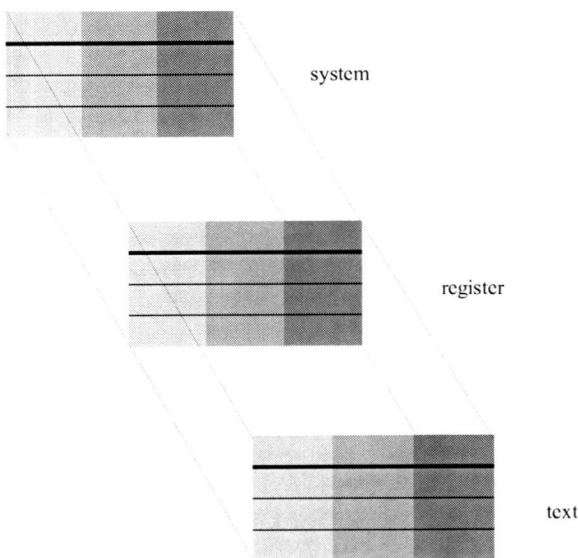

system

register

text

FIGURE 2.3   Text seen along the dimension of instantiation

framework of language indicates that **text** is inherently both multi-functional and multi-stratal; therefore, text cannot be properly modelled without reference to a register or the overall system, nor can it be modelled at a single stratum or within a single metafunction. This is exactly the view on text, and on a model of text, that is being adopted in the present study.

However, it should also be pointed out that in the SFL architecture of language, text is mainly represented as a product rather than a process. Halliday does make a distinction between text as product and as process, as this quote shows:

> The text is a product in the sense that it is an output, something that can be recorded and studied, having a certain construction that can be represented in systematic terms. It is a process in the sense of a continuous process of semantic choice, a movement through the network of meaning potential, with each set of choices constituting the environment for a further set. (Halliday 1985b: 10)

This distinction, however, is made to elaborate on the notion of instantiation: text is the product of going through the network of meaning potential. It is a process only in the sense of being a trip along multiple paths in the network, with some paths being the entry conditions of further paths; whereas the process of taking such trips successively as the text unfolds before its completion, is taken as given. In other words, Halliday interprets the process of text basically as a single trip into the system network, rather than as successive trips that constitute a whole text through to its end.[3]

Besides, it should be noted that neither is register – of which text is an instance – represented in dynamic terms in the SFL architecture of language. Register is seen as the intermediate semiotic region between the system (potential) and text (instance), and hence can be viewed either from the system end as a subsystem or subpotential, or from the text end as a text type or instance type (see Halliday 2004: 27). In this sense, register is indeed both a way into a general description of the semantic system of a language,[4] and a way into a specific description of an individual text. In other words, register has an unavoidably important place in any model of text. However, register in this sense is merely an existing subsystem, and text type is all texts instantiating the same subsystem while realizing the same situation type. As such, register is by no means a construct for the dynamic flows of meaning that run through texts of the same type.

Thus it can be said that the unfolding process of text is not represented in the SFL architecture. Halliday is aware of the problem: 'The major problem perhaps is that . . . of representing both the system and its instantiation in dynamic as well as in synoptic terms' (Halliday 1985a: 10). He is also aware why a dynamic representation is difficult to achieve in a grammar-based linguistic theory:

> Since grammatical theory evolved as the study of written language, it is good at synoptic-type 'product' representation, with constituency as the organizing concept, but bad at dynamic-type 'process' representations, which is what are needed for the interpretation of speech. (Halliday 1994: 224)

More recently Halliday again stresses that 'it is important to be able to think of text dynamically, as an ongoing process of meaning' (2004: 524). But how to represent text both as a finished product and as an ongoing process of meaning, and how to represent register as both a synoptic and a dynamic subpotential, remain questions to be addressed fully and explicitly in SFL; hence they become the concerns of the present study. And the data used in this study, i.e. EFL classroom discourse, constitutes an appropriate site for a study of text as process, since it is in spoken language that the meaning potential is most richly explored and expanded, and since spoken language in particular calls for 'dynamic-type "process" representations'.

Chapter 3

Review of Existing Models

This chapter presents a review of major models of text as process within the SFL school, with a view to bringing out existing descriptions of text as process – both the insights they offer, and their inadequacies if there are any. Since EFL classroom discourse is the object of analysis in this study, special attention is given to models that are both pertaining to text as process and oriented towards spoken discourse in general or classroom discourse in particular. The chapter is divided into four sections: (1) models of genre, (2) models of spoken discourse, (3) models of classroom discourse and (4) summary.

3.1 Models of genre

There have been a number of approaches to text as process in the structural-functional tradition of SFL,[1] which all examine the process of text in terms of its **global structure** in an attempt to set up some kind of dynamic subpotential for a given text type. These approaches, however, are more concerned with text structure, i.e. how a text unfolds from one stage to another (often referred to as 'staging'), than with text as an instantiation of the linguistic system. That is why the term 'genre' is more often used than 'text type'. Reviewed in this section are three major models of genre in the SFL tradition which, apart from offering frameworks of one kind or another for analysing text structure, provide insights into text as process. (For a comprehensive review, see Fang 1998, 2002; Qin 1997, 2000; Zhang 2002a, 2002b.)

3.1.1 Hasan's genre model

Hasan (1985) offers a model of genre as an attempt to deal with text structure. She is mainly concerned with how text does its job in its context, i.e. the textual function of language that is related to the mode of discourse. She believes that the most outstanding characteristic of text is unity – unity of **texture** and unity of **text structure**. While Halliday and Hasan (1976) explain texture 'from below', in terms of semantic ties realized by lexical or grammatical devices, known as COHESION; Hasan (1985) explains text structure 'from above', in terms of a genre-specific semantic potential predicted by the context of situation.

In Hasan's model, genre is a semantic concept, referring to texts that are embedded in the same situation type – defined as a contextual configuration (CC) – and share the same text structure. It is the specific values of a CC that predict the shared text structure of a genre, including what elements must occur in the genre, what elements can occur, where they must or can occur, and how often they occur. Hasan argues that 'an ELEMENT is a stage with some consequence in the progression of a text' (1985: 56). That is to say, the description of text as process can be achieved by analysing the structural elements in texts of the same genre.

Hasan proposes to describe the text structure of a genre, also called generic structure, in terms of generic structure potential (GSP), i.e. 'the total range of optional and obligatory elements and their order' (1985: 64). She uses a formula[2] to represents GSP, as illustrated in Figure 3.1 (which is the GSP for service encounter, see ibid. for details). GSP as such is not only a framework for describing the text structure of a genre, but also a kind of subpotential for the process of a given text type.

$$[(G) \cdot (SI)^\wedge] [(\overset{\frown}{SE} \cdot) \{SR^\wedge \overset{\frown}{SC^\wedge}\} ^\wedge S^\wedge] P^\wedge PC (^\wedge F)$$

G=greeting   SI=sale initiation   SE=sale enquiry   SR=sale request
SC=sale compliance   S=sale   P=purchase   PC=purchase closure   F=Finis

FIGURE 3.1   An example of GSP formula

But unlike Halliday who looks at subpotential from the system end, Hasan, who is concerned with the unity of text as reflected in text structure, is looking at subpotential from the text end – and solely in terms of the textual function. Consequently, while Halliday takes subpotential as both multi-functional and multi-stratal, Hasan does not feel the need to relate GSP either to the stratum below, i.e. grammar (see Zhang 1998), or to every metafunction.

Regarding the role of grammar, Hasan believes that GSP contains meanings of two categories: (1) structural elements (e.g. SR, S, P), which are specific to the genre concerned; (2) components of structural elements (e.g. reference of goods or quantity in SR), which are defined in grammatical terms but are irrelevant to the generic status of a text. She concludes:

> ... the statement of genre specific 'language' is best given in terms of the semantic categories, rather than the lexicogrammatical ones, since (1) the range of meanings have variant realisation; and (2) the more delicate choices within the general area is not a matter of generic ambience. (Hasan 1985: 113)

However, as Yang (2007b) observes, if one analyses text structure merely 'from above', without any evidence 'from below' as support, the conclusions thus reached can be subjective and shaky, especially with a genre (such as public speech) that constitutes the field of discourse.

Regarding the place of the three metafunctions in GSP, as can be seen in Figure 3.1, the obligatory elements specific to the genre of service encounter are in fact all meanings of the ideational kind predicted by the field of discourse (i.e. buying and selling), so that the GSP amounts to a statement of the organization of ideational meanings. This allows the GSP model to work well with genres like service encounter, or appointment-making (see Hasan 1977), where texts unfold in the same sequence as the social activity they accompany. But it is unlikely to work equally well with genres where texts play a constitutive rather than ancillary role in the field. In public speech, for example, the values of FTM vary from element to element, making it unlikely to define the genre based on structural elements predicted by a single CC (see Yang 2007b). And in a nursery tale, the text structure does not even depend on the situation, but on a culture's 'array of existing conventions' (Hasan 1984/1996). This is why Martin (1992: 572) says Hasan's model 'is one which derives text structures in two fundamentally different ways, depending on mode', and why Harris (1987) articulates a similar critique.

In sum, from a practical point of view, Hasan's genre model provides a useful framework for analysing the text structure of some genres. And her GSP formula is useful metalanguage for describing all genres. From a theoretical point of view, Hasan defines text structure as a semantic structure predicted by a CC, throwing light on the nature of text as process. But her GSP is a range of meanings detached from grammar and associated only with the textual and perhaps also the ideational function, thus being neither multi-stratal nor multi-functional. As such, GSP is hardly a subpotential as defined in the SFL architecture, nor is it applicable to the analysis of the process of all text types.

3.1.2 Martin's genre model

While Hasan examines genre at the semantic stratum, Martin examines it at the contextual stratum. In fact, Martin's genre model (Martin 1984, 1985, 1992, 1999; Martin and Rose 2003) is a part of his 'language based theory of context' (1992: 493) developed out of two research needs: (1) a practical need for a model of context to be used with teachers to inform literacy teaching; (2) a theoretical need for a reconciliation of Halliday's three contextual variables that match the three metafunctions, with Gregory's (1967, 1987; Gregory and Carroll 1978) four variables – field, personal tenor, functional tenor[3] and mode – that do not mesh as nicely with the metafunctions.

Martin (1999) traces the path he went through modelling context. He had found **functional tenor** to be different from the other three variables because it ranged across metafunctions in realization and could be used to talk globally about a text's social purpose in relation to its organization So he decided that it was 'the appropriate contextual variable to associate with text structure (which we later referred to as schematic structure)' (ibid.: 28), and renamed it **genre** 'to avoid confusion with personal tenor and to consolidate the association with text structure' (ibid.). Thus context is split into two parts: (1) FTM, collectively called 'register'[4] by Martin; (2) genre, defined as 'a staged, goal-oriented, purposeful activity in which speakers engage as members of our culture' (Martin 1984: 25). He also refers to genre as the context of culture and 'register' as the context of situation (see also Eggins 1994).

As to the relationship between the two kinds of context, Martin treats genre as a stratum above 'register' and realized by 'register'. This is obviously deviant from the SFL architecture, or as Hasan (1995: 148) says, 'inconsistent with the systemic functional model'; but it is useful in practice. With genre being elevated to a stratum above FTM, it is possible to distinguish the unfolding phases of a text from the activity sequences of its field, thus making it possible to account for the global structure of texts whose mode is either ancillary or constitutive (for details see Yang 2007b).

Meanwhile, Martin treats both 'register' and genre as the content plane expressed by language, viewing them as two complementary perspectives on context, and as 'semiotic systems manifested in whole or in part through language' (Martin 1992: 493). 'Register' is context seen from the perspective of language, thus being organized into FTM that engender meanings manifested 'in part', that is, through the clause in a metafunctionally diversified manner (as specified in Halliday's Functional Grammar). Genre is context seen from the perspective of culture, thus being a social process manifested 'in whole', that is, through a whole text where meanings engendered by FTM are realized in a metafunctionally unified manner (as specified in Martin's discourse semantics; see Martin 1992). Although it may not be sound to interpret this complementarity as two strata related through realization, the two perspectives themselves are both useful since they can be applied to different kinds of analysis. The cultural perspective is useful in genre analysis that focuses on text structure, and the language perspective in 'register' analysis that focuses on grammatical choices in a text at the clause level.

It should be noted, however, that genre analysis of this kind is actually a culture-meaning-wording approach, leaving out the 'register' stratum (see Martin and Rose 2003), and it implies two alternatives. One is 'outside-in'[5]: to begin by dividing a text into sections that reflect shifts of meaning phases, and then look for patterns of meaning choices from the 'discourse semantic systems' (Martin 1992) that are both correlated with those sections in text structure and realized in grammar. The other is 'inside-out': to begin by looking for foregrounded semantic motifs realized in grammar, and then correlate the discourse semantic patterns with any possible sections in text structure. Although the approach is inconsistent with the realizational relationship between genre and 'register' as defined by Martin himself, it has proved useful to analysts with socio-cultural concerns, especially those working with teachers to design literacy materials and programs (see a collection of articles in Christie and Martin 1997).

Regarding the representation of the schematic structure of a genre, Martin prefers system network to structural formula. He represents a genre (e.g. service encounter) as a system of features characterizing the type of activity (e.g. appointed vs. unappointed, goods vs. information, display vs. across counter, and so on). It is choices from the system that generate specific stages of the activity, i.e. elements of the schematic structure (e.g. 'appointed' generates 'Wait' while 'unappointed' generates 'Service Bid'). In this light, two things become clear. First, text structure is the structural realization of a genre system; therefore it is not a semantic concept, but a contextual one. This should more or less explain why Martin prefers the term 'schematic structure' to 'text structure'. Second, Martin's genre system is also meant to be a subpotential, just like Hasan's GSP. But while the latter generates one type of text structure that defines one genre, the former generates a set of agnate genres whose schematic structures are both similar and different. The strength of deriving text structure from a genre system rather than from a single CC is that it enables an account of texts whose FTM values vary from one stage to another.

In sum, Martin's genre model is in theory multi-stratal – covering genre, 'register', (discourse) semantics, and grammar; and multi-functional – with genre and 'register' both realized in metafunctionally organized semantic systems that in turn are realized in grammar. It is also, as Eggins and Slade (1997: 56) put it, 'a theory of the unfolding structure texts work through to achieve their social purpose.' The question left unanswered is how to relate the schematic structure of a genre to FTM if they are two strata of context realizing each other.

3.1.3 Swales' genre model

Swales (1990) offers a model of genre analysis that is much in line with the structural-functional tradition of SFL, although Swales himself cannot be called a systemicist. He acknowledges in his book many sources of influence on him, among which are Halliday's (1978) framework and categorizations, Miller's (1984) and Martin's (1985) view on genre as a means of social action, and the socio-rhetorical approach in the field of L1 writing that takes discourse as a vehicle to achieve rhetorical goals.

Swales is interested in the teaching of a particular type of text, i.e. English for Academic Purposes, hence his concern with 'the roles texts play in particular environments' (Swales 1990: 7) rather than texts *per se*. He interprets text-role in text-environment as 'communicative purpose/goal'; text environment as 'discourse community', i.e. 'sociorhetorical networks that form in order to work towards sets of common goals' (ibid.: 9); and genre as 'communicative vehicles for the achievement of goals' (ibid.: 46). He argues that the communicative goals constitute the rationale behind a genre, which shapes genre conventions – including the rhetorical organization (schematic structure) of texts along with the linguistic means of its accomplishment. In other words, it is the communicative goals that determine the text structure of a genre.

Based on the above interrelated concepts he has defined, Swales proposes a model of genre analysis, i.e. a framework for analysing the rhetorical organization of texts. According to the model, text can be divided into rhetorical sections based on their function in the furtherance of the communicative goals of the genre. Each section can be further divided into 'Moves' based on their function in the section, and a Move in turn into 'Steps'. In the case of the genre of research articles, Swales has identified four sections: Introduction, Method, Result and Discussion. He has also identified a Move-Step structure in the Introduction section, as follows (adapted from Figure 10, ibid.: 141):

Move 1	Establishing a territory	
	Step 1	Claiming centrality
and/or	Step 2	Making topic generalization(s)
and/or	Step 3	Reviewing items of previous research
Move 2	Establishing a niche	
	Step 1A	Counter-claiming
or	Step 1B	Indicating a gap
or	Step 1C	Question-raising
or	Step 1D	Continuing a tradition
Move 3	Occupying the niche	
	Step 1A	Outlining purposes
or	Step 1B	Announcing present research
	Step 2	Announcing principal findings
	Step 3	Indicating research article structure

Furthermore, the Moves and Steps are said to have their own linguistic exponents or signals. For example, Move 2 is said to be signalled, in an order of decreasing frequency, by (1) negative or quasi-negative quantifiers, (2) lexical negation, (3) negation in the verb phrase, (4) questions, (5) expressed needs/desires/ interests, (6) logical conclusions, (7) contrastive comment and (8) problem-raising (see ibid.: 155–6).

Swales' genre model clearly shares a number of features of the structural-functional tradition of SFL. First, like Hasan, Swales examines genre in terms of the global structure of text and gives ideational labels to the structural elements, such as 'establishing a territory' and 'claiming centrality' (comparable to 'sale', 'purchase', 'closure', etc.). Moreover, he correlates the structural elements with their linguistic signals. So his model is both like the GSP model, in that it describes text structure in semantic terms; and unlike the GSP model, in that it covers the grammatical stratum as well, thus allowing analyses 'from below'.

Second, when looking 'from above', although Swale does not relate text structure to a CC as Hasan does, he relates it to a set of communicative purposes of a given genre, which is comparable to Gregory's functional tenor. However, Swales does not make a distinction between context and language as Martin does; he actually combines them into one concept, i.e. genre. As he says, 'I propose to view genres as rather more than texts' (1990: 6). Thus the concept of genre in Swales' model is multi-stratal – though not in a strictly SFL sense – covering the rhetorical organization of a genre (semantic/functional), which is motivated by and meant to achieve a set of communicative purposes (contextual), and is at the same time signalled by lexical and syntactic choices (grammatical).

Third, Swales represents text structure as a rank scale (Article – Section – Move – Step), a method applied in SFL both in grammar and in the description of some discourse types (see 3.3.1 below). He also includes, in the representation, the sequence of structural elements (e.g. Move 1, Step 1) and a distinction between obligatory and optional elements (e.g. Step 1A or 1B). This indicates that Swales is also aiming at some kind of potential that can exhaust the possibility of text structure for all texts of a given genre.

In sum, Swales' genre model can be said to be multi-stratal, enabling an analysis of text structure both 'from above' and 'from below'. It may also be said to be concerned with the textual and ideational functions of language, offering a practical method of text analysis that can lead to the establishment of a genre-specific potential, i.e. a resource for producing and recognizing the rhetorical organization of texts of a specific genre. But, of course, it is not the kind of subpotential for a text type as defined in the SFL architecture of language.

3.2 Models of spoken discourse

While the genre models reviewed above describe the process of an unfolding text in terms of the **global** structure of a certain text type, the models reviewed in this section examine the process of a spoken text in terms of its **local** structure.

3.2.1 Halliday's Speech Function model

Halliday's (1994, 2004) Speech Function model is multi-stratal: it is a semantic system within the interpersonal metafunction, associated with the tenor of discourse in the context of situation, and realized through the Mood system in grammar.

From the perspective of the tenor of discourse, Halliday (1994: 68) interprets the clause in its interpersonal function as an 'exchange' – in the sense of 'an interactive event involving speaker, or writer, and audience', or simply an 'interact'. In fact, he first identifies two fundamental speech roles, i.e. giving and demanding; as well as two general types of commodities being exchanged, i.e. goods-&-services and information. With these two distinctions cutting across each other, he then identifies four primary speech functions that are manifested in the clause as an interact: (1) offer, (2) command, (3) statement, and (4) question. He refers to the first two as 'proposal' and the last two as 'proposition'. Meanwhile, he relates the speech functions to the Mood system in grammar: it is variations in the mood structure of the clause that constitute typical realizational forms of different speech functions. The declarative clause realizes a statement, the interrogative a question, and the imperative a command; whereas an offer is somehow less grammaticalized. See Table 3.1 for a multi-stratal representation of Halliday's Speech Function model. Although Halliday has been criticized for infusing grammar with semantics (Butler 1985a; Fawcett 1987; Martin 1985, 1992), his Speech Function model is perhaps where he is closest to a distinction between the two.

In order to account for the process of spoken discourse, Halliday expands his semantic system of Speech Function by adding an opposition between 'initiation' and 'response'. See a brief representation of the system in Figure 3.2 (adapted

Table 3.1 A multi-stratal representation of Halliday's Speech Function model

speech role (tenor of discourse)	exchange of commodities			
	goods-&-services		information	
	demanding	giving	demanding	giving
speech function (interpersonal meaning)	**command**	**offer**	**question**	**statement**
	proposal		proposition	
Mood system/structure (grammar)	imperative: (−Subject) −Finite	[less gram- maticalised]	interrogative: (WH^) Finite ^Subject	indicative: Subject^ Finite

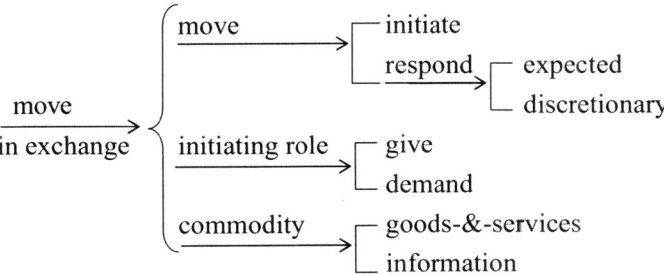

FIGURE 3.2 A brief representation of Halliday's Speech Function system

Table 3.2   Initiating/responding speech functions and their typical realizations

initiating speech function	responding speech function	
	expected	discretionary
offer ↘ Shall I ? I'll...(+moodtag)	acceptance ↘ yes; no	rejection ↘ no; don't
command ↘ imperative (+moodtag)	undertaking ↘ yes; I will	refusal ↘ no; I won't
statement ↘ declarative (+moodtag)	acknowledgement ↘ oh; is it?	contradiction ↘ no; it isn't

question ↘ interrogative:
      yes/no; WH-
	answer ↘ yes; no;
	      group/phrase
		disclaimer ↘ won't say;
		      don't know

from Fig. 4–2 in Halliday 2004). Thus the system will engender not only the four primary speech functions that are found in the initiating move, but also speech functions found in the responding move – either expected or discretionary[6].

And to strengthen the tie between meaning and wording of clause in its interpersonal function, Halliday argues that the responding speech functions are also realized through negotiation of meaning as manifested in the mood structure (present or elliptical). See Table 3.2 for details (adapted from Tables 4(1) and 4(2) in Halliday 2004; here the right downward arrow indicates a relationship of realization).

In sum, Halliday's Speech Function model focuses on the interpersonal metafunction of language, but multi-stratally – covering speech roles (tenor of discourse), the speech function of clause (semantics), and the mood structure of clause (grammar). It gives a multi-stratal account of the basic facts about a dialogue, that is, why and how moves are tied into adjacency pairs. However, as the system is clause-based, it is not likely to apply to the analysis of a long sequence of moves. Nor is it readily applicable to real-life spoken discourse, which necessarily entails constant shifts of topic, many turns that are longer than a single move, and various supporting and challenging moves.

3.2.2 Martin's Negotiation model

Martin (1992: Ch. 2) offers a model of dialogue that he calls Negotiation. In fact, it is an expansion and revision of Halliday's Speech Function system, so that the system can operate at the rank of both move and exchange (i.e. a sequence of moves)[7].

Martin argues that minor clauses, in spite of lacking Mood elements (Subject / Finite), can function as moves such as greeting, calling and exclaiming. He

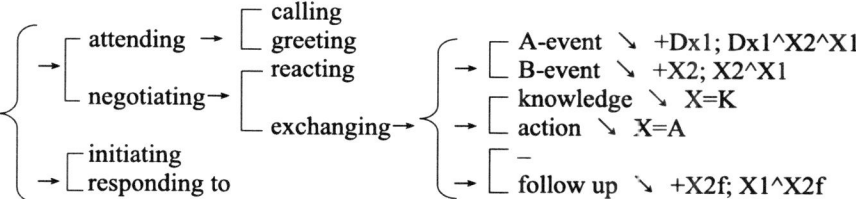

FIGURE 3.3 A summary of Martin's Negotiation system

therefore expands the Speech Function system so that it engenders seven adjacency pairs (for details see Martin 1992: 44–5) instead of four pairs as described in Halliday's model. The three additional pairs are (1) Call/Response to Call, (2) Greeting/Response to Greeting, (3) Exclamation/Response to Exclamation. As the first two pairs are non-negotiable, Martin introduces into his Negotiation system (network) an opposition between (a) the Attending system which engenders the first two pairs, and (b) the Negotiating system which engenders the third one through the Reacting system, and those four originally proposed by Halliday through the Exchanging system. See a summary of the Negotiation system in Figure 3.3 (adapted from Figures 2–10/11 in Martin 1992; the plus sign indicates presence and the minus sign absence).

Actually, Martin gives more attention to the Negotiating system (hence Negotiation), in particular the Exchanging system where he extends an adjacency pair at the move rank to a sequence of moves at the exchange rank. The Exchanging system is based on the work of Berry (1981c), who makes three distinctions: (1) between exchanges concerned with information and with action; (2) between X1, i.e. the primary knower (K1) or actor (A1), and X2, i.e. the secondary knower (K2) or actor (A2); and (3) between A-event and B-event that are initiated respectively by X1 and X2 (for details, see 3.3.2). Besides, Martin incorporates Ventola's (1987) X1f into the system, so that it may engender a sequence of up to five moves, as illustrated by this invented A-event action exchange (D = delaying; f = follow-up):

DA1	Can I get you a beer?	A2	Yes please.
A1	Here you go.	A2f	Thank you.
A1f	You are welcome.		

As for multi-clause moves that may extend into a passage Martin proposes to treat them as a 'move complex', i.e. a univariate structure realized by a paratactic clause complex, following Ventola (1987, 1988). As to moves not predicted by an initiation such as tracking (e.g. check, clarification, etc.) or challenging (e.g. aborting, querying), he proposes to view them as dependent moves, drawing on the concept of 'dependency' in Fawcett et al. (1988). Thus in an actual analysis, Martin describes an exchange as a multi-variate structure that

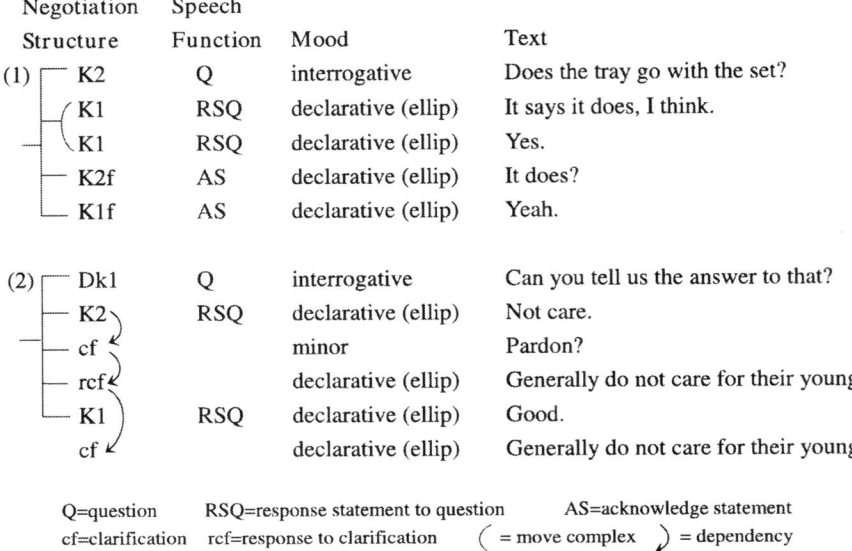

Negotiation Structure	Speech Function	Mood	Text
(1) ┌─ K2	Q	interrogative	Does the tray go with the set?
┌ K1	RSQ	declarative (ellip)	It says it does, I think.
└ K1	RSQ	declarative (ellip)	Yes.
├─ K2f	AS	declarative (ellip)	It does?
└─ K1f	AS	declarative (ellip)	Yeah.
(2) ┌─ Dk1	Q	interrogative	Can you tell us the answer to that?
├─ K2	RSQ	declarative (ellip)	Not care.
├─ cf		minor	Pardon?
├─ rcf		declarative (ellip)	Generally do not care for their young.
└─ K1	RSQ	declarative (ellip)	Good.
cf		declarative (ellip)	Generally do not care for their young.

Q=question   RSQ=response statement to question   AS=acknowledge statement
cf=clarification   rcf=response to clarification   (= move complex   ⟩ = dependency

FIGURE 3.4   Synoptic-dynamic analysis of conversational exchange

accounts synoptically for a sequence of moves, at the same time introducing univariate and dependency structures to account dynamically for move complexes and tracking/challenging moves respectively. See Figure 3.4 for an illustration of the synoptic-dynamic analysis of two conversational exchanges: (1) service encounter, (2) classroom discourse (for details see Martin 1992: 89/79).

Martin's Negotiation model is closer to dialogue in the real world. It enables identification of different types of conversational exchanges based on a functional interpretation of their exchange structures. It also enables – through an introduction of the concepts of 'move complex' and 'dependency' into the exchange structure – a description of the process of real-life dialogue in both synoptic and dynamic terms. However, as his dynamic description is subsumed into the synoptic description of the exchange structure, it does not apply to the global structure of a text. Besides, as Martin (1992: 76) admits, his model 'is especially weak in the area of turn-taking', which is most obvious where dependency structures or move complexes are involved (see the examples above). And his modular strategy in building up discourse semantics forces him to set aside as far as possible the logical, textual and experiential metafunctions when concerned with interpersonal meanings. Yet how to integrate semantic systems associated with different metafunctions into the dynamic description of the process of a dialogue remains an issue, especially where the ideational content of the dialogue becomes more complicated than that in a service encounter or a dialogue in a primary school classroom.

3.2.3 Eggins and Slade's Interactivity model

Eggins and Slade (1997: Ch. 5) offer a framework for analysing the process of unfolding exchanges in casual conversation. The framework is here referred to as Interactivity because it is said to be designed for the purpose of analysing 'interactivity', namely, patterns of conversation that are jointly constructed by the interactants and at the same time enable the interactants to adjust their alignment or distance and hence to establish and/or maintain their social identities and interpersonal relations.

Actually, the so-called Interactivity model is an expansion of the Speech Function system proposed by Halliday and further developed by Martin (as reviewed above). Since Eggins and Slade are interested in casual conversation, which is not motivated towards completion, they are not much concerned with how exchanges vary according to how they open and close, as Berry and Martin are. Instead, they are concerned with how an exchange continues before another opening move occurs, so that the exchange structure is merely 'one opening move followed by all related continuing and sustaining moves' (ibid.: 222). Therefore, they place emphasis on the responding speech functions rather than the initiating ones. Figure 3.5 is a brief summary of their Interactivity system.

While the Open system here is largely inherited from Halliday's and Martin's model, the Sustain system is new, and the React system within the latter is in fact an enormous system network composed of more than 30 different subclasses of supporting and confronting speech functions[8] (for details see ibid.: 195–213). Meanwhile, Eggins and Slade relate each speech function upward to its 'discourse purpose' (i.e. speech role) and downward to its 'congruent mood' (i.e. grammar). For example, 'offer' is defined as intended to give goods and services and realized by modulated interrogative, and 'disagree' as intended to provide negative response to question and

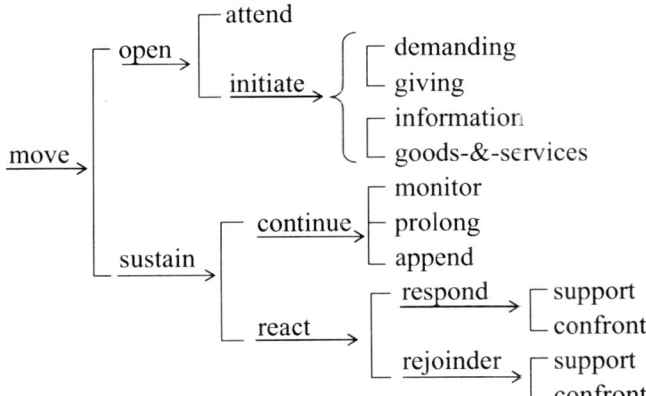

FIGURE 3.5 A summary of Eggins and Slade's Interactivity system

realized by negation of proposition. As such, their model is not only a resource for negotiating relationships of support and confrontation, but also a framework for analysing multi-stratally the process of unfolding exchanges in a text.

Regarding the speech function analysis of texts, Eggins and Slade propose two perspectives: synoptic and dynamic. Synoptically, the analysis can be done by quantifying choices of various speech functions per interactant, which will reveal the kind of role the person plays in the interaction, such as an initiator, a reactor, a supporter or a challenger. Dynamically, the analysis can be done by tracing the choices of speech functions throughout an unfolding text, which will lead to identification of all exchanges in the text as well as a functional account of each exchange, which in turn will reveal the interpersonal relationships being constructed through 'interactivity'. Eggins and Slade also claim that a dynamic interpretation of discourse structure can be achieved through an exchange-by-exchange analysis of the text.

The Interactivity model is a significant attempt to apply Halliday's Speech Function system to the analysis of real-life spoken discourse. Particularly, the model is characterized by **subclassification** of speech functions according to their role in the context, which not only enables an analysis of how various types of moves sequence into interpersonal patterns during the interactive process of casual conversation, but also points to a way of modelling interactive patterns of a specific text type. Additionally, the model allows interactive patterns to emerge out of speech function choices instead of setting ahead of time a few exchange structures for a dialogue to fit into, which is of course more suitable for analyses of real-life conversation. Furthermore, being multi-stratal, the model can be applied either 'from above' or 'from below'.

However, as the Interactivity model is designed for casual conversation, which is motivated essentially by interpersonal goals, the model is not equally applicable to spoken discourse in general, especially where complicated ideational and textual goals are involved, such as in EFL classroom discourse. To analyse lengthy, multi-move turns merely in terms of speech functions may not work, while an exchange-by-exchange interpretation of discourse structure will hardly reveal complicated patterns such as topic development. Thus how to combine dynamic descriptions of ideational, textual and interpersonal meanings, again, remains an unanswered question.

3.3 Models of classroom discourse

Classroom discourse is one of the discourse types most widely studied.[9] Reviewed in this section are only major models of classroom discourse within the SFL tradition, which also describe the process of text in structural-functional terms.

3.3.1 Sinclair and Coulthard's rank-scale model

Sinclair and Coulthard (1975, 1992) offer a model of classroom discourse that is often seen as a pioneering effort in the area. They were actually attempting a descriptive apparatus that would cope with all types of spoken discourse, but started with classroom discourse and based their study on the linguistic theory of Firth (1957; see also Palmer 1968), particularly as further developed by Halliday in his early scale-and-category grammar (Halliday 1961; Halliday and McIntosh 1966). So their model is sometimes characterized as a 'structuralist-functionalist' approach to conversation (see Taylor and Cameron 1987).

The 'structuralist' side of the model can be seen from the way Sinclair and Coulthard describe classroom discourse, i.e. in the form of a 'rank scale' – with its usual hierarchical implications (units at all ranks except the lowest can be defined in terms of a structure composed of units at the rank below). They recognize five ranks of classroom discourse (from the highest downward): lesson, transaction, exchange, move and act. See Table 3.3 for a summary of the discourse structures of units at all ranks except the lowest as described by Sinclair and Coulthard. In this table, following Hasan (1985), the caret sign indicates sequence and brackets indicate optionality; while a slash is used to indicate an alternative (same hereinafter).

Sinclair and Coulthard do not treat these ranks equally. They define 'lesson' briefly and vaguely. As for 'transaction', they specify its structure but not how an unlimited number of teaching exchanges are ordered. What they describe extensively and explicitly is 'exchange' and 'move', so that the former becomes the substantial structure of classroom discourse and the latter the minimal free

Table 3.3 A summary of the structures of lesson, transaction, exchange and move

discourse unit	discourse structure
lesson	an unordered series of transactions
transaction	Boundary$^\wedge$ Teaching ^{n} $^\wedge$ (Boundary)
exchange	Boundary: (Frame$^\wedge$) (Focus) Teaching: Initiation$^\wedge$ (Response$^\wedge$) (Feedback)
move	Frame: marker$^\wedge$ silent pause Focus: (marker$^\wedge$) (starter$^\wedge$) metastatement / conclusion$^\wedge$ (comment) Initiation: 1. (marker$^\wedge$) (starter$^\wedge$) elicitation / directive / informative / check$^\wedge$ (prompt / clue$^\wedge$) (cue / bid$^\wedge$) (nomination) 2. (cue / bid$^\wedge$) (nomination$^\wedge$) (starter$^\wedge$) elicitation /directive /informative /check Response: (acknowledge$^\wedge$) reply / react / acknowledge$^\wedge$ (comment) Feedback: (accept$^\wedge$) (evaluate$^\wedge$) (comment)

interactive unit, since acts making up a move are mostly bound units, as can be seen in the following teaching exchange (in IRF structure).

Initiation   Teacher: John [nomination], what's the capital of France
                             [elicitation]?
Response   Pupil: Paris [reply].
Feedback   Teacher: Paris [accept], that's right [evaluate].

The 'functionalist' side of the model can be seen from both the functional labels assigned to discourse units at various ranks, and the relationship between the discourse function of acts and their grammatical realizations. Sinclair and Coulthard relate the 21 acts they have identified to four clause types: declarative, interrogative, imperative and moodless. Where there is a lack of match between discourse and grammar, they bring in the notion of 'situation', which enables knowledge about schools, classrooms or a particular moment in a lesson to reclassify items already labelled by grammar into such 'situational categories' as statement, question and command (comparable to speech functions); so that an interrogative can be either a question or a command, depending on the situation. Besides, they bring in the notion of 'tactics', which enables syntagmatic patterns of discourse to reclassify items already classified by 'situation' futher into different categories; so that a question in an initiating move can be either a starter or an elicitation, depending on its syntagmatic position in discourse.

Obviously, this 'structuralist-functionalist' model demonstrates at least two strengths in describing the process of classroom discourse. First, by representing text structure as a rank scale, the model allows integration of the local structure (exchange) into the global structure (transaction). Second, by relating acts to their grammatical realizations, the model operates on the strata of both semantics and grammar, offering a rigorous framework for describing classroom discourse 'from below'; and through the notion of 'situation', the model incorporates the context (informally, though) into the descriptive framework, offering explanations for some of the acts 'from above'.

However, this model cannot be said to be multi-stratal in a full sense, since only units at the lowest rank of discourse are interpreted from the perspective of the context of situation.[10] Nor can the model be considered as multi-functional. Even if the transaction structure may be informally deemed textual and the exchange structure interpersonal (see Turner 1987), the experiential meanings are basically ignored in the model. And the logical meanings, such as those treated by Halliday (2004) as continuatives (e.g., *well*, *OK*, etc.) or as logico-semantic relationships (e.g. [reply ^ comment] in a response), are all treated as acts forming a move structure. In this way, the ideational meanings are incorporated into the interpersonal structure of a move, which not only blurs the distinction between move and act (e.g. 'answering' vs. 'reply'), but also puts too much pressure on the move structure. So how to integrate different types of meaning into the description of text as process remains a question.

3.3.2 Berry's exchange structure model

Immediately following its appearance, Sinclair and Coulthard's model was applied, adapted and extended – most notably by Burton (1978; 1980; 1981), Coulthard and Brazil (1981), and Berry (1981a, b, c; 1987). Berry has extended the model, particularly the exchange structure, in two directions by following Halliday's (1978) socio-semiotic theory of language.

The first direction has to do with multi-functionality. Arguing that an account of discourse in terms of a single linear structure does not show similarities and differences between texts, Berry (1981a, b, c) proposes a 'multi-layered' approach to the exchange structure, by describing the exchange structure in terms of interpersonal, ideational and textual meanings simultaneously.

Interpersonally, Berry classifies what is being exchanged into two categories: information and action; and the speech roles (x) related with both categories also into two types: the primary knower (k1) who already knows the information as against the secondary knower (k2) to whom the information is imparted, and the primary actor (a1) who is going to carry out the action as against the secondary actor (a2) who is getting the other person to carry out the action. For both information and action exchanges, Berry identifies a 4-slot exchange structure potential – ((dx1) ^ x2) ^ x1 ^ (x2f) – with one obligatory move and three optional ones. This is clearly an extension of Sinclair and Coulthard's 3-move IRF structure. More importantly, it enables Berry to distinguish two kinds of exchanges, namely, those initiated by x1 and by x2, which Berry calls respectively A-event (about which A knows but B does not) and B events (about which B knows but A does not), following Labov (1972; Labov and Fanshel 1977). As such, the model can be used to reveal similarities and differences among exchanges in classroom discourse. For example:

A-event (1)	dk1	In England, which cathedral has the tallest spire?
	k2	Is it Salisbury?
	k1	Yes.
	k2f	Oh.
A-event (2)	k1	Salisbury is the cathedral with the tallest spire in England.
	k2f	Oh.
B-event	k2	Do you know which cathedral in England has the tallest spire?
	k1	Salisbury.

The ideational structure of an exchange, according to Berry (1981a), is concerned with the amount of information in an exchange, and the minimum amount is a 'completed proposition'. She identifies three structural elements: (1) propositional completion (pc), which conveys the information; (2) propositional base (pb), which provides the basis for and predicts pc; (3) propositional support (ps), which supports the pc. The structure is represented as (pb) ^ pc ^ (ps). For action exchanges, p is replaced by a(ction). The textual structure, on the other hand, is much simpler, concerned merely with turns and represented as ai^ bi^ aii^ bii ... an^ bn, which is the same for both types of exchange. So, the above example of A-event (1) can now be assigned both an ideational and a textual structure:

A-event (1)   pb   ai   In England, which cathedral has the tallest spire?
              pc   bi   Is it Salisbury?
              ps   aii Yes.
                   bii Oh.

But it should be pointed out that such an ideational structure mainly has to do with negotiation of a proposition, and the textual structure has to do with turn-taking. So they are both handled by Halliday (1994, 2004) in the Speech Function system.

The second direction in which Berry has extended Sinclair and Coulthard's model has to do with multi-stratality. Pointing out that their model fails to relate facts about the structure of classroom discourse to the social context, Berry (1987) proposes to relate discourse features to relevant social roles. She chooses three facts: 3-move exchanges, evaluates, and frames; and tries to find distinctive features of the teacher's role that will predict and account for the presence of these facts. She then identifies three features of the teacher's role, some of which are shared by a doctor in doctor-patient interviews and/or a chairman in committee talks (see Table 3.4 for a summary of the relations between the three role features and the three discourse features). She argues that these role features can be used both to analyse the concept of 'teacher', and to predict the distribution of different discourse features in different social contexts.

Table 3.4   A summary of role features relatable to discourse features

role feature	expected behavior	role	acquired role feature	discourse feature
(1) +HIGHER	be in control of the discourse; be responsible for marking off stages in the discourse	teacher doctor chairman	(1)	frame
(2) +PRIMARY KNOWER	have greater knowledge about the general field	teacher doctor	(1) (2)	initiate 3-move exchanges
(3) +primary knower	have greater knowledge about propositional content of exchange	teacher	(1) (2) (3)	evaluate

This approach to text-context relationship certainly helps to link interpersonal features of discourse with features of the social role of the speaker (i.e. tenor of discourse), which in turn enables a multi-stratal account of discourse. Besides, it offers an explanation for the behaviours entailed by being a teacher, which is clearly relevant in the educational context, including the EFL teaching context.

3.3.3 Christie's curriculum genre model

Christie's (1997, 2002) model of classroom discourse is both linguistic and sociological, in line with a concern within the SFL school about the role of discourse in constructing values and ideologies in a given culture (e.g. Martin 1992; Fairclough 1992; Lemke 1995). In fact, her model is built upon both SFL – in particular Martin's genre model and Halliday's Functional Grammar – and the sociological theories on pedagogic discourse by Bernstein (1986, 1990, 1996).

Following Bernstein's view that schools are an agency of symbolic control that shapes consciousness through pedagogic discourse, Christie views classroom discourse as social practice that shapes consciousness through shaping pedagogic subject positions. And following Martin, who explains social processes in terms of genre, she proposes to examine classroom discourse as 'curriculum genre', defining it as 'staged goal-driven activities devoted to the accomplishment of significant educational ends' (2002: 22). She describes a curriculum genre in terms of its schematic structure, which she considers to be more suitable than the IRF structure, as the latter cannot be equally revealing about the social meanings constructed. Meanwhile, she proposes to describe elements of the schematic structure in terms of language choices relatable to the three metafunctions. For example, in her analysis of an early childhood curriculum genre called 'morning news', Christie (1997) identifies six structural elements: [Lesson Initiation^ Morning News Nomination^ (Morning News Greeting^) Morning News Giving^ Morning News Finis^ Lesson Closure]; and she describes Lesson Initiation as follows:

Textual:	textual theme *okay* (a continuative that features teacher talk at initiation or closure); teacher monologue
Experiential:	repetition of lexical items (e.g. *manners*); relational process of attribution (e.g. *manners are very very important*)
Interpersonal:	declarative mood (children are obliged to listen); imperative (softened by *please*); modal Adjuncts

Thus Christie's curriculum genre model can also be viewed as a culture-meaning-wording approach to texts, although her approach to meaning is different from that of Martin and Rose (2003). She does not apply in her analysis those discourse semantic systems as set up by Martin (1992), but applies Halliday's Functional Grammar instead. Moreover, she applies Halliday's notion of register (as subsystem), grouping all lexicogrammatical choices found in classroom discourse into two registers: regulative and instructional. Following Bernstein (1986, 1990), she defines the two registers as follows:

> ... regulative register refers to sets of language choices which are principally involved in establishing goals for teaching-learning activities, and with fostering and maintaining the direction of the activities until the achievement of the goals ... instructional register refers to language choices in which the knowledge and associated skills being taught are realized. (Christie 1997: 136)

In this sense, the language choices in Lesson Initiation as given above can be said to belong to the regulative register, which is foregrounded in this element for the purpose of creating a sense of acceptable behaviour for the coming activity. So, Christie's concept of 'register' is not entirely the same as Halliday's. On the one hand, the two registers she has identified can be viewed as subsystems since they cover a range of lexicogrammatical options organized around the three metafunctions and associated with a given situation type. On the other hand, they are distinguished according to their difference in pedagogic purposes rather than in FTM values. This raises the theoretical question of how to explain the existence of two registers – and most probably two sets of FTM values as well – within one single text.

Christie also argues that the regulative register (RR) and instructive register (IR) operate in all curriculum genres. Sometimes they are singly foregrounded in a specific structural element, and sometimes they converge in the same element. A typical pattern of their operation can be shown as follows (adapted from descriptions in Christie 1997: 149):

RR^   RR/IR   ^   IR   ^   RR/IR   ^   IR (RR tacit)

As can be seen, RR is dominant, especially in the initiating stage, but may not need explicit expression by the end of a genre when the pedagogic subjects are already on track. Besides, the changing of registers tends to correlate with the unfolding of the stages of a genre. This is why Christie says 'the elements of structure are built through changing sets of register choices' (ibid.: 158). In other words, it is the operation of the two registers in a patterned way, along with their different lexicogrammatical realizations, that constructs the various stages of a specific curriculum genre. In this sense, Christie's model is multi-stratal, although like Martin and Rose (2003) she does not explain the relationship between a curriculum genre and the context of situation. The model can also be said to be multi-functional since both RR and IR are described as metafunctionally organized.

3.4 Summary

In this chapter, a few relevant and influential models pertaining to text as process are reviewed in the light of the SFL architecture of language. While the models all follow the structural-functional tradition of SFL in their approach to text as process, they differ in focus owing to variations in the aim of the researchers and in the theoretical perspective thus taken. Some focus on the global structure of text and take the structure as either semantic or contextual; others focus on the local structure; still others try to combine the global with the local structure. Besides, while most of the models explain text structure from the perspective of context, their interpretations of the context vary, and so do their treatment of such inherent features of the text as multi-stratality and multi-functionality. Table 3.5 is a summary of all models reviewed above (brackets indicate what is not true to its label in a strictly SFL sense; grey background indicates unsystematic treatment).

Clearly, these models display both similarities and differences. In terms of similarities, two groups can be identified: (1) the models of genre by Martin and Christie, which take the global structure of text as the structural realization of a cultural/institutional system; (2) the models of speech function by Halliday, Martin, and Eggins and Slade, which take the local structure of a spoken text as the realization of interpersonal meanings that in turn realize the tenor of discourse.

The models in the first group are concerned with the process of a whole text, offering multi-stratal and multi-functional descriptions of patterns of staging in the text; although Martin focuses on the semantic patterns throughout the text (i.e. discourse semantics) while Christies focuses on semantic features (i.e. registers) characterizing various elements of the schematic structure. Because they both consider text structure as driven by a social purpose rather than by a configuration of FTM, they explain meanings by reference to the role of text in furthering institutional (e.g. business, educational) goals rather than in constructing FTM values. In other words, they take text as the **realization** of the context of culture; whereas Halliday views text as an **instantiation** of a register and the **realization** of a situation type, and the situation type as an instantiation of the context of culture. So this group, while providing practical frameworks for analysing text structure, is theoretically deviant from the SFL architecture. It has raised but has not answered the following questions:

1. If text structure is associated with the context of culture as Martin thinks, how to relate the various structural elements to FTM?
2. If a text type is associated with only one register as Halliday says, how to explain the co-existence of two registers in one text type as discovered by Christie?
3. If register resources have a role to play in the dynamic process of a text as Christie shows, how to represent such resources as a dynamic potential?

Table 3.5 A summary of the reviewed models of text as process

	models reviewed	context	multi-stratality sem.	gram.	multi-functionality id.	int.	tex.	text as process global structure	local structure
genre	Hasan	configuration of FTM	√		(√)		√	semantic	
genre	Martin	social purpose	√	√	√	√	√	contextual	
genre	Swales	communicative purposes	(√)	(√)	(√)		(√)	rhetorical (semantic)	move / step
spoken discourse	Halliday	tenor	√	√		√			move
spoken discourse	Martin	tenor	√	√		√			exchange/move
spoken discourse	Eggins and Slade	tenor	√	√		√		exchange-by-exchange	exchange/move
spoken discourse	Sinclair and Coulthard	(situation)	√	√	(√)	(√)	(√)	transaction–exchange–move	
spoken discourse	Berry	role features	√	√	(√)	√	(√)		exchange/move
classroom discourse	Christie	educational ends	√	√	√	√	√	contextual	

Those models in the second group, on the other hand, are concerned with the process of a spoken text locally, offering multi-stratal accounts of how speech moves are realized in grammar and how they sequence into interactive patterns in a dialogue. While Halliday's Speech Function system serves as a theoretical foundation, its development and extension by Martin and by Eggins and Slade provide frameworks that more readily and more explicitly describe real-life conversational exchanges, apart from explaining how talk can construct social reality. Berry's exchange model may also be included in this group since it is essentially interpersonal in spite of her proposal for a multi-layered approach. This group further proves that the semantic patterns of an unfolding text can be explained both 'from above' and 'from below'. But as these models focus only on the interpersonal metafunction, they take move as the basic unit of analysis without giving answers to such questions as:

1. Do local interactive patterns composed of moves serve to compose the global structure of text, and if so, how?
2. If multi-functionality is an inherent feature of text, how to integrate ideational and textual patterns with interpersonal patterns when describing the dynamic unfolding of a text?

Not mentioned in either group are the models by Hasan, Swales, and Sinclair and Coulthard. Hasan's genre model is also concerned with the process of whole texts, just like those in the first group, but differs from them in that Hasan views text structure as a semantic structure expressing a text's role in its context of situation. Her model becomes weak when detached from grammar, and she has not answered the following questions:

1. If text structure is a semantic structure, how to integrate interpersonal meanings into the structure?
2. When variations of FTM are identified in relation to a single text, how to explain their relationship with GSP and with specific elements in a GSP?

Sinclair and Coulthard's model differs from all others in that it combines the global structure with the local structure of texts, allowing a focus on patterns of the whole text as well as the intermediate patterns. This feature of their model seems more or less shared by Swales' genre analysis model. However, the mechanisms linking the global with the local structures are revealed neither in Swales' nor in Sinclair and Coulthard's model.

All in all, the models reviewed in this chapter have brought insights into the issue of text as process which this study is concerned with. Some of them will serve as part of the basis upon which a number of theoretical assumptions are made before a new model is proposed (see Chapter 4). Many others, especially those of spoken discourse in general and classroom discourse in particular, will be drawn upon in one way or another in the course of establishing dynamic systems of EFL classroom discourse (see Chapters 6, 7 and 8). Nevertheless, these models have left unexplored quite a number of questions concerning the modelling of text as process, especially when viewed in the light of the SFL architecture of language. It is these questions that have brought about a great many efforts of further enquiry into the issue, which have led to the development of a new model of text as process, that is, the TEXT TYPE model.

Chapter 4

Development of the TEXT TYPE Model

As seen in Chapter 3, text as process has been approached within the SFL school generally by following its structural-functional tradition. It has been described in terms of either the global or the local structure of texts, with explanations being given from the perspective of the context. However, as those structural descriptions must go beyond the level of **clause**, where Functional Grammar has proved to be a sufficient tool, uncertainties arise as to (1) how to use the same tool at the level of **text**, (2) how to relate the structure of texts simultaneously to the three metafunctions and to the various strata of language, and (3) how to represent the structural descriptions as a dynamic as well as a synoptic subpotential. These uncertainties apparently have to be solved before any further substantial efforts can be made to properly model text as process.

In this chapter, a number of theoretical assumptions are first made as an attempt to solve the above-mentioned uncertainties, and then a new model of text as process called TEXT TYPE is proposed based on the assumptions, followed by a description of the specific method of analysing text as process as suggested by the new model.

4.1 Theoretical assumptions

The theoretical assumptions made here are concerned with the nature of text as process, the method of describing text as process, and the way to represent the description as a subpotential. They are based on the SFL philosophy of language (explored in Chapter 2), on insights drawn from some of the existing models of text as process (reviewed in Chapter 3), and on a few concepts newly developed in SFL.

4.1.1 Nature of text as process

Assumption 1: Text as process can be viewed as the semantic structure of text.

As indicated by the philosophical framework of SFL, language is **functional** as it is a lower-order semiotic system, while culture is the higher-level semiotic system. As such, language is a mode of expressing social meanings, or a means to an end – although the end and means actually co-exist (that is, they realize each other). In this light, the term 'semantic', which is used interchangeably with 'functional' in SFL, is by no means associated with such concepts as sense and reference, denotation and connotation, and so on. Instead, it is equivalent to creating, making or constructing meanings by means of language – or simply 'languaging', as Halliday (1985a: 7) phrases it. The linguistic system is called a semantic system because it can be used to construct meanings as defined by a given culture, while text is called a semantic unit because it is produced to construct meanings as defined by a given situation type.

It is in this special sense as defined in SFL that the term 'semantic' is used in the first assumption made here. That is, text as process is, first of all, viewed as **semantic** in nature, just as text itself is viewed as semantic in nature. Then, following the structural-functional tradition of SFL, as well as drawing on Hasan's (1985) semantic perspective on text structure (see 3.1.1 above), it is assumed that text as process can be described in structural terms – as the **semantic structure of text**. In other words, text structure is at the semantic stratum: it is the semantic structure of all texts embedded in the same situation type, motivated by specific values of FTM and at the same time realized in lexicogrammar.

There have been two different positions within the SFL school regarding the actual stratum that text structure should be mapped onto (see 3.1 above). Martin's position is that text structure be elevated to the stratum of the context of culture and be defined as the process of a social activity. This position easily incurs theoretical uncertainties regarding the culture-situation relationship, which is evident in Martin's culture-meaning-wording analysis of texts. Hasan's position, on the other hand, is that text structure be mapped onto the semantic stratum and be defined as an expression of the specific values of a given situation type. The latter position is adopted here, because it is held that the context of situation, being an instance of the context of culture, does not exclude the process of a social activity. As a configuration of FTM, a situation type necessarily includes the actual process of a particular social activity (field), along with the kind of role relationship involved in the activity (tenor) and the role of language in the situation (mode). When summarizing the differences between dialect and register, Halliday clearly states that 'register reflects social order in sense of social *process* (types of social activity)' whereas 'dialect reflects social order in sense of social *structure* (type of social hierarchy)' (1985b: 43, original emphasis). The questions that need to be further answered include: how to describe phases of meanings in an unfolding text in terms of the three metafunctions simultaneously, how to relate the meanings to their lexicogrammatical realizations, and how to explain variations of FTM associated with different phases of meaning in the same text, especially texts whose mode is constitutive rather than ancillary.

Such inter-stratal as well as inter-metafunctional relations are not very well handled in Hasan's model of text structure, nor are they fully explained in any other models as reviewed in Chapter 3. Here, guided by the first theoretical assumption, i.e. *text as process can be viewed as a semantic structure*, those relations will be addressed first through other assumptions to be made in the rest of Section 4.1, then through the TEXT TYPE model to be proposed based on all of the assumptions, and finally through the method of text analysis as suggested by the TEXT TYPE model.

4.1.2 Description of text as process

Assumption 2: The semantic structure of text can be described as a pattern of logogenetic patterns.

'Logogenesis' is a concept more recently developed by Halliday and Matthiessen (1999) and further interpreted by Halliday (2004). Halliday and Matthiessen (1999: Ch. 1) stress that meaning is constructed in grammar, and propose to view the meaning potential of language as the outcome of the processes by which meanings are constructed in grammar, called 'semogenic processes'. They recognize three time frames of the semogenic processes: (1) phylogenetic, i.e. the evolution of human language; (2) ontogenetic, i.e. the development of the individual speaker; (3) logogenetic, i.e. the unfolding of the act of meaning itself. That is to say, phylogenesis takes place in the maximum time frame, during which grammar emerged to create meaning and keeps expanding the meaning potential by grammaticalizing more and more meanings. Ontogenesis takes place in a shorter time frame, during which an individual's meaning repertoire expands from a bi-stratal protolanguage system gradually into the multi-stratal system of the community. Logogenesis takes place in the shortest time frame, during which choices from within the grammatical systems are made successively until a complete unit of meaning, i.e. a text, is formed.

The concept of **logogenesis** is particularly relevant here, because it highlights at least two points. First, text is the outcome of the process of meanings being created through instantiation of the grammatical systems. Secondly, instantiation should be viewed as actual processes that 'are explicitly located in time' and 'unfold in time' (Halliday and Mattiessen 1999: 382), that is, as processes that take place along with the unfolding of the text. Therefore, instantiation is not merely the process of one systemic option turned into one actual choice; it is also the processes by which a system is turned into a succession of choices that show up one after another as the text unfolds in time. As Halliday further says:

> . . . it [the concept of logogenesis] allows us to explore how *local* grammatical selections accumulate to create logogenetic patterns that become part of the **systemic history** of an unfolding text . . . we can identify phases of selections within such logogenetic patterns; and we can then match them up with contextual and semantic structures of a more global nature. (Halliday 2004: 531; original emphasis)

This further suggests that the concept of logogenesis can be used to talk about the semantic structure of text (i.e. text as process): the successive grammatical choices in a text will create logogenetic patterns, which in turn are relatable to phases of meaning in the global structure of the text. What is more, although the concept stresses the ongoing process of the systems being instantiated in a text within a time frame, it does not change the nature of instantiation. Since the successive grammatical choices that create a logogenetic pattern all come from the same metafunctionally organized system of a language, and since the grammatical, semantic and contextual strata of the system all co-exist, the ongoing process of instantiation must also be multi-functional and multi-stratal. As Halliday (2004: 530) further says, 'Logogenesis pertains to the entire meaning potential – all the strata and all the metafunctions.' In this sense, the concept of logogenesis, when used to talk about the semantic structure of text, will not incur theoretical uncertainties regarding the inter-stratal and inter-metafunctional relations as defined in the SFL architecture of language.

Thus by drawing on the concept of logogenesis, it is here assumed that the semantic structure of text can be described in terms of logogenetic patterns formed by successive choices from the grammatical system. Matthiessen (2002a: 94) also points out, 'For any text we analyse, the process can be reconstructed out of an analysis of the product by showing how successive selections within the linguistic system form patterns.' Moreover, since all the strata and all metafunctions are inevitably involved in the description, it is further assumed that logogenetic patterns found within different strata and different metafunctions would co-articulate certain kinds of common logogenetic patterns in a text, so that eventually *the semantic structure of text can be described as a pattern of logogenetic patterns.*

A further question that arises now would be how to analyse logogenetic patterns that are formed by successive choices from the grammatical system. If a clause-based grammatical analysis does not readily work in the description of text structure, will it work in the description of logogenetic patterns? So here comes the third assumption.

4.1.3 Grammatical analysis of text as process

Assumption 3: Logogenetic patterns can be analysed grammatically in terms of UNIVARIATE.

While explaining the relationships among components of the semantic system as seen 'from below', Halliday (1978) points out that the logical component is distinct in that it is realized through **univariate** structures whereas the experiential, interpersonal and textual components are all realized through **multivariate** structures (for details see ibid.: 129–31). That is to say, when those different types of meaning are realized in lexicogrammar, two kinds of structure can be distinguished.

1. The univariate structure, which realizes the logical meaning, is a structure involving one single variable that recurs one or more times, hence also called a 'recursive' structure. It is found at the rank of clause complex, with the clause functioning as univariate.
2. The multivariate structure, which realizes the experiential, interpersonal and textual meanings, is a structure involving several variables that each have a distinct function with respect to the whole and hence occur only once, thus also called a 'non-recursive' (or constituent) structure. It is found at the rank of clause (or group), with elements within the clause (or group) functioning as multivariate.

It is held here that the two kinds of structure imply two different methods of grammatical analysis. One focuses on how grammatical choices serve as elements within the multivariate structure of a clause; the other focuses on how grammatical choices enable clauses themselves to sequence into a univariate structure. And it is the latter method that is relevant here, in that the successive choices forming logogenetic patterns can now be defined as UNIVARIATE – capitalized to indicate that Halliday's notion of univariate has been stretched.

Whereas Halliday uses the term univariate to refer to successive clauses combined through 'interdependency' or 'taxis' (see Halliday 1994, 2004 for details) into a clause complex, the term UNIVARIATE is here used to refer to a particular grammatical choice that recurs in successive clauses to form a **logogenetic pattern** and hence link all these clauses into a semantic phase. Taking a simple example from EFL classroom discourse in an Intensive Reading class (for more, see discussions in Part II of this book), the choice of material process (e.g. *get, pass, stand, arrive*) being repeated in a number of clauses in succession creates a logogenetic pattern of 'event', which in turn helps to define this span of text as a phase of story retelling; while the choice of relational process (e.g. *be, mean, suggest, imply*) being repeated in another span of text creates a logogenetic pattern of 'elaboration', which in turn helps to define this text span as a phase of linguistic explanation. In other words, under the notion of UNIVARIATE, a number of clauses can be viewed as related, not because a conjunction can be found between them, but because a pattern of meaning choices – i.e. a logogenetic pattern – can be detected across these clauses.

The real significance of the notion of UNIVARIATE lies in the fact that it enables an examination of grammatical choices, not as multivariate coming from several **different** systems to make up the semantic structure of a clause (e.g. transitivity structure), but as UNIVARIATE coming from the **same** system to link successive clauses into a logogenetic pattern with a particular meaning feature (e.g. 'event' or 'elaboration'). And the logogenetic patterns, as such, not only construct meanings locally in different text spans, but also in effect form semantic phases functional in the global semantic structure of a text (e.g. phases of story-telling and linguistic explanation in an Intensive Reading class). Thus based on the newly developed notion of UNIVARIATE, it is assumed that *logogenetic patterns can be analysed grammatically in terms of UNIVARIATE.*

4.1.4 Representation of text as process

Assumption 4: Text as process can be represented as a dynamic subpotential in system-structure terms.

So far, it is assumed that text as process can be viewed as the *semantic structure of text* that can be described in terms of *logogenetic patterns* that can be analysed lexicogrammatically in terms of *UNIVARIATE*. The question left unanswered is how to represent the description of text as process.

There have been a number of ways of representing the global structure of text in the SFL school. For example, Hasan (see 3.1.2 above) uses a structure formula, and Ventola (1984; 1987; 1989) uses a flow chart. The latter can better accommodate real-time happenings such as recursions, abortions, and so on; but it can also be overwhelming in size. It is held here that a system-structure representation has an advantage, in that a system only specifies the 'order' but not the actual 'sequence' of the structural elements (see Halliday 1966), so its size will not be so overwhelming and yet it leaves enough room for any possible real-time flows of meaning.

In fact, SFL has a system-structure tradition initiated by Firth, who holds that 'the first principle of linguistics is to distinguish between system and structure' (Firth in Palmer 1968: 200). While 'system' is defined in terms of paradigmatic relations, as a network of interrelated sets of options for making meanings (hence called meaning potential or a resource for making meanings), 'structure' is defined in terms of syntagmatic relations, as the realization of the systemic options in the form of a constituent structure. In other words, system is the potential while structure is its realization: the two are inseparable (though system is given priority in SFL, hence 'systemic' linguistics). Drawing on the system-structure tradition of SFL, it is assumed here that *text as process can be represented in system-structure terms* – that is, as a **system** (network) of logogenetic patterns, with the systemic options being realized in the semantic phases that constitute elements in the semantic **structure** of the text.

This system is considered as a **dynamic** system. For one thing, the system is made up of logogenetic patterns that are identified in an unfolding text and defined by successive selections from the system. For another, the structural realization of a system of logogenetic patterns is found at the text level, extending over the entire text. In contrast, the structural realization of a system of grammar is found at the clause/group level, restrained within a grammatical element. Thus the former kind of structure is the semantic structure of text, revealing the dynamic process of meaning creation in an unfolding text; whereas the latter kind is the semantic structure of clause/group, revealing the static meaning features in a finished text. In this sense, the former is dynamic, whereas the latter is synoptic.

The system of logogenetic patterns is also considered as a **subpotential**. Halliday and Matthiessen (1999: 384–5) point out that 'logogenesis builds up a version of the system that is particular to the text being generated.' That is, the ongoing process of instantiation will result in an 'instantial system' specific to the text in question. However, as text is an instance of a register and a register is instantiated in a text type, the instantial system specific to one text but repeated in many other texts of the same type will inevitably lead to a system specific to a text type or register. Halliday states:

> The logogenetic patterns that emerge as a text unfolds form a **transient system** that is specific to that text; but from repeated patterns over many such transient systems may in turn emerge a **generalized system** characteristic of a certain type of text or register. (Halliday 2004: 586; emphasis added)

Thus a system of logogenetic patterns may be transient at first, as it results from an analysis of the UNIVARIATEs found in an individual text. But through repeated analyses of many texts of the same type, the transient systems of the texts can be generalized into a system common to the text type. And this generalized system is in fact the system of a register, i.e. a subpotential. In this sense, the successive UNIVARIATEs forming logogenetic patterns in texts should be considered as choices made from within a given register rather than the overall linguistic system, that is, from a subpotential rather than the entire meaning potential. So the assumption in full will be: *Text as process can be represented as a dynamic subpotential in system-structure terms.*

4.2 The TEXT TYPE model

Based on the theoretical assumptions made above, a new model called TEXT TYPE is proposed here to describe text as process. Since Assumption 4 given above already raises the issue of dynamic subpotential, this section begins by drawing attention again to the notion of register – as subpotential or subsystem – in order to highlight the need for a dynamic subsystem. Then, 'register' is reinterpreted from both a synoptic and a dynamic perspective. Finally, the TEXT TYPE model is presented, along with the method of analysing text as process as suggested by the new TEXT TYPE model.

4.2.1 Register: synoptic or dynamic?

In the SFL architecture of language, register is seen as a subsystem between the overall system and text, or subpotential between the entire meaning potential and an instance; and it is defined as a configuration of meanings typically associated with a particular situation type and instantiated in the text type embedded in that situation type. Now that instantiation can be viewed as processes that take place successively along with the unfolding of a text, is it possible to interpret register in dynamic terms, or is it merely a synoptic subsystem?

Halliday has long been stressing the need for a **probabilistic** interpretation of linguistic systems (see Halliday 1991; Hu 2005), so he often defines register in probabilistic terms:

> A register is a functional variety of language – the patterns of instantiation of the overall system associated with a given type of context (a situation type). These patterns of instantiation show up quantitatively as adjustments in the systemic probabilities of language; a register can be represented as a particular setting of systemic probabilities. (Halliday 2004: 27)

When talking about the use of corpus in linguistics that makes it possible to attach probabilities[1] to options in the systems of language, he again says:

> I would define a register as being a skewing or shifting of the probabilities, because not many registers actually close off bits of the system. What they tend to do is to shift the probabilities, so it is the same system but with a different set of probabilities, not only in the vocabulary but also in the grammar. (Halliday in Thompson and Collins 2001)

In other words, register can be distinguished from the overall system, not because it is a different system, but because the same systemic options – when associated with a given context of situation – would shift their probabilities.

In line with this kind of definition, register is often interpreted **synoptically** as a set of linguistic variations that tend to occur more **frequently**[2] in texts embedded in a specific context of situation. This can be easily seen in the early register studies in the 1970s and 1980s, especially in ESP studies (see a collection of papers in Trimble et al. 1978). Also, it can be seen in the studies of the so-called varieties of language (including both registers and dialects), which started to draw attention from the ELT circle in China in the late 1980s and early 1990s (see Hou 1988; Cheng 1989; Xu 1992). Furthermore, it can be seen in the more recent corpus-based register studies (e.g. Biber and Conrad 2001). Such studies typically focus on the distributional frequencies of linguistic variations in specific registers; but they are not always adequate, as pointed out by Swales (1990).

Actually, with more attention being drawn to genre and to the global structure of text since the 1990s, questions inevitably arise as to whether register can be interpreted in dynamic terms, or simply whether the notion of register is enough for an account of the global structure of text. Here is Halliday's answer when the question was put to him (see Thompson and Collins 2001, emphasis added):

> GT – But then if we take a more practical angle, the term genre is sometimes used when you are looking at the text as a whole, without necessarily projecting right up onto the culture. Do you find a need for a term to talk about how texts utilize **register resources** within a particular overall organization or patterning?

> MAKH – I've always seen that as a part of the notion of **register**. Let me put it this way. Suppose you collect instances: if you stand at that end, then you will arrive at groupings of text types, bodies of texts that are in certain respects like each other and different from others. If you then shift your observer position to the system end, then that text type becomes a subsystem, and that's what we call register. That's the way I would see it: it's the semantic analogue of what in the context of culture would be an institution of some kind, a recognized body of cultural practice, or institutionalized cultural forms; and that semantic entity, to me, would fall within the concept of **register**.

Obviously, since Halliday always uses the term system to 'cover both system and process: both the potential and the instances that occur' (1996: 4), he is also using the term register to cover both subsystem and text type – the same thing seen from two different standpoints (i.e. from the system end as against the text end).

However, it is held here that, in order to 'talk about how texts utilize register resources within a particular overall organization or patterning', it is not enough just being able to describe systemic options that shift their probabilities in the situation type in question; it is also necessary to be able to describe the dynamic processes by which such systemic options turn into a succession of choices that show up one after another until the text is complete. In other words, it is held that register resources – which engender texts – need to be interpreted explicitly in both synoptic and dynamic terms, so as to enable a description of text both as product and as process. And it is this view that has led to the following reinterpretation of 'register'.

4.2.2 Reinterpretation of 'register'

The reinterpretation of 'register' given here is also inspired by Martin's (1985) argument for both a synoptic and a dynamic potential. Martin was first intrigued by the two sets of terms used by Hjelmslev (1961): (1) system vs. process, used with semiotic systems in general, and (2) language vs. text, used with one of the semiotic systems, i.e. language. His speculation goes as follows:

> So little is accidental in Hjelmslev that one cannot help speculating on his use of these terms to distinguish language from the semiotic systems which in general comprise our culture. Is there a sense in which linguistic manifestations are products rather than processes while the realization of other semiotics is action rather than a thing? (Martin 1985: 248)

Then he came to the conclusion that 'text' and 'process' simply reflected two different perspectives on linguistic manifestation. From a static perspective, it is 'text', i.e. a product or a thing; from an active perspective, it is 'process', i.e. an action. He points out the need for both a synoptic and a dynamic system – as 'two distinct but symbiotically interacting potentials' that generate text and process (ibid: 259). He argues that 'once any attempt at an exhaustive description is made, the need for both perspectives becomes clear' (ibid: 249), although he is aware that

> [t]he difference between the product and process perspectives is unfortunately not easy to illustrate with reference to grammar or phonology . . . This is presumably why linguists have been so happy to live without the distinction. (Ibid: 248)

And this is presumably also why Martin (1992; Martin and Rose, 2003) has made enormous efforts to reformulate lexicogrammatical systems into discourse semantic systems. As he claims, 'this kind of semantics focuses on text-size rather than clause-size meanings' (1992: 1), and it is certainly meant to accommodate the process rather than the product perspective.

Inspired by Martin's argument, it is here proposed that 'register' be reinterpreted – from two different perspectives – as two distinct but symbiotically interacting subsystems, one synoptic and the other dynamic. From a static perspective, text is a finished product that can be analysed in terms of frequencies of grammatical choices functional in clause structure, so the system generalized from transient systems of texts is a system of grammatical options that have shifted their probabilities in a given situation type. This is the **synoptic** subsystem oriented towards text as product. From an active perspective, text is an ongoing process that can be observed in terms of logogenetic patterns – formed by the same grammatical choices that now function as UNIVARIATE – that sequence the successive clauses into a semantic phase functional in text structure, so the generalized system is a system of logogenetic patterns that characterize the development of text. This is the **dynamic** subsystem oriented towards text as process. See Table 4.1 for a representation of 'register' as reinterpreted here.

Table 4.1　Reinterpretation of 'register'

perspective	text	register
static	product	synoptic subsystem
active	process	dynamic subsystem

In order to avoid confusion between register as a synoptic subsystem and as a dynamic subsystem, they are here termed respectively REGISTER and TEXT TYPE – capitalized to indicate that (1) they are both systems and (2) the two terms are defined differently from how Halliday defines them. The following are the definitions of the two new concepts:

REGISTER:　It is a system network of lexicogrammatical options that are organized metafunctionally, expressed phonologically, and associated with a certain situation type through adjusted probabilities of occurrence. It is a synoptic subsystem realized in the semantic structures of clause (or group) that are found to be common in a certain text type.

TEXT TYPE:　It is a system network of logogenetic patterns that are formed by lexicogrammatical UNIVARIATEs chosen from the REGISTER system, hence also organized metafunctionally, expressed phonologically, but associated with a certain situation type through adjusted sequences of occurrence. It is a dynamic subsystem realized in the semantic structure of text that is found to be common in a certain text type.

Obviously, the two concepts are different from what Halliday calls 'register' and 'text type'. While 'register' is here split into two systems, 'text type' is reduced to a subordinate position – referring to all texts embedded in the same situation type. The reason why Halliday's terms are retained while redefined (indicated by capitalization) is two-fold. First, both REGISTER and TEXT TYPE are here viewed as subpotential – subpotential in the same sense as defined in the SFL architecture of language; using totally different terms would hinder their association with the notion of subpotential. Second, the term 'text type' is commonly used in SFL in two senses: (1) as a theoretical construct in the SFL architecture, equivalent to 'instance type'; (2) as a type of texts identified through a shared text structure (see Hasan 1985; Martin 1984, 1985, 1999). The second sense – including such related concepts as staging, text structure, etc. – is also associated with the description of text as process, so the term TEXT TYPE is adopted in order to retain that association.

It should also be pointed out that, although the distinction between REGISTER and TEXT TYPE is influenced by Martin's argument for both a synoptic and a dynamic potential, the objective of the present study is different from Martin's.

Martin's efforts are aimed at 'potential', i.e. an overall discourse semantics that can serve as a tool in analysing any individual texts in terms of how they manifest aspects of culture (see Martin and Rose 2003: Ch. 1) – hence his culture-meaning-wording approach to text analysis; whereas the present efforts are aimed at 'subpotential', i.e. a dynamic subsystem specific to a given text type, which can be applied in the analysis of the ongoing process of all texts embedded in the same situation type. Martin's work, as he claims, 'has been pursued within the framework of critical linguistics' from the start (Martin 1992: 2); whereas this study is pursued within the framework of the SFL architecture of language as defined by Halliday and reviewed in Chapter 2 above.

4.2.3 Presentation of the TEXT TYPE model

Based on the above definitions of the two subsystems as well as the theoretical assumptions made in 4.1, a new model of text as process is now proposed within the philosophical framework of SFL, i.e. the SFL architecture of language. The model is given the name TEXT TYPE in order to highlight the process perspective as distinguished from the product perspective, which is indeed the essence of the TEXT TYPE model. See Figure 4.1 for a representation of the TEXT TYPE model (T = text).

The model can be further described through the following ten statements. Although some of them have been given earlier in this chapter either implicitly or explicitly, either in part or in whole, they are included in the following list, and are restated, for the sake of describing the model.

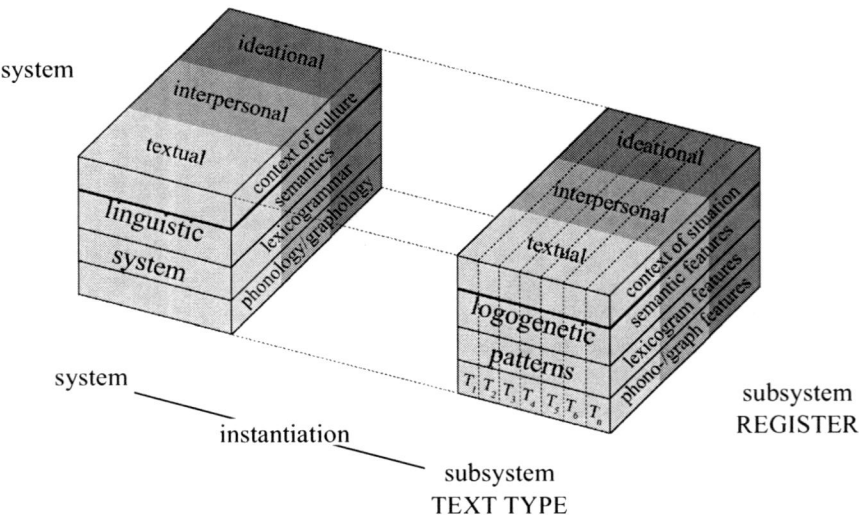

FIGURE 4.1   The TEXT TYPE model

Statements: general

1. The relationship between system and subsystem is one of instantiation. The linguistic system is a semantic system defined by the context of culture, encoded in lexicogrammar, and expressed in phonology/graphology. A subsystem is a configuration of semantic features defined by the semiotic configuration of a certain context of situation, encoded in a configuration of lexicogrammatical features, and expressed in a configuration of phonological/graphological features.

2. The relationship between subsystem and text is one of accumulation as well as instantiation. A text is also a semantic system, though a transient one, built up through instantiation of a certain subsystem and hence sharing its semantic, lexicogrammatical, and phonological/graphological features. A subsystem is generalized from repeated transient systems of texts embedded in the same context of situation, thus being common to the text type in question.

3. Instantiation can be viewed from two perspectives. From a static perspective, text is a product where the lexicogrammatical choices can be quantified, so the subsystem – generalized from many transient ones – is a system characterized by shifted probabilities of lexicogrammatical options functional in clause structure. From an active perspective, text is a succession of processes where lexicogrammatical choices can be observed as UNIVARIATE, so the generalized subsystem is characterized by meaning features of logogenetic patterns that link clauses into semantic phases functional in text structure.

4. The two subsystems seen from different perspectives, i.e. REGISTER and TEXT TYPE, are different as well as similar. Both of them instantiate the overall system and are instantiated in a text type, so they both are multi-functional and multi-stratal. But the TEXT TYPE system is oriented towards text as process, realized in the semantic structure of text; while the REGISTER system is oriented towards text as product, realized in the semantic structure of clause (or group).

5. REGISTER and TEXT TYPE interact symbiotically. REGISTER is a system of lexicogrammatical options whose probabilities of occurrence are adjusted to a certain situation type. TEXT TYPE is a system of logogenetic patterns formed by the same lexicogrammatical options – viewed as UNIVARIATEs – whose sequences of occurrence are adjusted to the unfolding of the text. The UNIVARIATEs are choices from within the REGISTER system, and the REGISTER choices are made to produce a whole text as well as clauses in the text.

Statements: operating

1. TEXT TYPE is a semantic system that can be represented as a network of logogenetic patterns pertaining to the entire meaning potential, i.e. all the metafunctions and all the strata.[3]

2. The lexicogrammatical logogenetic patterns emerge along metafunctional lines, for they are formed by the successive UNIVARIATEs in a text, i.e. choices from the REGISTER system but examined from an active (process) perspective.

3. The semantic logogenetic patterns are meaning features realized by lexicogrammatical logogenetic patterns, articulating or even co-articulating semantic phases – either within the same metafunction or across metafunctions – that are functional in the semantic structure of text.

4. The contextual logogenetic patterns[4] are realized by semantic logogenetic patterns and tend to match up with the semantic phases within or across metafunctions, constituting contextual stages that are defined by variations of FTM values either within one of the variables or across the three.

5. The multi-stratal and metafunctionally organized logogenetic patterns that are found to be common in texts embedded in the same situation type form the TEXT TYPE system of the text type, which in turn can be applied to the analysis of the ongoing process of other texts of the same type.

4.2.4 Suggested method of analysis

As can be seen from the above statements, the newly proposed TEXT TYPE model is by no means suggesting that Halliday's Functional Grammar be abandoned in the analysis of text as process. Instead, it is suggesting a new method of using Functional Grammar, which involves the establishment of both the REGISTER system and the TEXT TYPE system. The method is specified in the following steps of analysis.

Establishing the REGISTER system

Step 1. Observation and selection: make close observations (plus quantifications where necessary) of lexicogrammatical choices in texts embedded in the same situation type, while keeping in mind all the systems of Functional Grammar, so as to select those systems that shift their probabilities in the situation type in question and are more revealing about the given text type.

Step 2. Analysis and generalization: apply the selected systems to a detailed analysis of the texts, noting down and sorting out the realizational forms of the systems, and at the same time relating the systems to the FTM values of the context of situation, so as to generalize the transient systems of the texts into the REGISTER system of the text type.

Step 3. REGISTER description: give a multi-stratal and multi-functional description of the established REGISTER system.

Establishing the TEXT TYPE system

Step 4. Coding and identification of lexicogrammatical logogenetic patterns:
use the established REGISTER system to code the texts, while observing
closely how lexicogrammatical choices from the same system show up one
after another as the text unfolds, so as to identify the lexicogrammatical
logogenetic patterns in the texts in terms of UNIVARIATE.

Step 5. Identification of lexicogrammatical-semantic relationships: re-examine
the lexicogrammatical logogenetic patterns thus identified, so as find out
how they construe semantic logogenetic patterns (i e. meaning features)
within each of the metafunctions, as well as how the semantic patterns
articulate semantic phases functional in the semantic structure of the texts
either within or across metafunctions.

Step 6. Identification of semantic-contextual relationships: relate the semantic
phases in the texts to the context of situation in terms of FTM, so as to find
out whether and how the semantic phases correlate with variations in
FTM values that define contextual stages either within or across the three
contextual variables.

Step 7. Generalization and TEXT TYPE description: sort out the multi-stratal
logogenetic patterns thus identified in the texts analysed, so as to generalize
the transient systems of the texts into the TEXT TYPE system of the text type,
and to give a multi-functional and multi-stratal description of the established
TEXT TYPE system.

These steps of analysis may seem to be going only in two directions: (1) from
the grammatical stratum up to the semantic stratum, and then to the contextual
stratum; (2) from transient systems specific to individual texts being analysed,
to a generalized system of the text type. Actually, the steps can also be taken
from opposite directions, hence in four directions altogether, as illustrated in
Figure 4.2.

The four directions are: (1) from below (i.e. bottom-up); (2) from above
(i.e. top-down), (3) from specific, and (4) from generalized. Directions 1
and 3 are more useful at the present stage, where a multi-stratal as well as
multi-functional description of text as process is rarely found. Once an
established TEXT TYPE system of a certain text type can be found (this will
come true by the end of this book), direction 4 can be adopted, which would
enable the analyst to tell whether a text's specific system is far from or close
to the generalized system, or even how far or how close it is. The 'from-
generalized' approach is particularly useful if the analysis is meant to be
prescriptive, such as in teaching writing or in evaluating teachers' verbal
behaviours in the classroom; meanwhile the approach may also give feedback
to the established system, as either challenges or further developments.
Direction 2, i.e. the top-down approach, can almost always be adopted where

	specific	→	generalized	
above	contextual logogenetic patterns: stages within / across FTM variables		contextual logogenetic patterns: stages within / across FTM variables	**above**
↑ ↓	semantic logogenetic patterns: phases within / across metafunctions		semantic logogenetic patterns: phases within / across metafunctions	↑ ↓
below	lexicogrammatical logogenetic patterns: UNIVARIATEs		lexicogrammatical logogenetic patterns: UNIVARIATEs	**below**
	specific	←	generalized	

FIGURE 4.2　　Four directions in analysing text as process

direction 1, i.e. the bottom-up approach, is needed; but it can be more useful where the concern is less linguistic and perhaps more sociological or educational, since it encourages arguments to be made at the contextual stratum. In Part II of this book, the method will be demonstrated 'from below' and 'from specific'.

Part II

Applying the TEXT TYPE Model to EFL Classroom Discourse

Chapter 5

Design of the Application

In order to test the applicability of the TEXT TYPE model, it has been applied to an actual analysis of EFL classroom discourse. Part II of this book presents the analysis as a demonstration of the model and its feasibility. While the analysis itself will be presented in Chapters 6, 7 and 8, the design of the application is presented in this chapter, by focusing on the specific questions being addressed, the data used, the method of analysis, and the method of presenting the analysis.

5.1 Questions addressed

The application addresses a number of specific questions, which fall into the following two categories.

Theoretically-oriented questions:

1. Which lexicogrammatical systems tend to shift their probabilities in the EFL classroom situation, so that they form the REGISTER system network of EFL classroom discourse?
2. What kinds of lexicogrammatical logogenetic patterns can be identified in EFL classroom discourse, so that they form the TEXT TYPE system network of EFL classroom discourse?
3. Do these lexicogrammatical logogenetic patterns articulate semantic phases in a text within one single metafunction, or do they resonate across metafunctions so as to allow a multi-functional interpretation of the semantic phases?
4. Do FTM values in the EFL classroom situation vary and form contextual stages relatable to the different semantic phases in a text, so that the logogenetic patterns thus identified can be said to be multi-stratal?

Practically-oriented questions:

1. How do variations in the contextual values of EFL classroom discourse (in terms of FTM) reveal the EFL classroom environment in the Chinese context?

2. How do various kinds of meanings identified in EFL classroom discourse (in terms of multi-stratal logogenetic patterns) reveal the process of EFL classroom teaching and learning in the Chinese context?
3. Are those meanings expressed appropriately (in lexicogrammatical terms) by the Chinese EFL teachers and students?

Admittedly, the theoretically oriented questions are primary while the practically oriented questions are secondary, since the application is meant as a demonstration of the newly proposed model while EFL classroom discourse is used as data in the application. In effect, questions of the former kind served to guide the entire process of the application, leading to a multi-functional and multi-stratal description of the TEXT TYPE system of EFL classroom discourse. Nevertheless, questions of the latter kind were being kept in mind throughout the application, leading to a description of various features of the EFL classroom environment, the process of EFL teaching and learning in the classroom, and the discourse strategies of EFL teachers and learners, all within the Chinese context.

5.2 Data collecting and processing

The data used in the analysis is authentic EFL classroom discourse. Altogether ten EFL classes, each lasting 45 or 50 minutes (i.e. one class hour), were audio-recorded between 2002 and 2005.[1] The recordings were then transcribed into ten texts, and the first substantial question asked in each class was used as the title of the text. Here is a list of the text titles, together with the name of the course being taught in each class (given in brackets).

Text 1:   *What is a Disaster?* (Extensive Reading)
Text 2:   *How can History be Taught and Learned?* (Intensive Reading)
Text 3:   *Are you Ready?* (Oral Interpretation)
Text 4:   *What does 'Regime' Mean?* (Intensive Reading)
Text 5:   *Can we Trust Strangers?* (Intensive Reading)
Text 6:   *Do you Share the Same Idea with the Writer?* (Comprehensive English)
Text 7:   *What will Sue do if the Trains are Delayed?* (Comprehensive English)
Text 8:   *When and Where did the Story take Place?* (Intensive Reading)
Text 9:   *Anybody Like to Read it?* (Intensive Reading)
Text 10:   *Can you Tell the General Idea of the Text?* (Extensive Reading)

These ten classes were taught by ten different teachers from eight well-known universities in Beijing. The teachers were chosen on account of (1) their outstanding records in the teaching evaluation conducted each semester or annually in their universities, and (2) their reputation as a "good" EFL teacher among both their students and colleagues. The decision was made out of

Table 5.1 Teacher differences involved in the data

academic title	lecturers: 3	professors: 2	associate professors: 5	
age	20–30: 2	30–40: 3	40–50: 3	over 50: 2
gender	male: 3	female: 7		
affiliation	general university: 2		normal university: 2	
	foreign language university: 2		special college: 4	
course type	Intensive Reading: 5		Comprehensive English: 2	
	Extensive Reading: 2		Oral Interpretation: 1	

consideration of the ELT situation in China (see 1.1.3). Given the level of average EFL teachers in China, it was assumed that the "good" teachers would be more likely to manage the classroom process well, and that their classes would therefore promise a more fruitful analysis from the point of view of ELT research. In addition, the classroom behaviours of "good" teachers would be more likely to suggest strategies to be followed by average EFL teachers. However, differences among the ten teachers came out quite strongly in terms of academic title, age, gender, type of university affiliated to, and type of course being taught. See Table 5.1 for a detailed description.

To guarantee consistency in data treatment, a one-person-responsibility policy was adopted. That is, it was always the same person who went into a classroom to do the recording, to take notes of relevant body language where necessary, and then to complete the transcription.

In transcribing the recordings, all of the turns were numbered, and so were the moves within the same turn. Here, a **turn** is defined as the speech produced by one speaker before another speaker gets in. A **move**, following Halliday (2004), is defined as a discourse unit that performs a specific speech function. As for the grammatical realization of a move, while Halliday (2004: Ch. 4) claims that a speech function is realized in the mood structure of the clause, the data indicates that it can be realized by several linked clauses instead of a single clause (see Example 5–1). So, the realization of a move is here extended, following Martin (1992: 40), to 'a clause selecting independently for mood'. That is, all clauses that are non-finite, embedded or dependent are taken as part of the same move, performing the same speech function. Also taken as part of the same move are: (1) a false start, (2) an identical clause that is produced a second time in the same turn, and (3) a clause that is slightly paraphrased without changing the mood and is produced in the same turn. Both **turn** and **move** are applied here as units of discourse because they are both useful in the analysis. While the former is useful in identifying the speaker (teacher or student), the latter is an appropriate unit as long as the analysis covers the lexicogrammatical stratum.

The following is the transcription key:

1. **Arabic numerals [1, 2, 3]** are used to number the turns and moves.
2. **Letters** are used to represente the speakers, including:
   T = teacher
   S = an individual student
   22-T/2 = Teacher's second move in Turn 22
   Sn = several students or the whole class
   S(n) = one student currently holding the floor plus many others joining in
   S/a, S/b = different students who speak one after another to answer the same question
   Xxx = the Chinese name of a student
3. Utterances that are not understandable, especially those produced simultaneously by more than one student, are represented as **[confusion]**.
4. **Period [.]** marks termination of a sentence with falling intonation, whether complete or elliptical.
5. **Question mark [?]** indicates termination of a sentence with rising intonation, whether interrogative or declarative in form.
6. **Dots [. . .]** indicate hesitation within a sentence and hence often incompletion of the sentence, while **fillers** are represented orthographically as **er, en** or **ern.**[2]
7. **Comma [,]** indicates a spontaneous pause in the middle of a sentence, whether syntactically significant or not.
8. **Dash [–]** marks a sudden stop in the middle of a sentence, which indicates either incompletion of the sentence due to interruption, or an attempt to end a false start or to insert an explanation.
9. **Double quotation marks ["”]** enclose a certain part quoted from the text currently being taught in class, whether it is a complete sentence, or part of it, or a series of sentences.
10. **Single quotation marks [']** enclose a word, group or clause selected from the textbook and currently being explained, which originally can be any part of speech but is now made to function as a nominal group in the sentence being produced.

Here are three examples in which most of the above-presented symbols can be found.

Example 5–1 [from Text 2]
82-T/3:   And ". . . are usually introduced to the study of history by way of" – by means of – "a fat textbook" – a very thick, a thick or a big textbook – "and become quickly immersed in a vast sea of names, dates, events, and statistics" – the hard facts, we call hard facts, er, like when this event took place, and who actually played the role, and when and where did it happen, right, and things like that.

Example 5–2 [from Text 4]
12-T/5:   山上一棵树都不长, how to say?
13-S: The hill . . .
14:T: The hill is
15-S: . . . bare of, of trees.
16-T/1:   bare of trees.

Example 5–3 [from Text 4]
16-T/7:   And, so ern, "except appetite and racial domination", 'appetite' –
           what does 'appetite' mean?
17-Sn: [confusion]
18-T: Desire, right, desire for what?
19-S(n):   Territory.
20-T/1:   For territory, for more and more territories, and for ruling, for
           controlling more and more civilians, more and more peoples.

There was, however, a kind of self-repetition (see underlined parts in Example 5–4) that was not transcribed. This is a repetition of part of the sentence being produced by the same speaker, and the repetition seems quite unintentional. It is more like a personal habit than a strategy (compare Example 5–5) that is employed to make sure that all students can hear and understand the words being spoken.

Example 5–4 [from Text 8]
it seems that, say, you stand here, looking down, well, no path at all, <u>er, no path at all</u>, no foot path, <u>no foot path</u>, maybe just mountain path, <u>er, mountain path, mountain path</u>.

Example 5–5 [from Text 6]
25-T/2:   OK, from the list, what can you tell, from the list, what can you tell?

5.3 Method of analysis and of presentation

In accordance with the suggested method of analysis as described in 4.2.4, the analysis of the ten texts[3] was done 'from below' and 'from specific' by following the seven steps of analysis, which eventually led to the establishment of both the REGISTER system and the TEXT TYPE system of EFL classroom discourse. The presentation of the analysis in the rest of Part II of this book will also be given 'from below' and 'from specific', and will basically follow the same seven steps. See Figure 5.1 for an illustration of analysis 'from below', i.e. a bottom-up analysis.

For the sake of clarity, the presentation of the analysis is organized into three parts, i.e. Chapters 6, 7 and 8. Each chapter centres upon one of the three

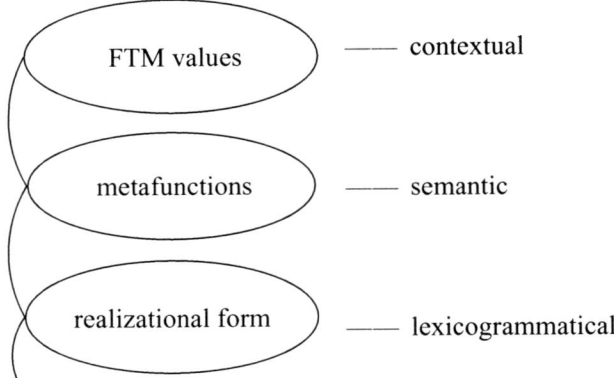

FIGURE 5.1   A bottom-up analysis of EFL classroom discourse

metafunctions: interpersonal, ideational and textual; while co-articulations across metafunctions will be pointed out wherever they occur. And each chapter is further divided into three sections.

Section 1 focuses on the REGISTER system network of EFL classroom discourse within the metafunction in question, which is established through the analysis in Steps 1 and 2, and is here given a multi-stratal description (Step 3) 'from below' and illustrated with numerous examples taken from the data.

Section 2 focuses on the logogenetic patterns within the given metafunction, which are identified and found as pertaining to all the strata during the analysis in Steps 4, 5 and 6, and are here given a multi-stratal description (Step 7) also 'from below' and again illustrated with examples from the data.

Section 3 gives both a complete representation of the TEXT TYPE system network of EFL classroom discourse that is organized around the given metafunction (Step 7), and an illustration of the network – by applying it to a detailed analysis of the process of a whole text taken from the data.

It is expected that the analysis of EFL classroom discourse as presented in the rest of Part II will lead to (1) a clear demonstration of the TEXT TYPE model, (2) a data-informed dynamic system network that can be applied in the analysis of the process of EFL classroom discourse, and (3) an understanding of features of EFL teaching and learning in the classroom, particularly in the Chinese context.

Chapter 6

Interpersonal Analysis
of EFL Classroom Discourse

This chapter presents the interpersonal part of the analysis of EFL classroom discourse. In accordance with the steps of analysis described in 4.2.4, this chapter – and the following two chapters as well – is divided into three sections: (1) REGISTER network, (2) logogenetic patterns, and (3) TEXT TYPE network.

6.1 REGISTER network: interpersonal

As a result of close observations of lexicogrammatical choices in each of the ten texts in the light of all interpersonal systems of Functional Grammar, four systems were found to shift their probabilities in, and reveal more about, EFL classroom discourse: (1) mood, (2) Subject person, (3) deicticity[1] and (4) modal assessment. When these systems were applied to the analysis of the ten texts, however, some of the systems proved inadequate in describing facts about EFL classroom discourse and hence had to be extended or revised, while the delicate options in some other systems proved dormant in the analysis and hence were left out. Thus the interpersonal systems in the REGISTER network of EFL classroom discourse have been set up based on both the above four systems as developed by Halliday (2004), and their structural realizations as actually found in the data.[2]

In this section, each of the interpersonal systems in the REGISTER network of EFL classroom discourse will be presented multi-stratally. That is, it will be described lexicogrammatically, explained semantically in interpersonal terms, and related to the values of the tenor of EFL classroom discourse (i.e. the role relationship between the teacher and students). Typical examples taken from the data will be provided as illustrations.

6.1.1 The MOOD system

The Mood system, according to Functional Grammar, is realized in the mood structure of the clause (see a brief description in Table 6.1, summarized from

Table 6.1   The mood structure of the clause

Mood		Residue		
Subject	Finite	Predicator	Complement	Adjunct
nominal group/ nominalization/ pronoun	verbal operator (temporal/ modal)	verbal group (non-finite)	nominal group/ nominalization/ pronoun/	adverbial group/ prepositional phrase

Table 6.2   Metaphors of mood in EFL classroom discourse

	declarative	interrogative
command	I'd like/want you to… * you can/may/need to… (*infer, guess*) * you will (*read it and then tell me…*) * you (*read it and then tell me…*)	would you like to…? would / can you…? * how can you (*explain it*)? * how do you say (要不是有你的帮助…)?
statement	you know that… you can imagine / see that…	can you imagine that…?
question	you can tell us whether / how…	could/can you explain/tell me how…? do you mean that…? * do you know/have any idea/ remember whether/how…

Halliday 2004: Ch. 4). Variations in the mood structure serve to classify clauses into different mood types (declarative, interrogative and imperative) that constitute the congruent realizations of four primary speech functions, two propositions and two proposals (for details see Table 3.1).

As found in the analysis of the data, the Mood system is realized both congruently and metaphorically. Metaphors of mood include a shift of the realizational domain (e.g. a command realized by an indicative instead of imperative clause: *Can you give an example?*) and 'interpersonal projection' (Halliday 2004: 626). The latter is in fact the ideational resource of verbal or mental projection being made to do an interpersonal service. A common example found in the data is *Do you know what the word means?*, where the projecting clause (*do you know*) is not a proposition in its own right but serves to specify the subjective orientation of the proposition in the projected clause (*what the word means*). Table 6.2 presents the various types of mood metaphors as found in the data (* indicates an instance not described by Halliday, and a simple example is given in italics within brackets).[3]

Besides, many elliptical clauses are found in the data, where either the Mood elements (e.g. *What do you think are the causes?* **Population**.) or the whole clause (e.g. *Did your parents give you any advice? Yes*.) is absent. Regarding ellipsis, Martin (1992) proposes that an Ellipsis system be subsumed into the Mood system as a resource for tying a responding move to an initiating move. The view held here, however, is that the role played by ellipsis in sequencing moves in a dialogue is a matter of textual meaning rather than interpersonal meaning. As found in the data, ellipsis also occurs in initiating moves, playing several different textual roles (see 8.1.1). Moreover, the structure of EFL classroom dialogue is far more complicated than an Initiation ^ Response pair or a ((dx1) ^ x2) ^ x1 ^ (x2f) structure, so its description necessarily involves – apart from ellipsis – several other textual resources such as repetition and textual Theme (see Chapter 8 for details). In relation to the structural realizations of the Mood system, ellipsis is relevant only to the extent of making the mood type of a clause **implicit** and the route of identifying the mood type indirect. And it is relevant only to the indicative (declarative and interrogative) mood, since in the imperative the Mood element is absent by default rather than by choice. Thus in the MOOD system of EFL classroom discourse, a contrast between 'explicit' and 'implicit' is subsumed into the indicative mood, while both the congruent and metaphorical forms of realization are recognized for every mood. See Figure 6.1 for a representation of the system.

Here are two examples of explicit mood, in either congruent or metaphorical form.

Example 6–1 [from Text 8]
21-T/2:   And the Democratic Party was founded in eighteen-twenty-three.

Example 6–2 [from Text 5]
101-T/3:   xxx, do you know what a motto is?
102-S: ern, it means a short sentence or phrase chosen and used as a guide or rule of behaviour, or as an expression of the aims or ideals of a family, a country, an institution.

Both explicit mood and metaphorical mood, as indicated by the data, are more often found in teachers' than in students' speech, and both occur in the teachers' statements or questions, construing the teacher's role as an initiator. The metaphorical mood, through a syntagmatic extension of wording, increases the semiotic distance between meaning and wording: it gives the responder

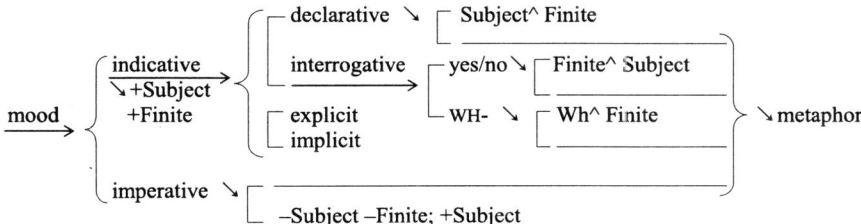

FIGURE 6.1   The MOOD system of EFL classroom discourse

more room for negotiation and makes it possible to reject naturally and politely. In terms of the tenor of discourse, mood metaphors create a more comfortable social distance between the teacher and students.

Implicit mood, on the other hand, can be found in both the teachers' and students' speech. In the former, it usually occurs in questions (typically *why? why not? what else?*). In the latter, it generally occurs in responding statements, which sometimes display negligence of grammatical correctness, for example (⬚ indicates implicit Mood element):

Example 6–3 [from Text 1]		*Example 6–4 [from Text 6]*	
201-T/2:	So when did it start?	122-T:	Well, what do we have to do with
202-S:	Maybe, er, ⬚ Monday.		[about] population?
203-T/1:	Monday, okay.	123-S:	⬚ Control the increase.
203-T/2:	Why ⬚ Monday?		

In sum, presented above is a data-informed MOOD system of EFL classroom discourse. While it may be used to make a quantitative analysis (following Eggins and Slade 1997: Ch. 3) of a teacher's or the students' mood choices in order to find out their respective status, it is meant to be used to code EFL classroom discourse move by move, so as to observe emerging logogenetic patterns that articulate phases of interpersonal meaning in the text.

6.1.2 The SUBJECT PERSON system

The Subject Person system is newly introduced into the Mood system network (see Fig. 4–15 in Halliday 2004), made up of only two options: interactant and non-interactant. Actually, Halliday (2004) presents this system merely in figure, without giving explanations about the interpersonal meaning of either the system or its options. But when applied to the analysis of the data, the system is found to be salient as well as revealing about EFL classroom discourse.

As found in the analysis, the interpersonal meaning of the system lies essentially in what may be called the **principle of engagement**, a concept developed based on the 'principle of responsibility' mentioned by Halliday (2004: 117) when he defines the Subject element. He takes the Subject as the 'responsible element' in a clause, i.e. the one 'responsible for the functioning of the clause as an interactive event' (ibid.). In a proposal, it is the one held responsible for realizing the offer or command (*I'll call him, shall I? Call him, will you?*); in a proposition, it is the one based on which the information being exchanged can be affirmed or denied (*He didn't come, did he? No, he didn't*). In other words, the Subject is not just a grammatical category; it is the one responsible for the performing of the interpersonal function of a clause. With Subject person, then, the question is not just **which element** is responsible, but **who** is responsible; or more precisely, whether the interactants, i.e., the speaker

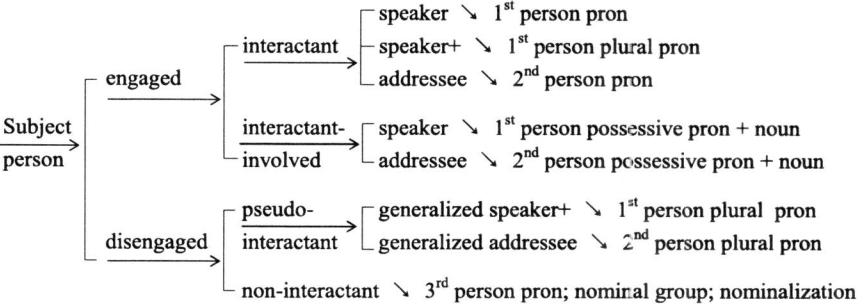

FIGURE 6.2 The SUBJECT PERSON system of EFL classroom discourse

and addressee, are responsible or not. In other words, the person of the Subject will reveal whether the interactants themselves are engaged in the interactive event or not. And this **principle of engagement** is clearly found to be in operation in the data of EFL classroom discourse. Thus driven by the data, the SUBJECT PERSON system of EFL classroom discourse is organized around two major options: engaged vs. disengaged. See a representation of the system in Figure 6.2.

As indicated by the data, when the Subject of a clause is 'interactant', the teacher or the student producing the clause is not just making a move, but also personally engaged in the interactive event, be it a proposal or a proposition. With a proposal, the unmarked form of an imperative clause has no Mood element, hence no Subject; yet the clause may also be marked for person, hence a Subject in second person (*you*) or first person (*let me*) or first person plural (*let's*) – which all indicate that the speaker and/or addressee are the one(s) to be engaged in the action being demanded:

Example 6–5 [from Text 10]
69-T/6:   First <u>you</u> read the question, and
                then, give the correct answer.

Example 6–6 [from Text 8]
1-T/4:   Alright, now, <u>let's</u> take
              up the text.

With a proposition, on the other hand, when the Subject is 'interactant', the students are engaged in an information exchange to such an extent that they become the ones to determine the validity of the information:

Example 6–7 [from Text 1]
21-T/2:   All right, have <u>you</u> ever
                experienced any disaster
                in your life?
22-S/a: Yes.
23-S/b: No.

Example 6–8 [from Text 6]
71-T/2:   Do <u>you</u> have worries?
72-S(n):   Yeah.
73-T: What worries do <u>you</u> have?
74-S: Whether <u>I</u> can find a good
            job in the future.

However, it is found in the data that the Subject is more often 'non-interactant' with propositions:

— non- interactant

Example 6–9 [from Text 8]

11-T/2:   So the American Civil War broke out in 1861, ended in 1865; it lasted four years.

11-T/3:   Er, and then, which side won the war?

12-S: North.

— non-interactant

Example 6–10 [from Text 4]

25-T/1:   What is Nazi regime – what Nazi Germany did in the Second World War, when they invaded other countries, what did they do?

25-T/2:   They killed people, destroying their home, suppressed their resistance.

25-T/3:   So they were very cruel.

As can be seen, a 'non-interactant' Subject has a strong orientation towards the outside world, detached from the speaker or addressee. Here, neither the teacher nor the students are responsible for the validity of the information being exchanged about *the American Civil War* or *they*; hence they are much disengaged from the interactive event.

Apart from the systemic contrast between 'interactant' and 'non-interactant', which is identified but not described by Halliday in his Subject Person system, two other options have been newly identified in the data, i.e. 'interactant-involved' and 'pseudo-interactant'. They can be seen as the intermediate degrees between the above two poles, although they are in effect each closer to one of the poles.

The option of 'interactant-involved' is realized by a nominal group that takes on a first or second person possessive pronoun as a Determiner:

Example 6–11 [from Text 1]

33-S/b: Where is your hometown?

34-S/a: 山东，青岛.

Example 6–12 [from Text 5]

5-T/2:   Now, what did your parents say to you?

6-S: My parents said that the only one you can depend on is yourself.

Here, the Subject is in third person: the interactants do not seem to be the resting point of the validity of the information being exchanged. But the Subject – *your hometown*, *your /my parents* (note also the pronoun *you* and *yourself* that are not in the Subject position, though) – does involve one of the interactants, a student in both cases, who is therefore unlikely to avoid being engaged in the interactive event. In fact, it is up to this student to determine the validity of the information. That is why the option is named 'interactant-involved' and included in the Engaged system.

The option of 'pseudo-interactant' is realized by a generalized personal pronoun, i.e. a first or second person plural (*we, you*) that in fact refers to everyone, including the speaker and addressee of course:

Example 6–13 [from Text 3]
12-T/1:   Can <u>we</u> say 'ton coal'?
12-T/2:   No, when <u>we</u> use the measurement, <u>we</u> always have to say 'tons of' something, all right, 'tons of' something.

Example 6–14 [from Text 5]
29-T/2:   Now, if <u>you</u> want to 'get a ride' – that means to get a ride from somebody, from a driver, from a car or a truck passing by – what do <u>you</u> do?
29-T/3:   Anyone – xxx.
30-S: I think <u>you</u> wave your hands.

Here, the Subject does not really engage the speaker or addressee. This is clearly proved by Example 6–14 in which the student says *you wave your hands* instead of *I wave my hands.* In other words, either *we* or *you* used in this way is comparable to the general person *one,* though they sound somewhat closer to the interactants than a 'non-interactant' Subject. This is why it is called 'pseudo-interactant' but taken as an alternative to 'non-interactant' in the Disengaged system.

In sum, the SUBJECT PERSON system of EFL classroom discourse is a data-driven extension of Halliday's Subject person system. In the classroom situation, it is an important resource a teacher can make use of in order to engage the students in classroom interaction (see Yang 2007a).

6.1.3 The DEICTICITY system

The term 'deicticity' used here does not have to do with the Deictic element in a nominal group, nor with the cohesive function of a reference item, but with the Finite element in an indicative clause, i.e. a clause that functions as an exchange of information (a proposition). Actually, 'deicticity' refers to a specific temporal or modal space being **pointed to** by the choice of primary tense or modality in an indicative clause. The concept is recently put forward by Halliday (2004: 116), when he interprets the interpersonal meaning of the Finite element in a clause. He argues that what primary tense and modality have in common is 'interpersonal deixis':

[T]hat is, they locate the exchange within the semantic space that is opened up between speaker and listener. With primary tense, the dimension is that of time: primary tense construes time interpersonally, as defined by what is 'present' to you and me at the time of saying. With modality the dimension is that of assessment: modality construes a region of uncertainty where I can express, or ask you to express, an assessment of the validity of what is being said. (Halliday 2004: 116)

That is to say, interpersonally, temporal or modal Finite points to a semantic space between the interactants within which the clause as an interactive event is located. And this space is defined within the immediate context of the speech event, in terms of either the time of speaking, or the interactants' involvement – i.e. the speaker's judgement in a giving move and the addressee's judgement in a demanding move.

As found in the analysis of the data, variation of deicticity is very common in EFL classroom discourse, sometimes even within one single turn:

Example 6–15 [from Text 2]
1-T/1:   All right, let's resume our class, OK?
1-T/2:   And, so a university student <u>can</u> comment on how history should be taught, and now, we'<u>ll</u> comment on it.
1-T/3:   Now, what about the rest of you – <u>did</u> you come across, er, an interesting history teacher?
2-S/1:   Yes, when I <u>was</u> in primary school, ern, I . . .

Here, the teacher makes three moves in her first turn of speaking. The first move is an imperative clause having no Finite element, hence no deicticity. But in the rest of the clauses, it is quite clear that deicticity flows from a modal Finite (*can*) that points to a judgement voiced by the teacher, to a temporal Finite (*'ll*) that points to a time ahead of 'now', and then to another temporal Finite (*did*) that points to a time in the past. In this way, the teacher is leading the students (note also the interactant Subjects *we, you, I*) from one semantic space to another, near or remote, certain or uncertain.

At other times, a shift of deicticity occurs within the same move:

Example 6–16 [from Text 5]
41-T/7:   You <u>remember</u> what kind of journey <u>was</u> he going to make?
42-S: ⬜ From coast to coast.
43-T/1:   Yeah, he <u>was</u> going to make a coast-to-coast journey.

Here, the choice of past tense (*was*) runs through the moves. But in the first teacher's move, there can be found a shift of deicticity from the present time (*remember*) to the past time (*was*). This is considered to be a case of mood metaphor (see 6.1.1), where the shift of deicticity does not change the speech function of the move (i.e. question). The mood metaphor enables the teacher to orientate the question towards the students, and to reduce the distance between the immediate context and the information about a past event. Just compare *<u>You remember</u> what kind of journey <u>was</u> he going to make?* with a mere *What kind of journey <u>was</u> he going to make?*

Driven by such variations of deicticity frequently found in the data, the DEICTICITY system of EFL classroom discourse has been set up, as represented in Figure 6.3. On the whole, deicticity functions to limit the semantic space of

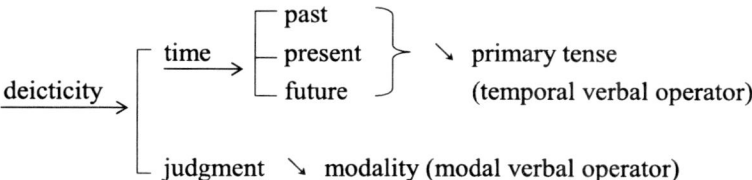

FIGURE 6.3 The DEICTICITY system of EFL classroom discourse

a proposition, anchoring the information in the immediate context of the speech event. In the classroom context, it enables the teacher and the students to find themselves at a certain distance – far or near – from the information that is being exchanged.

6.1.4 The ASSESSMENT system

In Functional Grammar, modality is viewed as an expression of (or request for) an interactant's judgement or attitude regarding a proposition, realized congruently by the modal Finite and/or modal Adjunct. In other words, modality is interpreted within the **clause** by reference to its speech function. This position has found a complement in the Appraisal system developed by Martin and his colleagues, a system of the interactants' attitudes (classified into Affect, Judgement and Appreciation) realized through **lexis** regardless of their function in the clause (see Martin 2000; Martin and Rose 2003; Martin and White 2005). More or less as a response to this complement, Halliday (2004) presents a huge system of Modal Assessment, which is summarized in Figure 6.4 (adapted from ibid.: Ch. 4).

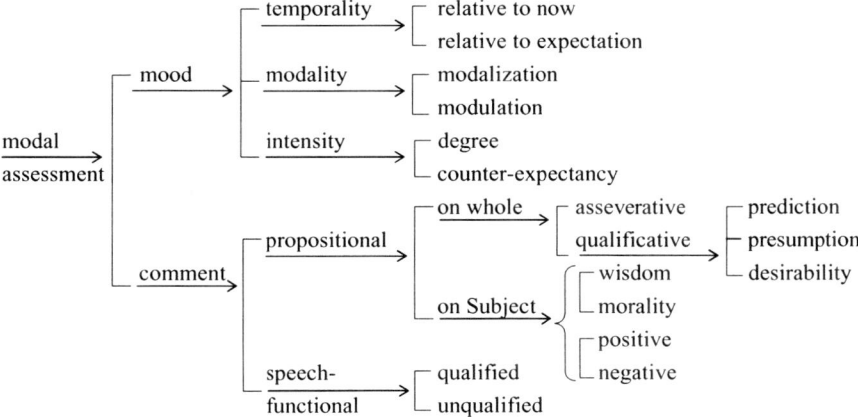

FIGURE 6.4 A summary of Halliday's Modal Assessment system

According to Halliday (2004: 607–12), this system has 'different realizational domains' including (1) modal Adjunct within the clause, e.g. *wisely* expressing comment on Subject, *obviously* expressing comment on the whole proposition, and *eventually* expressing temporality of the speech function; (2) metaphor of modality (also called 'interpersonal projection'), e.g. *I think / guess that . . .* as personal projection expressing probability subjectively, or *it seems that . . .* and *they say that . . .* as factual projection expressing probability and presumption objectively; (3) interpersonal Epithet in the nominal group, e.g. *wise, right, natural, happy, wonderful* expressing comment on the Subject or the whole proposition. It should be pointed out that Modal Assessment is a system that has not only incorporated as many modal resources as possible, but also allowed itself to remain a clause-based system.

When applied to the analysis of EFL classroom discourse, some of the options in the system appear prominent while others are hardly noticeable. Thus, up to the point reached in the data, the ASSESSMENT system of EFL classroom discourse has been established, as represented in Figure 6.5.

In this system, 'comment on Subject' refers to the interactant's comment on the person or thing in the role of Subject, realized by an evaluative adjective or adverb or noun[1] in the Residue of the clause. It is a resource for voicing evaluation, which is found to be frequently applied by the teachers. Here are some examples of 'capacity', a concept borrowed from Martin's Appraisal system where it is a feature of social esteem in the Judgement system (whereas Halliday calls it 'wisdom'):

Example 6–17 [from Text 10]
53-T: So, why false?
54-S: From the last question "different cultures enrich American culture", so I think there's no danger of immigration disuniting the USA.
55-T/1:   So, you are <u>very clever</u>: you think the last question explains this one . . .

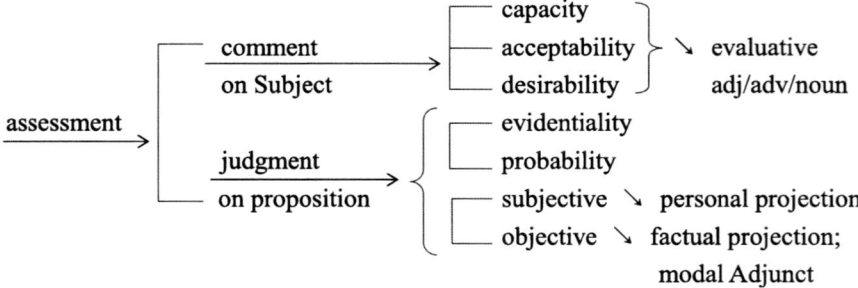

FIGURE 6.5   The ASSESSMENT system of EFL classroom discourse

Example 6–18 [from Text 7]
54-T/2: OK, any others?
55-S: I'll take some medicine.
56-T/1: I'll take some medicine, sounds <u>very wise</u>, yes.

'Acceptability' is a concept comparable to 'morality' used by Halliday, as well as 'propriety' used by Martin in the sense of social sanction in the Judgement system. But 'acceptability' has to do with both ethics and correctness. Common examples in the data include *that's right, you are right, (al)right, good*, and *very good*. Here are two more examples:

Example 6–19 [from Text 2]
34-S: Yes, he is <u>abnormal</u>.
35-T/1: Okay, you think he isn't <u>right</u> – NOT <u>abnormal</u> – you don't think he is <u>right</u>, okay, yes.

Example 6–20 [from Text 5]
87-T/5: All right, well, I think you can all answer [all answered] the questions <u>very well</u>, and you did a <u>very good</u> job, in previewing the lesson.

'Desirability' is a concept borrowed from Halliday's Modal Assessment system, and is comparable to 'reaction' used by Martin as a feature in the Appreciation system. For example:

Example 6–21 [from Text 3]
41-T/3: Well, go over the whole sentence again, please!
42-Sn: [confusion]
43-T/1: Alright, everything is <u>very clear</u>, alright, everything is <u>very clear</u>.

Example 6–22 [from Text 5]
41-T/2: OK, now, next question: what do you think, what do you think was the <u>biggest problem</u> during the journey?

As can be seen above, 'comment on Subject' is actually integrated into the proposition itself, since the realizational forms are indispensable elements of the clause. But 'judgement on proposition', which is realized by a modal Adjunct or a modalized projecting clause, is more like an added element to the proposition, since without them the clause is still complete. For example:

Example 6–23 [from Text 2]
11-T: OK, if <u>you say</u> he taught well, how, how can that be you didn't quite like him?

Example 6–24 [from Text 10]
51-T/4: <u>Do you think</u> it's right?
52-S: <u>I think</u> it's false.

Here, *you say* realizes 'evidentiality', i.e. the evidential status of a proposition (*you made the statement that he taught well*); while *do you think* and *I think* realize 'probability', i.e. the degree of likelihood of a proposition (*how likely it is right / false*). Clearly, both kinds of judgement can be added to a statement as well as a question, expressing or requesting the interactant's assessment. The subjective orientation (*do you think*), in particular, encourages the named addressee to give assessment, which in the EFL classroom context is a resource for engaging the students.

6.1.5 Summary

In sum, the four interpersonal systems in the REGISTER network of EFL classroom discourse, as presented above, are developed on the basis of relevant systems of Functional Grammar, as well as their structural realizations as actually found during the analysis of the data. See Figure 6.6 for a representation of the entire interpersonal REGISTER network of EFL classroom discourse.

6.2 Logogenetic patterns: interpersonal

Following the steps of analysis as described in 4.2.4, the four systems in the interpersonal REGISTER network of EFL classroom discourse were used to code the data move by move (see Appendix I). As a result, it is found that choices from the systems of MOOD, SUBJECT PERSON and DEICTICITY form most of the interpersonal logogenetic patterns in the unfolding texts. Choices from the ASSESSMENT system appear somehow interspersed in the texts,

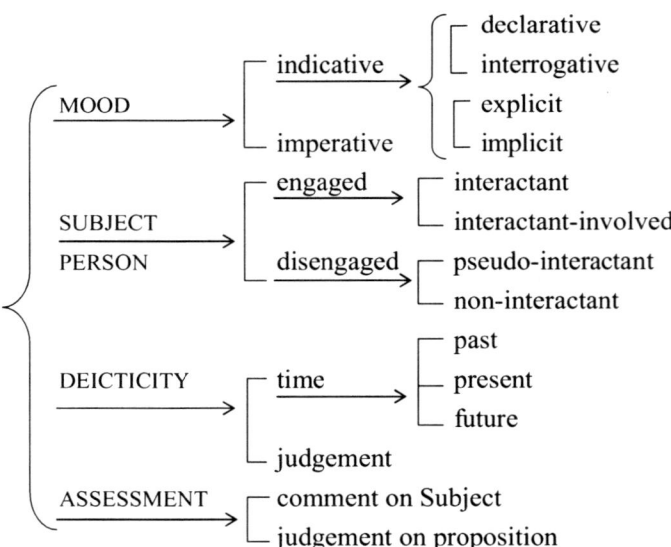

FIGURE 6.6   The interpersonal REGISTER system of EFL classroom discourse

forming what Martin (1992, 1997) calls a 'prosodic pattern' which, however, is not considered as a logogenetic pattern. Nor do metaphors of either mood or modality contribute to any specific logogenetic patterns, although they do seem to display the teachers' strategies to engage the students (see Yang 2007a for more).

This section presents those logogenetic patterns formed out of interpersonal choices as identified in the analysis of the data. The patterns fall into three categories: (1) boundaries, (2) information types, and (3) information or action sequences. They are here described in terms of UNIVARIATE, explained in terms of their interpersonal function, and related to the values of the tenor of EFL classroom discourse.

6.2.1 Boundary: in the move

With the texts being coded according to the interpersonal REGISTER network of EFL classroom discourse, the most easily noticeable logogenetic pattern is that found within a single move, which displays different interpersonal choices from the following and/or preceding moves and looks like a boundary line. The pattern occurs in three types of teachers' moves. See the following examples where the three types of moves are given grey background, and note how they differ in Subject person, deicticity and mood from the surrounding moves (t=turn, m=move, bold type is applied to highlight relevant choices while brackets indicate an 'implicit' choice; same hereinafter).

t-m	text	Subject person	deicticity	mood
Example 6–25 [from Text 3] ~statement~				
1-T/1	All right, last time, **we did** some practice from English to Chinese.	interactant: speaker+	past	decl
1-T/2	Today, **we'll** start from Chinese to English, and **we'll** again, similarly, **we will** start with single sentences and then get into a passage.	interactant: speaker+	future	decl: metaphor
1-T/3	Listen carefully, the first sentence. ~command~			imp
1-T/4	**Are you** ready?	interactant: addressee	present	interr
2-S	Yeah.	(interactant: speaker)	(present)	decl
Example 6–26 [from Text 5]				
95-T/11	Well, what is it, what **is the incident that's talked about?**	non-interactant	present	interr
95-T/12	OK, ☐ he did not stop for a hitchhiker.	(non-interactant)	(present)	decl
95-T/13	Now **let's** come to some of the words. ~suggestion~	interactant: speaker+		imp
95-T/14	er, "I came upon..." What **is the meaning of 'came upon'?**	non-interactant	present	interr
96-S	**It means** 'to find someone by chance'.	non-interactant	present	decl

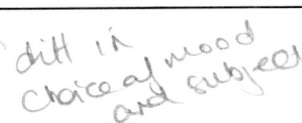

As can be seen, 1-T/1 is a statement, i.e. a proposition; while 1-T/3 and 95-T/13 are respectively a command and a suggestion, i.e. proposals. It should be pointed out that, while 'proposal' is defined by Halliday (2004: 111) as 'the semantic function of a clause in the exchange of goods-&-services' (vs. information), it is here redefined as a move in the semantic function of demanding or producing an **action** (following Berry, 1981c), because EFL classroom discourse is found to be specifically concerned with action – particularly verbal action – rather than goods-&-services in general. When seen from a logogenetic perspective, the two action moves, i.e. 1-T/3 and 95-T/13, both appear quite alone among successive moves: they both stand out against their preceding and following moves that display totally different choices of mood and Subject person. And they are not – nor are they meant to be – responded to by another move, though they do expect a non-verbal, psychological act to take place in the addressee, i.e. becoming alert (with the command) and watching for the coming words (with the suggestion). The statement move, on the other hand, does not stand in as sharp a contrast with its following move; but the two moves do differ in deicticity, as well as in mood since the choice of declarative in 1-T/2 is a mood metaphor realizing a suggestion rather than a statement (see 6.2.1.2 below for more).

As such, the three moves – command, suggestion and statement – each display a specific pattern which does not extend beyond the move but is recognizable only when placed among successive moves. Therefore, they are viewed as logogenetic patterns in the move, and as boundaries that are here named respectively as Direction, Orientation and Recapitulation.

6.2.1.1 Direction

The pattern of Direction is found in a command move (e.g. *listen carefully*). According to Halliday, a command is used to demand goods-&-services and is realized by the imperative mood. This description, however, proves inadequate for the commands found in the data. Actually, two types of command can be distinguished in EFL classroom discourse, both being produced by the teachers. They have the same grammatical realization, but differ in logogenetic positioning and hence in speech function.

One type of command expects another move, such as *Give me specific examples from the text* [Text 6: 35-T], which is followed by a student's complying move giving an example. The other type, such as 1-T/3 in Example 6–25, is meant to give directions for the coming action or information moves, expecting a non-verbal rather than verbal response. They are here viewed as two sub-classes of the speech function of command. The former is termed 'order', which places the speaker into the role of a commander; while the latter is termed 'direct', which construes the role of a controller. While the former fits into a logogenetic pattern above the move (see 6.2.3), the latter fits into a pattern in the move that can be called **Direction**. The following are a few more instances of Direction from the data (they are not presented with surrounding moves, to save space):

— logo genetic patterns

(1)   OK, turn to page fifty-seven. (Text 1: 99-T/5)
(2)   Well, if the text does not tell you directly, I think **you** can infer from what he said. (Text 5: 41-T/6)
(3)   First **you** read the statement and then **you** tell they are true or false. (Text 10: 16-T/3)

As can be seen, Direction is lexicogrammatically realized either congruently by the **imperative** mood (*turn to page* . . .), which may be marked for person (*you read . . . you tell* . . .); or metaphorically by the **declarative** mood combined with the choice of [**interactant: addressee**] in terms of Subject person plus the choice of **judgement** in terms of deicticity (*you can infer* . . .). Both realizational forms hold the addressee responsible for the carrying out of the action as specified in the 'direct' move. However, it should be noted that, because Direction is identified from a logogenetic perspective rather than merely based on its lexicogrammatical realization, it is considered as a logogenetic pattern instead of a mere move.

6.2.1.2 Orientation

The pattern of Orientation is found in a suggestion move (e.g. *let's move on to* . . .). Halliday (2004: 139) defines a suggestion as 'something that is at the same time both command and offer' and is realized by *let's do*. As revealed by the analysis of the data, a suggestion is realized not just congruently by the **imperative** mood marked for person, but also metaphorically by the **indicative** mood (either declarative or interrogative) combined with the choice of [**interactant: speaker+**] in terms of Subject person plus the choice of **future** in terms of deicticity (*we'll* or *we are going to*). In other words, instead of *let's come to some of the words*, the teacher may well be found saying *we'll come to some of the words*. Here are a few of the many instances found in the data:

(1)   Er, **shall we** go on, to the next paragraph? (Text 2: 95-T/8)
(2)   All right, today **we are going to** read *A Disaster in Dayton*. (Text 1: 99-T/4)
(3)   Today, **we'll** start from Chinese to English, and **we'll** again, similarly, **we will** start with single sentences and then get into a passage. (Text 3, 1-T/2)

In addition, since a suggestion is both command and offer, a clause that begins with *let me* – which would be called an 'offer' by Halliday – is here found to function the same way as those suggestion moves given above. Whenever the teacher offers to produce an action, the action inevitably involves both the teacher and students. For example:

Example 6–27 [from Text 6]
53-T: OK, what about your uncle?
54-S: My uncle, er, he is, **he has** lost his job, too.
55-T/1:   OK, what are other problems, what are other problems? – **let me** ask
           another question.
15-T/2:   Now **people have** lots of worries, but what **are the things** people are
           most worried, what are the things people are most worried about, do
           you know?

Here in Move 55-T/1 (*let me* . . .), although it is the **speaker** (instead of speaker+) who is proposing something for the speaker rather than for both the speaker and addressee to do, the action nonetheless involves both sides (*ask **you** a question*). What is more, the move is also found as standing out against the surrounding moves in terms of interpersonal choices in mood and in Subject person. Therefore, it is viewed as a move in the same speech function and the same logogenetic pattern as the earlier suggestion moves.

Admittedly, *let's* and *let me* sound somehow more pressing than *we'll, shall we* or *I'm going to*, especially when the latter is accompanied by a time Adjunct like *today*. But both forms are found in the same pattern from a logogenetic perspective. In terms of speech function, neither is found to be followed by an acceptance move such as *yes, let's* or *yes, please*. In other words, they are used not to propose an action for the addressee to consider, but to orientate all speakers present towards a new course of discourse, such as translating sentences in Example 6–25, or asking and answering questions in Examples 6–27. When produced by the teacher, the pattern places the teacher into the position of a controller.

Thus based on its interpersonal function as well as its role in the EFL classroom, the logogenetic pattern found in a suggestion move is named **Orientation**, and the suggestion move itself is renamed '**orientate**'.

6.2.1.3 Recapitulation

The pattern of Recapitulation is found in a statement move (*we did some practice* . . .). It is identified not only through the choice of declarative mood, but also through the choice of [**interactant: speaker+ / addressee**] in terms of

Subject person combined with the choice of **past** in terms of deicticity (*we did, you did*). For example:

Example 6–28 [from Text 1]

t-m	text	Subject person	deicticity	mood
162-T/2	So **snort is** not a typical sound made only by horse.	non-interactant	present	decl
162-T/3	All right, all right, just now **we talked** about the people, the animals.	interactant: speaker+	past	decl
162-T/4	And finally, what weather conditions, **what weather conditions appeared** in the text?	non-interactant	past	interr
163-S/a	**Rain.**	non-interactant	(past)	decl

As can be seen, it is the combination of the choices of [interactant: speaker+] and past that makes Move 162-T/3 stand out against both its preceding and following moves, which not only display different systemic choices but also form patterns of their own – [non-interactant + present] in the preceding move, and [non-interactant + past] in the following moves. Being alone between these two patterns, Move 162-T/3 is identified as a boundary pattern that allows the teacher to summarize what all speakers present (i.e. the whole class) did together previously. So this statement move is renamed '**recap**', while its logogenetic pattern is referred to as **Recapitulation**. Again, the pattern construes the teacher as a controller.

Meanwhile, as revealed by the data, Recapitulation is also found in a somehow formulaic statement, i.e. *so much for . . . / so much about . . . .*. For example, in Text 1, the teacher regularly uses this kind of statement: *so much about the people* (144-T/3), *so much for my questions* (170-T/2), and *so much for the exercises* (238-T/2); which all function the same way as Move 162-T/3 in Example 6–29. Just compare them with *just now we talked about the people / did questions-and-answers / did all the exercises*. Therefore, this kind of formulaic statement is also taken as a 'recap' move forming the logogenetic pattern of Recapitulation.

6.2.1.4 Summary

In sum, the logogenetic patterns of Direction, Orientation and Recapitulation are called boundaries because they tend to reflect shifts of meaning phases. They are formed by a single move – respectively a command, suggestion and statement, now renamed 'direct', 'orientate' and 'recap' – and hence described in terms of UNIVARIATE that occurs only once. Although these moves constitute speech functions identified through the choice of mood alone, the logogenetic patterns are identified through a co-articulation of choices from

Table 6.3　A summary of the interpersonal logogenetic patterns of Boundary

Boundary	lexicogrammatical UNIVARIATE			interpersonal function	value of tenor
	mood	Subject person	deicticity		
Direction — imperative	imperative			give directions for coming action or information moves	
Direction — declarative	declarative	interactant: addressee	modal		
Orientation — imperative	imperative	interactant: speaker/+		orientate all speakers present towards a new course of discourse	controller vs. controlled
Orientation — declarative/interrogative	declarative / interrogative	interactant: speaker/+	future		
Recapitulation — declarative	declarative	interactant: speaker+ /addressee	past	summarize what all speakers present did together previously	
		[formulaic] *so much ...*			

several different interpersonal systems in the REGISTER network of EFL classroom discourse. Table 6.3 is a summary of the three patterns.

6.2.2　Information Type: across moves

If the logogenetic patterns of Boundary, as described above, are pretty short in length, the patterns to be described below are much longer, because they feature the same systemic choice(s) running across many a move, up to a dozen or even more. Thus they are described in terms of UNIVARIATE that occurs repeatedly. Occasionally there can be one or two different choices inserted into such a pattern, but that will by no means change the pattern. These patterns are referred to as Information Type because they are found only with moves of the proposition type – which are used to exchange information – and because they serve to distinguish the information being exchanged into five types: (1) personal detail, (2) personal story, (3) story, (4) knowledge and (5) judgement. Therefore each pattern is named after a specific information type.

6.2.2.1　Personal Detail

Lexicogrammatically, Personal Detail is a logogenetic pattern identified through the choice of **interactant** (either speaker or addressee) in terms of Subject person, combined with the choice of **present** in terms of deicticity. That is, both types of choices are found to be absolutely dominant in successive moves over a certain stretch of discourse. For example:

Example 6–29 [from Text 6]

t-m	text	Subject person	deicticity
88-T	OK, **do you** have worries?	interactant	present
89-S/a	Yeah, **I'm** afraid I can't pass the exam.	interactant	present
90-T	You mean **the exam has** something to do with population?	non-interactant	present
91-S	Ern, maybe, I mean some other students, if **they can't** pass the exam, maybe **they will** end their life. (laugh)	non-interactant	modal
92-T	OK, **do you** have worries?	interactant	present
93-S/b	Yes, recently **I'm** worried about, about my study.	interactant	present
94-T	And **you're** worried about anything in the future?	interactant	present
95-S	In the future **I worry** about my job.	interactant	present
96-T/1	**Worry** about your job.	(interactant)	present
96-T/2	**Do you** have worries?	interactant	present
97-S/c	Job.	(interactant)	(present)

In this example, it can be seen that the same choice of either Subject person or deicticity runs through the entire stretch of discourse despite a couple of different choices in the middle (i.e. non-interactant and modal in Turns 90 and 91). Although the moves are produced by four different speakers (one teacher and three students), they display a consistent combination of two types of interpersonal choices that form a logogenetic pattern across moves.

Functionally, such a pattern indicates (1) the interactants are responsible for the validity of the information being exchanged, hence being personally engaged in the interactive events; (2) the information is located in the present time, hence being very close to the interactants themselves. These two features, when combined, specify the information being exchanged as details of the interactants themselves, hence 'personal detail'.

In terms of the contextual value of the tenor of discourse, the logogenetic pattern of Personal Detail seems to have an effect on the usual teacher-student relationship. During such a stretch of discourse, the teacher is for the time being seeking information that he really does not know, although the genuine purpose is to find connection between the unknown information and some other known information (*You mean the exam has something to do with population?*). The students (*you, I*), when being held responsible for the validity of the information demanded, are for the time being not speaking from their memory or from the textbook, but spontaneously relating a detail that is known to nobody else in the classroom except themselves. In this way, the relationship between the teacher and students becomes closer and less unequal, as if they were interlocutors in a conversation, which is more likely to enhance student participation.

6.2.2.2 *Personal Story*

Like Personal Detail, the logogenetic pattern referred to as Personal Story is identified, lexicogrammatically, through the choice of **interactant** or **interactant-involved** (e.g. *my village, my teacher*) in terms of Subject person; which, however, is here combined with the choice of **past** (instead of present) in terms of deicticity. For example:

Example 6–30 [from Text 1]

t-m	text	Subject person	deicticity
53-S	**I experienced** a small earthquake.	interactant	past
54-T	Earthquake, a small earthquake?	(interactant)	past
55-S	Yeah, below three. (laugh)		
56-T	Right, **what happened?**	non-interactant	past
57-S	Oh, just I, **I stayed** on my bed, after work, and **felt** . . .	interactant	past
58-T	**Felt** a bed shake?	(interactant)	past
59-S	Er, 特别小的一个 [a very small one].	(interactant)	(past)
60-T/1	Yeah, a small bed shake. (laugh)	(interactant)	(past)
60-T/2	OK, what's your reaction – what **did you** do?	interactant	past
61-S	I just – **I didn't** know, on that day, en, news, the experts say there's an earthquake, en . . .	interactant	past
62-T	So **you didn't** realize it was an earthquake?	interactant	past
63-S	Yeah –	(interactant)	(past)

Here, a combination of the same choices of Subject person and deicticity is found to run through the entire stretch of discourse, in spite of a choice of non-interactant (*what*) in 56-T and a few mistakes in tense (*on that day the experts say there's*) made by the student in 61-S.

Functionally, this pattern, like Personal Detail, indicates that the interactants are responsible for, or at least involved in, the validity of the information being exchanged, hence being personally engaged in the interactive events. Yet unlike Personal Detail, it indicates that the information is located in the past time, being far away from the interactants – and perhaps even farther from the information demander than its giver. These two features, when combined, specify the information type as an interactant's own story, thus 'personal story'.

In terms of the tenor of discourse, the logogenetic pattern of Personal Story also has an effect on the usual teacher-student relationship. Again, the teacher is seeking information unknown to him, although he may be using the unknown information to introduce a new topic. The student, for his part, is telling a story about himself, hence being so motivated as to talk at great length. In Example 6–30, the same student actually takes a total of six turns. So, if Personal Detail may encourage the students to participate in classroom interaction, Personal Story would help to increase the amount of their output – sometimes to such an extent that a student does more talking than the teacher, or at least no less. In this way, the relationship between the teacher and students, again, becomes closer and less unequal, similar to that in a conversation.

6.2.2.3 Story

Lexicogrammatically, the logogenetic pattern of Story is, like Personal Story, identified through the choice of **past** in terms of deicticity; which, however, is here combined with the choice of **non-interactant** (instead of interactant) in terms of Subject person. For example:

Example 6–31 [from Text 8]

t-m	text	Subject person	deicticity
5-T/4	Now, so, talking about American Civil War, when did it start, When **did the American Civil War** start?	non-interactant	past
5-T/5	Xxx		
6-S	April 12th, 1861.	(non-interactant)	(past)
7-T/1	Yeah, April 12th, 1861.	(non-interactant)	(past)
7-T/2	How long **did it** last?	non-interactant	past
8-S(n)	Four years.	(non-interactant)	(past)
9-T/1	Four years, good.	(non-interactant)	(past)
9-T/2	So **it started** in 1861 and **came** an end, or we say **ended**, in 1865.	non-interactant	past
9-T/3	Er, who **was the President** during that time?	non-interactant	past
10-S	**Lincoln.**	non-interactant	(past)
11-T/1	**Lincoln, Abraham Lincoln**, the sixteenth President of the US.	(non-interactant)	(past)
11-T/2	So the **American Civil War broke out** in 1861, **ended** in 1865; it **lasted** four years.	non-interactant	past
11-T/3	Er, and then **which side won** the war?	non-interactant	past

Here again, the same choice of either Subject person or deicticity, explicit or implicit, remains unchanged in the successive moves despite switches of turns.

Functionally, the pattern of Story is quite different from that of Personal Story. Although it indicates that the information being exchanged is located in the past time, the information is equally far from both the speaker and addressee. What is more, neither of the interactants is responsible for the validity of the information, hence being personally disengaged from the interactive events. This is why the information type is merely referred to as 'story'.

Contextually, the Story pattern construes a tenor that is quite typical of the classroom situation. The teacher knows but nonetheless demands certain information, in order to check the students' comprehension of the text they are learning, or just to find out if the students have learnt anything they are supposed to learn. What the students can do in response is just speak either from the textbook or from memory, so they tend to speak less, as in Example 6–31, either individually or collectively. If both Personal Detail and Personal Story may engage the students in one way or another, Story only places the students into the position of a testee and the teacher into the position of a tester, a relationship that is highly distant and unequal.

6.2.2.4 *Knowledge*

The logogenetic pattern of Knowledge is identified through the choice of **disengaged** in terms of Subject person – non-interactant or pseudo-interactant – combined with the choice of **present** in terms of deicticity:

Example 6–32 [from Text 8]

t-m	text	Subject person	deicticity
62-T/2	So, "one sunny afternoon in the autumn of the year 1861, a soldier lay in a clump of laurel", ok, 'a clump of' – a group of, a cluster of – 'laurel', what's **'laurel'**?	non-interactant	present
63-S	'月桂树'.	(non-interactant)	(present)
64-T/1	'月桂属植物', un-hun, 'a clump of laurel'.	(non-interactant)	(present)
64-T/2	Then, '一群羊', what **do we** say?	pseudo-interactant	present
65-S	'a flock of'	(pseudo-interactant)	(present)
66-T/1	'a flock of', and **we do not** use this one, 'a clump of'; **we use** 'a flock of sheep'.	pseudo-interactant	present
66-T/2	Er, '一丛树'?	(pseudo-interactant)	(present)
67-S	[confusion]		
68-T/1	'a cluster of trees', un-hun.	(pseudo-interactant)	(present)
68-T/2	'一束花'?	(pseudo-interactant)	(present)
69-S	'a bunch of flowers'.	(pseudo-interactant)	(present)
70-T/1	'一群牛'?	(pseudo-interactant)	(present)
71-S&T	'a herd of cattle'.	(pseudo-interactant)	(present)
72-T/1	So **we say**, a flock of sheep, a cluster of trees, a bunch of flowers, or a bunch of keys, and a herd of cattle.	pseudo-interactant	present

Here, while the choice of deicticity remains the same, the choice of Subject person is first non-interactant and then pseudo-interactant, which actually reveal two perspectives on the same thing: (1) the linguistic item itself, and (2) the language users in general.

Functionally, neither choice of Subject person holds the interactants personally responsible for the validity of the information being exchanged, although pseudo-interactant somehow seems less disengaging than non-interactant. But in either case, the information is located in the present time – i.e. close to the interactants – in spite of its irrelevance to them personally, thus constituting some kind of universal truth that is neither restricted in time nor targeted at anyone specifically. This type of information, therefore, is called 'knowledge'.

Like the pattern of Story, the pattern of Knowledge also construes a tenor typical of the classroom situation. The teacher, being the knower and the knowledge giver, asks students questions to test if, and how much, they know; while the students, in the course of gaining knowledge, are frequently made to display their growing knowledge repertoire. The speech they produce, as a result, often resembles blank-filling: they do not even need to produce a complete sentence (as shown by Example 6–32). So, the relationship between the teacher and students is again a tester-testee relationship, and obviously a hierarchical one.

6.2.2.5 *Judgement*

The logogenetic pattern of Judgement is, unlike the above four patterns, identified through the choice of **judgement** instead of time in terms of deicticity, realized by a modal rather than a temporal operator. The choice of Subject person found in combination with judgement is **disengaged**, either non-interactant or pseudo-interactant. It is also found that choices of **assessment** – mainly realized by an evaluative adjective, adverb or noun, or by the metaphorical form of personal projection (*do you think* / *I think . . .*) – tend to occur within this pattern. But these choices may also be found within other patterns such as Story (*was it **easy** to get a ride*), Knowledge (*the society is very **complex***), or Recapitulation (*you did a **good** job in previewing the lesson*); so they are not taken as defining UNIVARIANTS of this pattern at the present stage. See an example of Judgement (assessment being underlined):

Example 6–33 [from Text 2]

t-m	text	Subject person	deicticity
62-S	But <u>do you think</u> if we don't have any examination, **we can't** memorize all <u>very well</u>?	pseudo-interactant	modal
63-T/1	OK, **you have to** memorize something at least, before you come to your own conclusion.	pseudo-interactant	modal
63-T/2	OK, how <u>do you think</u> the examinations, I mean, **history could** be examined then, what way <u>do you think</u> history **can** be examined?	non-interactant	modal
64-S/1	**Anyone could** have his own opinion toward history.	pseudo-interactant	modal
64-S/2	But **you couldn't** do that in your examination.	pseudo-interactant	modal
65-T	That's right.		
66-S	If **the teacher** don't have very common standard, in our opinion, I mean, how **can** he judge your examination, how **can** he give you marks?	non-interactant	modal
67-T	Right.		
68-S	If **you** write your own opinion, then –	pseudo-interactant	
69-T	Right.		
70-S	then **the teacher can't**, tell whether you are <u>right</u> or you are <u>wrong</u>.	non-interactant	modal

As can be seen, a modal operator is consistently found throughout this stretch of discourse, in which the choice of Subject person is either pseudo-interactant or non-interactant.

Functionally, the pattern opens up a semantic space of uncertainty between the speaker and addressee, leaving considerable room for a personal judgement on the validity of the information being exchanged; that is why the information type is referred to as 'judgement'. Although the choices of Subject person indicate that the interactants are not directly engaged in the interactive events, it cannot be denied that the interactants are expressing their own judgement or opinion, and therefore being indirectly engaged.

In terms of the contextual value of the tenor, the pattern of Judgement allows the teacher to guide the students in their thinking and understanding of a certain issue, and it also gives the students an opportunity to think about and explore the issue for themselves. Consequently, the students can be better motivated and prepared to speak in class (note that in Example 6–33 the first question is raised by a student), and to talk at length (note that the student's turns in Example 6–33 are clearly longer than those in Examples 6–29 to 6–32). In fact, Judgement is different from any of the above four patterns across moves, in that it neither directly engages the students like Personal Detail or Personal Story, nor totally disengages the students like Story or Knowledge, but stays somewhere in between. While the teacher is in the role of a guide rather than a tester, the students are in the position of an explorer instead of a testee; so their relationship can be said to be neutral.

6.2.2.6 Summary

In sum, presented in this section are five interpersonal logogenetic patterns identified in the analysis of the data, which may now be further classified into two categories: (1) engaging, including Personal Detail and Personal Story that engage the addressee; (2) disengaging, including Story and Knowledge that do not. Judgement is on the borderline between the two. In spite of such differences, they all spread across successive moves over quite a stretch of discourse, are all identified through a combination of choices from the DEICTICITY and SUBJECT PERSON systems, and are all described in terms of lexicogrammatical UNIVARIATE that occurs repeatedly. See Table 6.4 for a summary of the logogenetic patterns of Information Type.

6.2.3 Information/Action sequence: above the move

In terms of length, the logogenetic patterns above the move, to be described below, are similar to the patterns across moves as described above, because they both spread over a considerable stretch of discourse. But while patterns across moves are identified through choices of Subject person and deicticity, those

Table 6.4 A summary of the interpersonal logogenetic patterns of Information Type

Information Type		lexicogrammatical UNIVARIATE		interpersonal function	value of tenor
		Subject person	deicticity		
engaging	Personal Detail	interactant	present	exchange personal info	interlocutor vs. interlocutor
engaging	Personal Story	interactant / interactant-involved	past	exchange each other's own story	interlocutor vs. interlocutor
disengaging	Story	non-interactant	past	exchange a story	tester vs. testee
disengaging	Knowledge	non-interactant/ pseudo-interactant	present	exchange universal truth	tester vs. testee
Judgement		non-interactant/ pseudo-interactant	modal	exchange judgement	guide vs. explorer

above the move are identified basically through the choice of **mood**. Consequently, the former are described in terms of UNIVARIATE that recurs in successive **moves** regardless of their speech functions; whereas the latter are described in terms of a pattern of UNIVARIATE that recurs in successive **sequences** of moves, with each sequence being nonetheless centred on **one** specific proposal or proposition – i.e. either an action move or an information move. In other words, these patterns are found, not across moves, but above the move – being either an action sequence or an information sequence.

Based on the specific types of sequences in which the patterns are identified, they are classified into (1) action exchange, (2) information exchange and (3) information chunk. But it should be pointed out that the three types of patterns are all created out of both interpersonal and textual resources. Therefore, only a partial description of the patterns – in interpersonal terms – is given here, while the textual description will be given in Chapter 8.

6.2.3.1 Action Exchange

In 6.2.1 above, such action moves as 'direct' (a sub-class of command) and 'orientate' identified in EFL classroom discourse are described as the logogenetic patterns of, respectively, Direction and Orientation. What is concerned here, then, is the other sub-class of command, i.e. 'order', which has been found in EFL classroom discourse as an action move that contributes to the logogenetic pattern of Action Exchange.

In fact, in the EFL classroom situation, an action move usually has to do with such verbal actions as giving an example, explaining a word, translating a word or sentence, reading aloud one of the paragraphs in a text, and so on. Consequently, an 'order' is never found to be responded to with a *here you are* or *yes, I will* and then followed up with a *thank you*, as in a typical exchange of goods-&-services. Instead, the responding move usually serves to accomplish the action being demanded:

Example 6–34 [from Text 8]
92-T/5:   Now, 'penalty', give me a synonym of 'penalty'.
93-S: 'punishment'.
94-T/1:   Good, 'punishment', 'punishment for his crime', '疏忽职守'.

Example 6–35 [from Text 5]
87-T/7:   Would you like to read the first paragraph?
88-S: OK. "One summer I was driving from my hometown of . . ."

Example 6–36 [from Text 10]
34-T/2:   Next one, Lyn, would you please?
35-S: True.
36-T/1:   Yes, it's true.

In each of the examples above, the first teacher move is an 'order', demanding a verbal action: giving a synonym, reading aloud a paragraph, and doing a true-or-false exercise. The responding move that follows it, produced by a student, is always used to accomplish the action specified in the 'order' move; it is therefore also considered to be an action move, whose speech function can be named 'comply'. Although a 'comply' may be realized, as can be seen in Examples 6–34 and 6–36, by a declarative clause (explicit or implicit in mood), the clause is nonetheless viewed as a compliance rather than a statement, since it is used to accomplish an action as ordered by the previous move rather than to give information. Besides, a complying move itself may be followed up with a third move, which is realized, not by a *thank you* for having received certain goods or a service, but by a repetition (e.g. *punishment, it's true*, see Chapter 8 for more) and/or a declarative (often implicit) clause containing either positive or negative comment (e.g. *good, that's right, alright, you can say that* or *not correct*). Thus the follow-up move is in the semantic function of acknowledging and/ or evaluating the action just produced, hence referred to as 'acknowledge' or 'evaluate'.[5]

In other words, although there is no obvious continuity in the lexicogrammatical choices across 'order', 'comply' and 'acknowledge'/'evaluate' (as in those patterns across moves) except for a shift of mood, the three moves are nonetheless linked through the action that is specified in the initial 'order' move. They respectively demand, produce and give a feedback to the same action. In this sense, 'order' is a **free** move, while the other two are **bound** moves; they together form a pattern that can be called Action Exchange. The pattern is viewed as a logogenetic pattern because it is identified during the unfolding of a text. It is viewed as a pattern above the move because, interpersonally, it is identified mainly based on the semantic function as well as lexicogrammatical realization of the first, free move – 'order'; and yet the pattern is larger than a move, being a sequence of moves all centred on the proposal made in the 'order' move.

Like those patterns across moves (such as Personal Detail, Knowledge, etc.), the pattern of Action Exchange may also extend over quite a stretch of discourse. But unlike the former, it has to be described in terms of a pattern of UNIVARIATE, i.e. [imperative ^ declarative ^ declarative], that recurs in successive exchanges rather than moves. Here are two successive action exchanges, both coded for mood and for the speech function of each move:

Example 6–37 [from Text 10]

t-m	text	mood	speech function
71-T/5	Now, number one, Daniel, would you please?	imperative	order
72-S	I think it's D.	declarative	comply
73-T	B – boy, right?		
74-S	D.		
75-T/1	Yeah, D, you are right: D is the correct answer.	declarative	evaluate
75-T/2	And number two, Emily, please.	imperative	order
76-S	I think the answer is B.	declarative	comply
77-T/1	B.	declarative	acknowledge

Here, the same pattern extends over two action exchanges (actually even more in the original text, i.e. exercises 3, 4, 5, etc.) and is identified mainly through the action move of 'order' realized in the imperative mood, and also through the sequence [order ^ comply ^ acknowledge / evaluate]. What has to be pointed out is that an action exchange of three moves is only its **simple** version, which may well be extended into an exchange of five or even more moves. The first exchange in the above example is a case in point. 73-T and 74-S are moves that occur accidentally; that is, they cannot possibly occur as an independent question-answer pair. But once they occur, they turn a simple exchange into a **complex** one (for a detailed description, see Chapter 8).

Contextually, the pattern of Action Exchange is consistent with the usual teacher-student relationship. It is the teacher who gives both an order and an evaluation, and it is the students who comply. Thus the teacher is the commander and the students the commanded. See Table 6.5 for a summary of this pattern.

Table 6.5 Interpersonal logogenetic pattern of Action Exchange

Action Exchange		lexicogrammatical UNIVARIATE	interpersonal function	value of tenor
order		imperative	demand action	
comply		declarative	produce action as ordered	commander
follow -up	acknowledge	declarative	acknowledge or evaluate the action produced	vs. commanded
	evaluate	declarative; comment		

6.2.3.2 Information Exchange

Another logogenetic pattern above the move is concerned with a proposition rather than a proposal, i.e. Information Exchange, which overlaps with those patterns of Information Type so that there can be a personal detail exchange, a story exchange, and so on. But the pattern of Information Exchange is identified mainly through the choice of **mood**, whether it is explicit or implicit. This is particularly true with the 'disengaging' types of information like story and knowledge. For example:

Example 6–38 [from Text 4]
31-T/12:   "No one has been a more consistent opponent of communism", and 'consistent opponent', what <u>does this mean, 'consistent opponent</u>'?
32-S: [] 'often compete'.
33-T/1:   [] 'often compete', and 'always compete'.

Example 6–39 [from Text 6]
15-T/2:   OK, can anyone tell me, say, at the time AD 1, how many people there were in the world – say, what<u>'s the population in AD 1</u>, remember?
16-S: [] 200 million.
17-T/1:   [] AD 1,200 million.

In both examples, there are three moves. The initiating move serves to demand information through an explicit interrogative clause, while the responding move serves to give information as demanded through an implicit declarative clause. The two moves are here respectively called 'ask' and 'answer', and it is held that they are not linked through ellipsis alone (see also 6.1.1).

As revealed by the data, the EFL teachers ask far more WH-questions than polar questions (which is easily seen in most of the examples given so far). The response to a WH-question is not a statement that only negotiates the information given in the question through polarity (e.g. *Yes, it is / No, it isn't*); instead, it serves to supply the missed part of the information as specified by the WH-element in the question. When the WH-element is conflated with the Complement (*what*) or Adjunct (*when, where, how, why*), which is very common in the data, there is simply **no** change of deicticity or Subject person in the responding move (e.g. *What does this mean? [It means] 'often compete'.*).

Therefore, what seems to tie 'ask' with 'answer' is indeed the specific proposition that is put forward in the former and remains incomplete until the latter occurs. In other words, it is the two moves that together generate a complete proposition (see also Berry 1981a). Thus it can be said that the two moves are linked not only through ellipsis (which is a matter of textual meaning), but also interpersonally through the same proposition that is set out in the 'ask' move. In this sense, 'ask' is a **free** move, just like 'order'; whereas 'answer', which is never produced without 'ask', is a **bound** move. Together they form a pattern above the move, which is called Information Exchange and is identified through a switch from an information-demanding interrogative clause to an information-giving declarative clause. Of course, if a question meets no response, or is responded to with a disclaimer, there occurs an information exchange failure.

Moreover, once a question is answered, another bound move may follow. It functions the same way as to the third, follow-up move in an action exchange; but here, it is used to acknowledge or evaluate the information given rather than the action produced in the responding move. As found in the analysis of the data, the teachers, being much concerned about truth-value in a 'disengaged' information exchange, tend to use 'acknowledge' more often than 'evaluate' (see Examples 6–38 and 6–39); they will not use 'evaluate' until they are satisfied with the student's answer (see Examples 6–17 and 6–18).

On the other hand, with the 'engaging' types of information like personal detail and personal story, the pattern of Information Exchange is identified through both choices of **mood** and the more delicate choices of **Subject person**. As an illustration, here are two brief exchanges taken from earlier examples.

(1)　92-T:　　OK, do **you** have worries?
　　　93-S/b:　Yes, recently **I'm** worried about, about my study.

(2)　5-T/2:　　Now, what did **your** parents say to you?
　　　6-S:　　　**My** parents said that the only one you can depend on is yourself.

In both exchanges above, there is a switch in Subject person from addressee (-involved) in the initiating move, to speaker(-involved) in the responding move. This not only indicates a turn transition characteristic of dialogic discourse, but also further proves that it is the two moves together that generate a complete proposition. Besides, it should be pointed out that the follow-up move in an information exchange is optional, and that it is even less common

Table 6.6   Interpersonal logogenetic pattern of Information Exchange

Information Exchange		lexicogrammatical UNIVARIATE		interpersonal function	value of tenor
		mood	Subject person		
disengaging	ask	interrogative	[unchanged]	demand information	initiator vs. responder
	answer	declarative		give information as demanded	
	follow -up (ackn)	declarative		acknowledge or evaluate the information given	
	(evaluate)	declarative; comment			
engaging	ask	interrogative	addressee	demand information	
	answer	declarative	speaker	give information as demanded	
	(follow-up: ackn)	declarative		acknowledge the information given	

in an exchange of the 'engaging' type of information than the 'disengaging' type. The 'evaluate' move, in particular, almost never occurs in the former (an issue that deserves further study).

In any case, the pattern of Information Exchange, as summarized in Table 6.6, would portray the teacher as an active initiator and the students as passive responders, a relationship quite typical in the classroom situation.

Again, like Action Exchange, Information Exchange may extend over quite a stretch of discourse, and hence has to be described in terms of a pattern of UNIVARIATE, i.e. [interrogative ^ declarative ^ declarative], that recurs in successive exchanges rather than successive moves; besides, it has a complex as well as a simple version. See an example:

Example 6–40

t-m	text	mood
53-T	Why do you think so [it was the biggest problem]?	interrogative
54-S	Because if he didn't get a ride in time, perhaps some, some dangerous things will happen, like some robbers, some thieves may do some harm to him.	declarative
55-T/1	Yes, they may attack him.	declarative
55-T/2	Now, do you think it is easy to get a ride, is it easy to get a ride from strangers?	interrogative
56-Sn	No.	declarative
57-T	Why not, do you think, why isn't it so easy to get a ride?	interrogative
58-S	I think it isn't easy to make people believe that you are innocent,	declarative

59-T	yes, un-hun	
60-S	you must, must make them believe that you are just a passer-by, you won't do any harm to them, so they will offer you a ride.	declarative
61-T/1	Yes, okay.	declarative

Finally, it should be stressed that a full description of Information Exchange – simple or complex – has to involve textual resources, and hence cannot be provided until Chapter 8.

6.2.3.3 Information Chunk

As the name suggests, Information Chunk is another logogenetic pattern above the move that centres on a proposition rather than a proposal. Like Information Exchange, it overlaps with the patterns of Information Type so that there can be a story chunk, a knowledge chunk, a judgement chunk, and so on. But unlike Information Exchange, which entails turn transition, Information Chunk is found within one single turn, composed of at least one move but most often a sequence of moves that all hang onto one central proposition. The pattern is identified through, apart from mood choices, an even higher proportion of textual choices to be discussed in Chapter 8. Presented here is the interpersonal description of the pattern, which is further classified into two sub-types.

One sub-type is identified through a consistent choice of **declarative** mood in the sequence, hence referred to as **Statement Series**. See an example, which is a knowledge statement series:

Example 6–41 [from Text 2]
93-T/9:   OK, "At other times, however, the same 'facts' are given different meanings by different historians and their conclusions therefore differ."
93-T/10:   In other words, they interpret the facts in different ways, okay?
93-T/11:   Or, they understand the facts, they explain the facts, in different ways, and they come to different conclusions.

Here, all the moves are produced by the teacher and are declarative in mood. While the semantic relations among them, such as conjunction, repetition, paraphrase, etc., have to be explained in terms of textual choices; it is apparent here that without the first move (a sentence quoted from the text currently being taught in class), there would not be any of the rest. In other words, it is the first move that gives information, setting out a proposition for the following moves to hang onto, thus a **free** move; whereas the other moves, which give no new information, are **bound** ones. In this sense, all of the moves here are seen as belonging to one statement series, forming one information chunk.

The other sub-type displays, initially, a switch from **interrogative** to **declarative** mood, like that found in an information exchange – but without actual turn transition. Therefore, it is referred to as **Pseudo Information Exchange**. See the following example, which is a pseudo story exchange:

Example 6–42 [from Text 4]
25-T/1:   What is Nazi regime – what Nazi Germany did in the Second World
           War, when they invaded other countries, what did they do?
25-T/2:   They killed people, destroying their home, suppressed their resistance.
25-T/3:   So they were very cruel.

Again, the semantic relations among the successive moves have to be explained textually. Interpersonnally, the chunk begins with a move in the interrogative mood, yet the clause is meant to raise a point for attention rather than demand information; whereas the following moves, all declarative in mood, go on to bring out that point. In other words, the interrogative clause functions as a rhetorical question rather than a genuine question. It is in fact the second move, i.e. the first among those in declarative mood (*they killed people . . .*), that offers a central proposition for the rest of the declarative clauses to hang onto, hence a **free** move; whereas the rest offer secondary propositions, hence **bound** moves. Together they form an information chunk.

Functionally, the pattern of Pseudo Information Exchange suggests an effort to involve the addressee, which should have a positive effect on classroom teaching (and deserves further study). But on the whole, it is like Statement Series in that both patterns serve to give rather than demand information. In this sense, they construe the teacher as an information giver and the students as information receivers. Table 6.7 is an interpersonal description of the pattern of Information Chunk.

In addition, three variants of the Information Chunk pattern have been identified in the data. They differ mainly in the **source** of the initial, central proposition in the chunk, i.e. who is the speaker. In Variant 1 (see Example 6–41),

Table 6.7 Interpersonal logogenetic pattern of Information Chunk

Information chunk	lexicogrammatical UNIVARIATE	interpersonal function	value of tenor
Statement Series	declarative	give information	information giver vs. receiver
Pseudo Information Exchange	interrogative	raise a point	
	declarative	bring out the point	

the initial proposition is quoted from a text in the textbook that is currently being taught in class, so that the teacher only produces secondary propositions that expand the information given in the text. In Variant 2, the central proposition is found in the initial move, but not in the initial clause in that move:

Example 6–43 [from Text 5]
97-T/2:   Now, "He <u>had</u> his thumb out. . . " This <u>means</u>, if you <u>want</u> to get a ride –
    I think we talked about this – if you <u>want</u> to get a ride, then you <u>stretch</u>
    your arm, and <u>wave</u> your thumb like this.
97-T/3:   This <u>means</u> that you <u>want</u> to get a ride.

Here, the first clause in the first move is also quoted from the textbook, but it is different from the rest of the clauses in its choice of deicticity: past vs. present (compare Example 6–41, where all clauses in the chunk display a consistent choice of present). So, it is a story statement, while the rest are all knowledge statements. It then follows that the first clause here plays a different role from that in Variant 1; that is, it cannot be seen as the central proposition in the statement series. Instead, it can only be taken as a textual Theme specific to EFL classroom discourse (see 8.1.3 for details), hence taken as part of rather than the entire first move. It is, rather, the second clause in the first move that offers the central proposition, so that this series is a knowledge chunk rather than a story chunk. Thus in Variant 2, it is the teacher who produces both the free and bound propositions, which are nevertheless all related to a point taken from the text being taught (*"he had his thumb out"*). To further prove that the initial quoted clause in this variant pattern functions as a textual Theme rather than a proposition, here is another example that goes so far as to begin the chunk with a partial rather than complete clause taken from the text:

Example 6–44 [from Text 9]
17-T/5:   And ". . . can play on either television or computer screens". So here
    you see, there's no difference actually between the television monitor,
    and the computer screens there.
17-T/6:   Ok, the television screen, and monitor could be used as a computer
    screen, ok, the same function there.

Variant 3 is an information chunk that does not begin with a quotation from the textbook; the chunk gives information related to, rather than on, (1) a specific sentence or point in the textbook (see Example 6–42) or (2) an action previously carried out (see Example 6–45, where the action was oral interpretation). But it is still the initial move that offers a central

Table 6.8   Three variants of the pattern of Information Chunk

Information Chunk	source of free proposition	interpersonal function
Variant 1	textbook	expand information given in the text
Variant 2	teacher	give information on a point in the text
Variant 3	teacher	give information related to the text or an action

proposition for the rest of the moves to centre on, and it is the teacher who produces all the moves.

Example 6–45 [from Text 3]

99-T/2:   Nowadays the world is kind of male-chosen, so normally we avoid that [his], even in written English.

99-T/3:   If you write essays or a paper, you have to write 'his' slash 'her'.

99-T/4:   But when you talk about it, you say 'his' or 'her'.

99-T/5:   But when you write it, 'his' slash 'her', right.

See Table 6.8 for a summary of the three variants, which are temporarily called Variant 1, 2 and 3 instead of being given names, because they are here only described interpersonally (and will be fully described in Chapter 8).

Finally, the pattern of Information Chunk may also extend over a stretch of discourse and therefore has to be described, interpersonally, in terms of a pattern of UNIVARIATE that recurs in successive chunks. Here is an example covering two pseudo knowledge exchanges:

Example 4–46 [from Text 4]

t-m	text	mood
27-T/6	What does this word ['efficiency'] suggest?	interrogative
27-T/7	Say, if you do your work with great efficiency, what does this mean, you do your work with great efficiency?	interrogative
27-T/8	You can do a lot of work in a very short time.	declarative
27-T/9	So here when 'efficiency' talks about the behaviour of Nazi Germany, what does this imply?	interrogative
27-T/10	It is not used to talk about, the work done by the Nazi Germany.	declarative
27-T/11	Instead, it's used to talk about their cruelty, and aggression.	declarative

6.2.3.4 Summary

In sum, presented in this section are three more interpersonal logogenetic patterns identified in the analysis of the data. They are referred to as

Information/Action sequence because they each entail a sequence of moves that all centre on one and the same information or action move. When the patterns are concerned with a proposition, they overlap with the patterns across moves such as Story, Knowledge, etc. But unlike the latter, all patterns above the move are described in terms of a pattern of UNIVARIATE that recurs in successive exchanges or chunks, and they cannot be fully described until Chapter 8.

6.3 TEXT TYPE network: INTERACTION

The previous two sections of this chapter present respectively (1) the interpersonal systems in the REGISTER network of EFL classroom discourse, established on the basis of relevant systems of Functional Grammar as well as their structural realizations as actually found in the analysis of the data; and (2) the interpersonal logogenetic patterns identified as a result of coding the data according to the interpersonal REGISTER systems. In both sections, the presentation is given multi-stratally in spite of a focus on the interpersonal metafunction. In this section, all the multi-stratal, interpersonal logogenetic patterns will boil down to an interpersonal TEXT TYPE network of EFL classroom discourse, referred to as INTERACTION. The section includes (1) a representation of the INTERACTION network, and (2) an illustration of how INTERACTION can be used to analyse and describe the interpersonal process of EFL classroom discourse.

6.3.1 Representation

Actually, when the three types of interpersonal logogenetic patterns in EFL classroom discourse as described in 6.2 were first identified, they were mainly distinguished according to how the lexicogrammatical UNIVARIATEs can be described in relation to a move. The patterns in the move are those in which the defining UNIVARIATEs do not extend beyond a single move, and which appear like a boundary line between phases of meaning, hence called Boundary. The patterns across moves are those defined by UNIVARIATEs that spread over quite a number of moves, and are found only with information moves classifying information into different types, thus called Information Type. The patterns above the move are those whose defining UNIVARIATEs occur in a pattern that repeats in successive sequences of information or action moves, with each sequence being centred on one particular proposition or proposal, hence called Information/Action sequence.

From the description of the three types of interpersonal logogenetic patterns, it can be seen that the patterns are all multi-stratal: the lexicogrammatical variations realize different interpersonal meanings, which in turn construe variations in the values of the tenor of discourse. And being multi-stratal patterns of interpersonal logogenesis, they are revealing about the **interpersonal process** of EFL classroom discourse. In particular, they reveal the kinds of discourse behaviours that mark EFL classroom **interaction**. For this reason, the interpersonal TEXT TYPE system they make up is named INTERACTION.

From the point of view of classroom interaction, which is defined by Alright (1984: 156) as 'live, person-to-person encounters', the interpersonal logogenetic patterns of EFL classroom discourse can be further classified into two categories: (1) **unilateral** interaction, realized by discourse behaviours of the teacher only; (2) **bilateral** interaction, realized by the teacher's plus students' discourse behaviours. Thus the primary options within the INTERACTION system are 'unilateral' and 'bilateral'. See Figure 6.7 for a representation of the entire system.

6.3.2 Illustration

To illustrate how the INTERACTION system can be used to analyse and describe the interpersonal process of EFL classroom discourse, an actual analysis of a whole text, i.e. Text 5, is presented in this section.

Text 5 is an Intensive Reading class, which is commonly understood in the Chinese context as an EFL class organized around a specific text in a textbook. In this case, the text is entitled *The Kindness of Strangers*.[6] The students had been given preview questions before this class, and this was the first class hour devoted to the text.

To make an analysis of the interpersonal process of Text 5, the text was first coded according to the interpersonal systems in the REGISTER network of EFL classroom discourse (see Appendix I). Then, as the interpersonal logogenetic patterns were found emerging out of the successive lexicogrammatical UNIVARIATEs, the text was further coded according to the INTERACTION

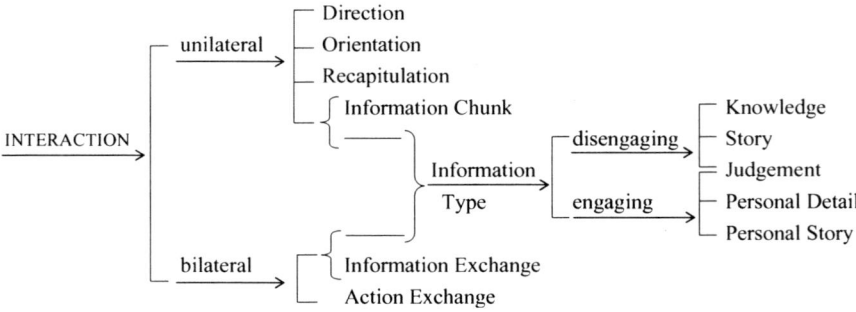

FIGURE 6.7 The INTERACTION system in the TEXT TYPE network of EFL classroom discourse

Interpersonal – Interaction (handwritten note on pink sticky)

sy
'i
th
p

...of EFL classroom discourse (see the
...IV). Admittedly, a few choices other than
...netimes be seen as mixed within a certain

...umorous.
...arcastic, the tone's sarcastic.
...his is the national motto, as *In God We Trust*
...cial, **was** adopted by Congress in 1956.
...writer is being very sarcastic, saying "I don't

...iter thinks, you know, er, the moral of the nation
...of helping other people, they say 'I don't want
...ve to protect myself.'

Here, the choice of past in terms of deicticity (*was* in 109-T3) can be found within the pattern of Knowledge Statement Series. Such occasional choices were ignored in the coding, as they generally would not affect the status of the pattern, nor change the type of information being exchanged.

Meanwhile, there could also be found instances of one pattern embedded in a stretch of discourse that features another pattern, such as in Example 6–48 below. Here, a judgement exchange is embedded in a stretch of personal story exchanges, with the status of both patterns being clear. The embedded pattern, therefore, was also coded.

Example 6–48 [from Text 5]

5-T/2	Now, what did your parents say to you?	personal story
6-S	My parents said that the only one you can depend on is yourself.	exchange
7-T/1	Depend on yourself, you can't depend, you know, you can't trust, you can't depend on anybody else, just yourself.	
7-T/2	But if you were badly in need of help, what would you do, suppose you are badly wounded?	judgement exchange
8-S	I'll call, call the police, or call the emergence agency. (laugh)	
9-T/1	OK, OK, that's right.	
9-T/2	Now, why do you think they advised you not to trust strangers, why did, did your parents advise you not to trust strangers?	personal story exchange

Once the whole text was coded for INTERACTION, several interpersonal phases could be seen emerging out of the interpersonal logogenetic patterns thus identified. While the pattern of Orientation – a suggestion that orientates the whole class towards a new course of discourse – tends to serve as a boundary line between different phases, those patterns either across moves or above the move tend to define the various phases. Altogether, five phases can be identified and are described as follows (please refer to Appendix IV).

Phase 1 [from 1-T/1 to 15-T/1]

Initiated by Orientation, this phase features personal story exchanges while embedding a judgement exchange. So, it is completely bilateral, with the teacher being the initiator. By inviting the students to tell their own story, the teacher is able to engage the students personally and to bring about student participation. Besides, by demanding judgement from the students – especially where the Subject person in the judgement exchange is interactant (*you, I*) – the teacher is able not only to encourage the students to think and to express themselves, but also to hold them responsible for the interactive events. Thus the teacher-student relationship is on the one hand somewhat equal: both the teacher and students are interlocutors. On the other hand, the relationship is hierarchical: the teacher is the controller, the initiator, and the guide; with the students being the controlled, the responder, and the explorer. In this sense, the phase is slanted towards a daily conversation, but clearly having its classroom style; hence referred to as **Classroom Conversation (CC)**.

Phase 2 [from 15-T/2 to 15-T/5]

This phase is not headed by Orientation, but it is set off against its preceding and following discourse in terms of both information type and interaction type: it is made up of a knowledge statement series (Variant 3), being completely unilateral. The teacher is the only speaker, giving the students information related to the text they are learning in class. So the teacher is the knowledge-giver; whereas the students, being disengaged from the interactive events, are passive knowledge-receivers. So the phase is referred to as **Teacher Monologue (TM)**.

Phase 3 [from 15-T/6 to 87-T/5]

This phase, again initiated by Orientation, is basically bilateral, featuring story exchanges while embedding a few knowledge exchanges. The Subject person remains non-interactant throughout, though occasionally replaced by pseudo-interactant. The teacher is demanding details of a story whose validity does not rest on the students, just in order to check if the students have comprehended the story or not. The students, for their part, are invited to give details of the story, while being personally disengaged from the interactive events. Equally disengaging is the briefly embedded Knowledge pattern that occurs where a mistake is made by a student, or where a question is difficult to answer; as well as a couple of embedded statement series (Variant 3, which gives information related to the text that is being taught) that are produced by the teacher in the wake of a story or knowledge exchange in order to revise and improve the student's answer. Finally, the phase ends with Recapitulation, in which the teacher makes positive comment on the performance of the whole class during the phase. Thus in this phase, despite students' participation in the interaction, the teacher-student relationship is essentially hierarchical. While the teacher is the initiator, tester, and occasionally knowledge-giver, the students are the responder, testee or knowledge-receiver. The phase, therefore, is referred to as **Teacher-Led Discussion (TLD)**.

Phase 4 [from 87-T/6 to 94-S]

This phase is once more initiated by Orientation. It is made up of one action exchange, in which the teacher demands an action through an 'order' move, and one of the students accomplishes the action through a 'comply' move. Thus the phase can be called **Student Action (SA)**, in which the teacher is clearly the commander, with the student being the commanded.

Phase 5 [from 95-T/1 to 109-T/8]

Actually, this phase, along with Phase 4, forms a recursive part in Text 5 (each time it is repeated, it focuses on a different paragraph of the text currently being taught). As can be seen, this phase is not headed by Orientation, but it clearly displays a switch from action to information, featuring unilateral knowledge chunks throughout. A slight change, though, can be found in the middle, caused by an Orientation that seems to cut the phase into two parts. Yet the two parts differ only in that the first part is entirely made up of statement series of Variant 2 (which gives information on a certain point in the text that is being taught); while the second part is slightly varied – featuring statement series but embedding pseudo exchanges, featuring Variant 2 but embedding Variant 3, and featuring chunks but embedding exchanges. In spite of that, in both parts the students are equally disengaged from the interactive events, and are assigned the same role as knowledge-receiver, with the teacher being the knowledge-giver. (See 7.3.2 for an interpretation of the differences between the two parts in ideational terms.) Therefore, the two parts are taken as forming one phase – a phase in which teacher talk is absolutely dominant; hence referred to as **Teacher Talk (TT)**.

With the above interpersonal phases being identified, the interpersonal process of Text 5 can now be described – in terms of the **interpersonal**

$$\overbrace{}^{CC}\quad\overbrace{}^{TM}\quad\overbrace{}^{TLD}\quad\overbrace{}^{SA}\quad\overbrace{}^{TT}$$

$$OR{}^\wedge PS\{J\}ex^n{}^\wedge Kss3{}^\wedge OR{}^\wedge[S\{K\}ex\{ss3\}]^n{}^\wedge[OR{}^\wedge Aex{}^\wedge[Kss2]^n{}^\wedge OR[Kex/ss/pex2/3]^n]^n$$

OR=Orientation	PS=Personal Story	S=Story	K=Knowledge	J=Judgement
A=Action	ex=exchange	pex=pseudo exchange	ss=statement series	2,3=Variant

FIGURE 6.8 The interpersonal structure of Text 5

structure of the text. Figure 6.8 represents the interpersonal structure of Text 5 (the formula is based on Hasan's, but revised: the caret sign ^ indicates order of phases; the slash / indicates an alternative pattern in the same order; the ^{n} superscript indicates iteration; square brackets [ ] enclose the domain of iteration; and braces { } enclose a pattern embedded within a dominant pattern).

As Figure 6.8 shows, Text 5, being an Intensive Reading class that is commonly understood as a type of EFL class focused on a specific text and on linguistic knowledge, proves to be teacher-dominant. Among the five phases identified, three are teacher-dominant: Teacher Monologue, Teacher Talk, and Teacher-led Discussion. Meanwhile, it can be seen that the interpersonal meaning in Text 5 is flowing

1. from exchanges to exchange-dominant, and then to chunk-dominant; that is, from bilateral interaction gradually toward unilateral interaction;
2. from Personal Story embedding Judgement, to Story embedding Knowledge, and then to Knowledge alone; that is, from the engaging kind of interaction gradually toward the disengaging kind.

These general flows of interpersonal meaning in Text 5 show that, in spite of an expected focus on a specific text and on linguistic knowledge, the teacher manages to introduce bilateral exchanges into classroom discourse, and to demand information whose validity rests on or at least involves the students (during the first phase of the class). This should more or less help to reduce teacher dominance and to engage the students. But, of course, further study is needed to prove the effect of any interpersonal strategies this teacher may be found to apply in organizing classroom interaction.

More importantly, the above analysis of Text 5 proves that the dynamic interpersonal process of an EFL class can be analysed by reference to the INTERACTION system, and can be described multi-stratally to reveal various features of EFL teaching and learning in the classroom. Furthermore, it proves that text as an ongoing process of making meaning may just as well be described by reference to Functional Grammar, as long as a dynamic approach is adopted such as the TEXT TYPE approach proposed here.

6.3.3 Summary

This section, being the last section in this chapter on the interpersonal analysis of EFL classroom discourse, has in fact brought out what the entire chapter is meant for, i.e. a multi-stratal description of EFL classroom discourse as a process of making interpersonal meaning. This is done in two steps. First, based on a description (given in 6.2) of the interpersonal logogenetic patterns identified in the data, this section brings all the patterns together into the interpersonal TEXT TYPE system of EFL classroom discourse called INTERACTION, i.e. a dynamic system organized interpersonally but recognizable multi-stratally. Then, the section presents an application of the INTERACTION system in an actual analysis of the interpersonal process of a whole text, offering a description of the interpersonal structure of the text. Thus the section not only demonstrates the applicability of the INTERACTION system, but also proves the feasibility of the TEXT TYPE model in interpersonal terms. The next chapter will be devoted to the ideational analysis of EFL classroom discourse.

Chapter 7

Ideational Analysis
of EFL Classroom Discourse

This chapter focuses on the ideational part of the analysis of EFL classroom discourse. Like the previous chapter, it presents (1) the ideational systems in the REGISTER network of EFL classroom discourse, (2) the ideational logogenetic patterns identified in the data, and (3) the ideational TEXT TYPE network of EFL classroom discourse, followed up with an illustration. In addition, the chapter will point out how the ideational logogenetic patterns resonate with the interpersonal ones.

7.1 REGISTER network: ideational

Following the steps of analysis as described in 4.2.4, observations were first made over lexicogrammatical choices in each of the ten texts, with all the ideational systems of Functional Grammar being kept in mind. However, fewer ideational systems than interpersonal systems were found shifting their probabilities in the EFL classroom situation.

Regarding the logical systems (concerning interdependent and logico-semantic relationships within clause-complexes), they neither stand out in the data, nor seem to be revealing about EFL classroom discourse. Even where some of the logical relationships do appear, such as the paratactic types of 'and', 'but' and 'so',[1] they tend to be applied as internal rather than external conjunction, and hence will be discussed in Chapter 8.

As for the experiential systems, the Transitivity system is found to stand out. More specifically, it is the process types that are found to shift their probabilities, while the participant roles are merely construed as part of a figure rather than in their own right. However, further examination indicates that, although the participant roles do not shift their probabilities in the EFL classroom situation; the **participant types** – namely, the types of Thing in the nominal group functioning as Participant – tend to display a strong association with certain process types, which is quite revealing about the experiential content of EFL classroom discourse. Thus the ideational systems in the REGISTER network of EFL classroom discourse as set up here include (1) PROCESS TYPE, and (2) PARTICIPANT TYPE. In the rest of this section, the two systems are described multi-stratally and illustrated with examples.

7.1.1 The PROCESS TYPE system

According to SFL, language is not only a resource for making interpersonal meanings, but also a resource for making experiential meanings, i.e. chunking experience into figures of happening/doing, sensing, being/having, saying, etc. (see Halliday and Matthiessen 1999). The grammatical system by which experiential meaning is made is **Transitivity**, which construes experience into a **figure**, i.e. a mental picture of a particular configuration of three elements: (1) Process, realized by a verbal group; (2) Participant (involved in the process), realized by a nominal group; and (3) Circumstance (such as time, space, cause, manner, etc.), realized by an adverbial group or a prepositional phrase. Obviously, Process is the centre of a figure.

Halliday (1994, 2004) distinguishes six types of process: material, mental, relational, behavioural, verbal and existential. As found in the analysis of the data, all of the six process types occur in EFL classroom discourse, yet they occur at different frequencies and some of them shift their probabilities significantly. For example, the most prominent process type here is relational rather than material. Table 7.1 presents the frequencies of the process types in the ten texts[2] (the percentages of both modes of the relational process, i.e. attributive and identifying, are provided, because they tend to construe distinct meanings in EFL classroom discourse); while a detailed description will follow.

Table 7.1 Frequencies of process types in the ten texts

text	percentage of each process type out of the total number of processes							
	relational	attributive	identifying	material	verbal	mental	existential	behavioral
1	42.1	25.0	17.1	39.0	7.9	6.7	1.2	3.0
2	50.0	35.7	14.3	23.8	4.0	18.3	0.8	3.2
3	43.4	24.1	19.3	30.1	22.9	1.2	1.2	1.2
4	69.0	25.3	43.7	20.7	5.7	2.3	2.3	0
5	39.9	21.7	18.1	27.8	15.1	12.1	3.0	2.0
6	29.2	25.8	3.4	20.2	13.5	25.8	11.2	0
7	60.5	57.9	2.6	18.4	15.8	5.3	0	0
8	53.6	27.2	26.5	21.2	13.2	1.3	9.3	1.3
9	75.0	37.5	37.5	15.0	2.5	3.8	2.5	1.3
10	55.1	42.4	12.7	11.9	13.6	12.7	5.1	1.7
mean	51.8	32.3	19.5	22.8	11.4	9.0	3.7	1.4

Relational process

The relational process is overwhelmingly dominant in the data, comprising over half of the total. This type of process represents a relationship of 'being' between two entities, which can be found in either the attributive or the identifying mode.

In the former, an entity has some class ascribed or attributed to it, so that an attributive clause has two inherent participants: Carrier and Attribute. As found in the data, the attributive process often serves to construe various states of entities:

Example 7–1: [from Text 8]
60-T/2:　Un-hum, his mother <u>was</u> seriously ill, and maybe her days <u>were</u> numbered – she <u>was</u> not long for this world; she <u>was</u> at the point of death maybe – so the news that he was going to join the Union Blue, would shock her, so maybe she will die very soon.

Meanwhile, as Halliday says, an attributive clause is also 'a central grammatical strategy for assessing by assigning an evaluative Attribute to the Carrier' (2004: 219). This is most evident in the 'evaluate' move (*you are right, that's right, right, alright, okay, that's good, (very) good,* etc.). For this reason, the percentage of the attributive process is even higher than that of the identifying process, particularly in Texts 6, 7 and 10 which involve a lot of action exchanges that require an 'evaluate'. Besides, attributive clauses are sometimes found within the interpersonal pattern of Judgement:

Example 7–2: [from Text 7]
36-T/2:　So, "what *will* Joe do when he *gets*", the first part <u>should be</u> in future tense, then the clause <u>should be</u> in present tense.

Thus the attributive process can be viewed as a resource for construing a relationship between an entity (*his mother, the first part, the clause*) and a class (*ill, numbered, long, at the point of death, in future tense, in present tense*). At the same time, it may also play a part in construing such interpersonal meanings as comment and judgement. As such, it clearly sets itself apart from the identifying process.

In an identifying clause, some entity has an identity assigned to it, hence two inherent participants – Identifier and Identified. As found in the data, the identifying process serves well to represent such relationships as naming, defining and symbolizing (cf. Halliday 2004: 234–5), which make up a fairly large proportion of the experiential content of EFL classroom discourse, especially in an Intensive Reading class (note its percentage in Texts 4, 8 and 9). Here are two examples:

Example 7–3: [from Text 4]
25-T/3:　And "in its cruelty and ferocious aggression", er, 'ferocious', and what, what <u>are</u> <u>the synonyms</u> for the word 'ferocious'?
26-S:　　'Fear'.

Example 7–4: [from Text 9]

9-T/2:   "The shows of the future . . ." – what we are talking about here, ok, the future – "may be the technological grandchildren of current CD-ROM titles", ok, 'CD-ROM' here (writes on the blackboard), what do the five letters here <u>stand for</u>?

10-S: 'Compact Disc Read Only Memory'.

It is also worth mentioning that the identifying process, as found in the data, may be **implicit** within a verbal or mental clause:

Example 7–5: [from Text 10]

4-T/3:   And so, do you think you can <u>tell</u> us the general idea of the text?

5-S: I think, the main idea <u>is</u> that although there are some disadvantages in New York, but there are still a lot of opportunities for you so seek your luck here.

Example 7–6: [from Text 9]

23-T/3:   Er, 'compatible', you <u>know</u> the word 'compatible'?

24-S: ∏ '兼容'.

25-T1:   Yeah, (writes on the blackboard) '兼容' 的意思.

In each example, the question is realized by a verbal (*tell*) or mental (*know*) clause, which could well be replaced by *what **is** the general idea* and *what does the word **mean**.* That is why the answer to the question is realized by an identifying clause: *the main idea **is** . . .,* (*it **means***) '兼容'. Once a student takes the clause literally as a verbal or mental clause instead of an identifying clause, the teacher will go out of his/her way to turn the implicit identifying clause into an explicit one:

Example 7–7: [from Text 5]

103-T/2:   So, ". . . a national motto", you <u>know</u> the national motto, of the United States – do you <u>know</u>, there is a national motto of the United States?

104-Sn: Yeah.

105-T/1:   But what <u>is</u> it?

Clearly, the verbal and mental clauses found in the above examples in fact serve as interpersonal projection, and the projected clause is an implicitly identifying clause. This kind of implicit clause is tentatively taken as an **ideational metaphor**, that is, a metaphorical variant of the congruent, explicit form of *what is it* or *what does it mean.*[3]

Material process

The material process ranks second in the data, although it occurs only half as often as the relational process. While the latter construes class-membership or identity, the former construes 'doing-&-happening'. So the material process has one inherent participant – the Actor – which brings about the unfolding of the process leading to an outcome. If the outcome is confined to the Actor, the process represents a 'happening' (intransitive); if it is extended to another participant, i.e. the Goal, the process represents a 'doing' (transitive).

Halliday (2004) takes one step further in delicacy to recognize a contrast between two sub-types of 'doing-&-happening', based on the meaning of lexical verbs functioning as Process in material clauses. They are the 'creative' type and 'transformative' type, distinguished according to whether the Actor in an intransitive clause, and the Goal in a transitive clause, existed prior to the unfolding of the process (for more, see ibid.: 5.2.3). Following Halliday's approach, a contrast relevant to EFL classroom discourse is drawn here according to the origin of the lexical verbs functioning as Process in material clauses, i.e. a contrast between what are here termed **daily-material** and **elevated-material**.

The daily-material type covers such verbs as *go, come, put, make, take, bring*, etc., which are of native English origin, often referred to as Anglo-Saxon words, making up the basic vocabulary of the English language. These verbs realize material processes that are common in daily life and do not require high-level reflection:

Example 7–8: [from Text 2]
93-T/8: Er, shall we go on, to the next paragraph?

Example 7–9: [from Text 7]
36-T/4: OK, now let's come back to No. 2.

The elevated-material type covers verbs that were borrowed at one time or another from other languages, principally from Latin and French, hence often referred to as Latinate words. These verbs realize material processes that are more abstract and much elevated from daily life, and hence require reflection at a higher level:

Example 7–10: [from Text 1]
129-T/2: OK, what else did people do?
130-S: They rescued, rescued a man.

Example 7–11: [from Text 8]
35-T/2: Shortly before Lincoln was elected President, South Carolina broke away from the Union, for the state had long been waiting for an event, ern, that will unite the south to fight against the anti-slavery forces . . .

While both sub-types of the material process construe events, activities and actions, their contrast suggests a distinction between material processes in EFL classroom discourse that require different levels of reflection.[4]

Verbal process

The verbal process ranks third in the data, but its percentage is actually pretty low (mean = 11.4). Being the process of 'saying', it has one inherent participant, the Sayer, representing the speaker, which may be a conscious being or anything that puts out a signal (e.g. *the text* says). Additional participant roles include (1) the Receiver, representing the addressee (*tell **the reader***); and (2) the Verbiage, representing the content of what is said (*tell **a story***) or the name of the saying (*ask **a question***).

Halliday (2004) discusses verbal clauses in the context of such specific types of discourse as narrative, news report and academic discourse, emphasizing their role of projection (quoting and reporting) and hence their role in providing the source of information. In the data used here, however, verbal clauses are found to be more straightforward; that is, they usually appear as a single clause rather than in a clause-complex. For example:

Example 7–12: [from Text 2]
1-T/2:   And, so, a university student can <u>comment</u> on how history should be taught, and now, we'll <u>comment</u> on it.

Example 7–13: [from Text 6]
1-T/3:   Now, let me <u>ask</u> you a question.

Example 7–14: [from Text 7]
8-T/2:   And normally you don't <u>say</u> 'I feel furious'; if you <u>say</u> so, you will sound very odd, very strange.

While these verbal clauses do not project, they share the same type of Sayer – *we, let me, you* – which refer to the teacher and students. Thus they serve well to represent verbal actions that are actually taking place in EFL classrooms.

Mental process

Excluding mental projection that functions as a metaphor of either modality (***do you think** it is easy to get a ride*) or mood (*so **you can imagine** what was the biggest problem*), mental clauses only account for an average of 9 percent of the total number of processes in the data. The mental process is the process of 'sensing', with one inherent participant, the Senser, along with an additional participant, the Phenomenon.

According to Halliday (2004), the Senser has to be endowed with consciousness, being either human (i.e. a person or persons) or human-like (i.e. any entity treated as conscious, e.g. *the **empty house** was longing for the children to return*). But as found in the data used here, the Senser is almost always human. As to the types of sensing, the most often found is the cognitive type (*know, realize*), while other types such as perceptive (*hear, feel*), desiderative (*want, decide*) and emotive (*like, enjoy*) can only be found from time to time. See a few examples:

Example 7–15: [from Text 1]
61-S: I just – I didn't <u>know</u>, on that day, ern, news, the experts say there's an earthquake, ern . . .
62-T: So <u>you</u> didn't <u>realize</u> it was an earthquake?
63-S: Yeah.

Example 7–16: [from Text 2]
9-T: So <u>you</u> <u>enjoyed</u> his teaching?
10-S: But – I didn't <u>like</u> him very much, but he really taught us very well.

Mental clauses serve well as an expression of what is going on in the human mind, which is highly encouraged in any classrooms, and particularly in EFL classrooms where both thinking and output are much stressed. But in reality, their percentage is fairly low (though interpersonal projection has a role to play in this regard and deserves further study).

Existential process

According to Halliday (2004: 257), existential clauses are not very common in discourse, comprising 3 to 4 per cent of all clauses. This is supported by the data used here: the average percentage of the existential process is 3.7. An existential clause has one inherent participant, the Existent, i.e. the entity or event taken as existent. There can also be found in the clause a circumstantial element of place or time, as well as the word *there* – which is neither a participant nor a circumstance but is needed interpersonally as the Subject. However, as found in the data, an attributive clause (e.g. *you **have** this word right below the word California, in different states they **have** towns with the same name [from Text 5]*) is often used in place of *there be*[5] and hence also taken as an existential clause.

   Halliday (2004) stresses the function of existential clauses in several different types of discourse, such as introducing a central character at the beginning of a story, introducing places of interest in a guide book, and so on. In EFL classroom discourse, existential clauses are simply used to reveal something that is obvious but may not have been recognized by the students:

Example 7–17: [from Text 6]
25-T/2:   OK, from the list, what can you tell, from the list, what can you tell?
26-S: The population <u>increases</u> very, very quickly.

Example 7–18: [from Text 4]
36-T/4:   Actually in the text, in Churchill's speech, <u>there is</u> another example, in the same paragraph, actually, <u>there is</u> another example, ern, in the next sentence in the same paragraph.

Although the existential process is not a major experiential resource, it is sometimes needed in the EFL classroom situation and serves well to represent certain aspects of the experiential content that require attention. This is why the process has a much higher frequency (11.2 per cent) in Text 6, which is concerned with the problem of over-population.

BEHAVIOURAL process

The behavioural process, as Halliday (2004: 248) says, is 'the least distinct of all the six process types'. For one thing, it construes physiological or psychological behaviour (*breathe, sleep, laugh*) as well as behaviour that is **near** a mental process (*look, watch, listen*), a verbal process (*murmur, grumble, mouth*), or a material process (*sing, sit, read*). For another, apart from Behaver as an inherent participant and Behaviour as an occasional second participant (such as *song* in *sing a song*), there is what Halliday (2004: 251) calls an 'anomalous' case of *I'm watching you* – in which *you* can be viewed as Phenomenon because the behavioural process *watch* is close to a mental one.

In other words, the behavioural process has both a **narrow** sense, in which it construes a clear-cut physiological or psychological behaviour; and a **broad** sense, in which it construes a process that overlaps with another process and hence may take on a second participant accordingly. To distinguish the two senses, they are here referred respectively as 'behavioural' and 'BEHAVIOURIAL'. And it is the latter that has been found in the data (at a low frequency, though) as quite revealing about EFL classroom discourse. For example:

Example 7–19: [from Text 5]
87-T/7:   Xxx, would you like to <u>read</u> [aloud] the first paragraph?

Example 7–20: [from Text 4]
1-T/1:   Now, let's <u>look at</u> page 71, the second line.

Here, both *read* and *look at* are BEHAVIOURIAL processes. The former is near a material process, taking on a second participant – Goal (*the first paragraph*); while the latter is near a mental process, also taking on a second participant – Phenomenon (*page 71, the second line*). Although the percentage of BEHAVIOURIAL process is low in EFL classroom discourse, it certainly represents a few very basic types of discourse behaviours in the EFL classroom.

7.1.2 The PARTICIPANT TYPE system

In order to find out more about the kinds of experience construed in EFL classroom discourse, it is not enough just to examine choices from the PROCESS TYPE system. The PARTICIPANT TYPE system can be equally revealing, especially regarding the kinds of experiential world in which the processes take place.

As an element in the transitivity structure, Participant is realized by a nominal group whose semantic core is the Thing, which in turn is realized by a common noun, proper noun or (personal) pronoun (Halliday 2004). The PARTICIPANT TYPE system, then, is a system of options that can be chosen as Thing in a nominal group functioning as Participant, realized by nouns or pronouns. The options are distinguished according to the types of experiential world they represent, rather than the participant roles they may enter into, and are thus called 'participant types'. It is found in the data that participant types, rather than participant roles, are revealing about the experiential content of EFL classroom discourse. For example, in identifying clauses such as *what are the synonyms for the word 'ferocious'* and *what do the five letters stand for*, the distinction between Identified/Value and Identified/Token is far less important than the meaning of 'language' as shared by the Things in both nominal groups (*synonyms, letters*). And in verbal clauses such as *normally you don't say 'I feel furious'* and *can we say 'millions publications'*, what stands out is, again, their shared choice of a generalized pronoun (*we, you*) along with the 'language' type of nouns (*'I feel furious', 'millions publications'*), rather than their shared choice of Sayer plus Verbiage – which is merely part of the figure. The system is composed of the following three major options.

On-spot participant

As one of the major options in the PARTICIPANT TYPE system, 'on-spot participant' refers to participants that are found in the immediate classroom world. It is further distinguished into three sub-types: person, language and textbook. See Table 7.2 for a detailed description.

An on-spot person refers to a human participant (individual or collective) present in person in the classroom world, i.e. the teacher and/or students. On-spot language refers to a linguistic participant. It is either a point, i.e. a specific word, group or clause quoted or selected from a text (enclosed respectively by a pair of double and single quotation marks); or a label given to a specific linguistic element. Either point or label is currently the object of teaching and learning in the EFL classroom. On-spot textbook refers to a textbook-related participant, including a part of or the whole text, an exercise item, a page number, etc. Sometimes a textbook participant may appear to be a person, especially in verbal clauses (e.g. *the writer / author says*), but it functions experientially in the same way as other textbook participants. Just compare **the writer** *here answers the question whether we can still trust strangers* with **this text** *answers the question whether we can still trust strangers*. So, this kind of person-like participant is taken as a textbook-related entity rather than an individual – except, of course, when it occurs in a material clause, e.g. *the writer traveled 14 states* (see 7.2.3.1 for more). These three sub-types of on-spot participant serve to represent different experiential aspects of the classroom world: (1) person, as the subject

Table 7.2 Sub-types of on-spot participant

sub-type		meaning	realization	examples
person		person(s) present in the classroom	1st/2nd person pronoun	I/you
			1st/2nd person plural pronoun	we/you
			proper noun; 3rd person pronoun	Jane/she (a student present in the classroom)
language	point	a language point currently being dealt with in class	a word/group/clause; demonstrative/ impersonal pronoun	'regime'/'came upon'/'might well'/'I feel furious'/"he lay at full length"/it/that
	label	a label given to a linguistic element	common noun; demonstrative / impersonal pronoun	letter/word/phrase/clause/ subject/predicate/synonym/ preposition/prefix/it/that
textbook		part/whole of a text/exercise/ textbook	common noun; impersonal (personal) pronoun	text/story/passage/paragraph/ sentence/(Exercise) No.2/ book/page/line/writer/he/it

in classroom teaching and learning; (2) language, as the object of teaching and learning in an EFL class; and (3) textbook, as an important medium for teaching and learning. While person and textbook can be found in all kinds of classrooms, language seems particularly relevant in a language classroom.

Relocated participant

The so-called 'relocated participant' refers to participants that are found out of the classroom, but relocated into the classroom by means of either the textbook or speech produced by the teacher and students. In other words, this type of participant is imaginary rather than real in the classroom world. It is further classified into three sub-types: person, animal and thing. See Table 7.3 for a detailed description.

A relocated person refers to a human participant that is found in a world away from the present classroom, but is currently being mentioned in the classroom. A relocated animal, similarly, refers to an animal participant found elsewhere and currently relocated into the classroom through speech. A relocated thing is more complicated than the other two sub-types. It refers to participant in a variety of experiential worlds, ranging from a natural disaster to a coast-to-coast journey, from immigration to the American Civil War, from population to cyber nation. As indicated by the data, such choices are generally pre-made by the textbook. To the extent that a relocated thing is revealing

Table 7.3   Sub-types of relocated participant

sub-type		meaning	realization	examples
person		person found in a world out of classroom	common noun; proper noun; 3rd person pronoun	wife/family/strangers/ driver/historians/ Churchill/Americans/ Lincoln/they/he
animal		animal found in a world out of classroom	common noun; impersonal pronoun	animals/rats/mule/ horses squirrels/donkey/ it/they
thing	concrete and general	thing in physical form, with multiple instances, existing out of classroom	common noun; impersonal pronoun	car/door/basins/bags/ job/boxes/clothes/ hometown/it/they
	concrete and special	thing in physical form, with a single instance, existing out of classroom	proper noun; impersonal pronoun	New York/Nazi Germany/ Civil War/Confederate/ Smithsonian/that/it
	abstract	an idea or conception	common noun; non-finite clause; impersonal pronoun	problem/cause/idea/ immigration/to get a ride from strangers/it/that

about EFL classroom discourse, it is classified into two categories – concrete and abstract – according to whether the thing has a physical form or is just a conception or idea. And then, a concrete thing is further classified into two categories – general and special – according to whether the thing has multiple instances or a single instance. The different sub-types of relocated participant serve to represent various experiential worlds – animate or inanimate, human or animal, abstract or concrete, general or special – which all exist elsewhere but are relocated into the classroom. This reveals, to a great extent, the varieties of the experiential content of EFL classroom discourse.

Generalized participant

The 'generalized participant' is on the borderline between the above two options. Lexicogrammatically, it is realized by a generalized personal pronoun such as *we, us, you* or simply *people*. Functionally, it represents people who can be said to be neither on-spot nor relocated, or as both on-spot and relocated. For example, in *normally you don't say 'I feel furious'*, the choice of *you* actually represents all speakers of the English language, including the students as learners of the language. In other words, a generalized participant construes an experiential world that may involve anyone concerned. In this sense, it represents a generalized rather than a specific entity, construing a universal rather than an individual world.

7.1.3 Summary

In this section, a description is given of the two ideational systems in the REGISTER network of EFL classroom discourse, i.e. PROCESS TYPE and PARTICIPANT TYPE. The former system is set up based on the Transitivity system, with a number of extensions in delicacy being made based on the data. The latter is a kind of expansion of the Transitivity system, which generalizes across rather than differentiates the participant roles, representing domain-specific features of the experiential content of EFL classroom discourse. Figure 7.1 is a summary of the ideational REGISTER network of EFL classroom discourse.

7.2 Logogenetic patterns: ideational

Following the steps of analysis as described in 4.2.4, the two systems in the ideational REGISTER network of EFL classroom discourse – PROCESS TYPE and PARTICIPANT TYPE – were used to code the data clause by clause. As a result, it is found that, as a text unfolds, successive choices from the two systems tend to combine in various ways marking off phases of the text. In other words, the combined choices co-articulate various ideational logogenetic patterns, which are actually found to construe four distinct types of content of EFL

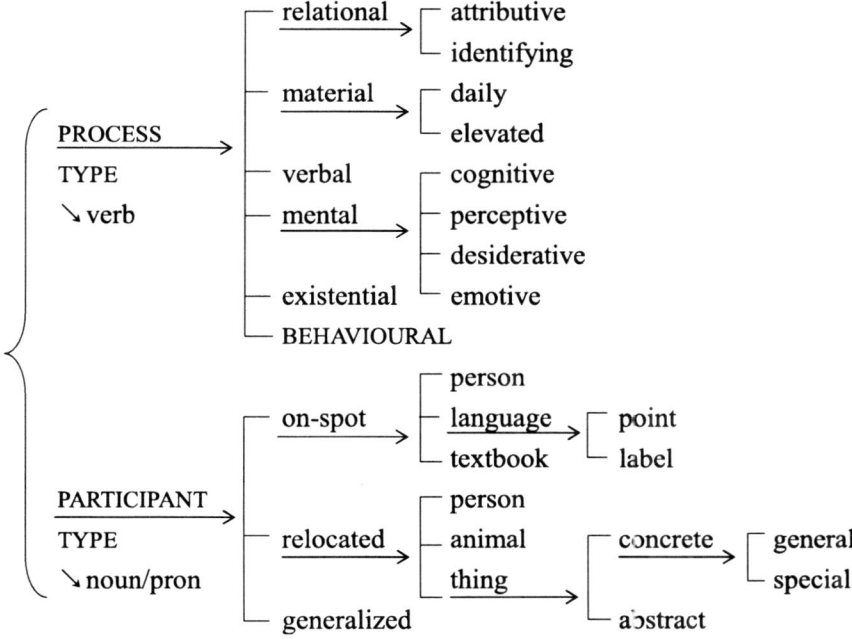

FIGURE 7.1   The ideational REGISTER network of EFL classroom discourse

classroom discourse: (1) classroom event, (2) life experience, (3) text, and (4) language. The patterns, therefore, are named after the content types.

In this section, the four ideational logogenetic patterns will be described multi-stratally. That is, they are described in terms of lexicogrammatical UNIVARIATE, explained in terms of their ideational function, and related to the contextual meanings they realize in terms of the field of discourse. Typical examples taken from the data are given as illustrations. Meanwhile, it should be stressed that PARTICIPANT TYPE is a system that generalizes across rather than differentiates participant roles. Therefore, where there are two participants involved in a clause, they are merely referred to as the **first** and **second** participant according to the linear order in which they appear. Usually, the first is an active participant, such as Actor, Sensor, Carrier and Sayer; but in the receptive (passive) variant of a material clause, the first participant is the Goal (e.g. *'ferocious' is used to* . . .), while the Actor is usually absent.

7.2.1 Classroom Event

The pattern of Classroom Event construes events actually taking place on the spot in classrooms, hence its name. Lexicogrammatically, it is identified through the choice of [**on-spot: person**] as the first participant, along with the choice of [**on-spot: textbook / language**] as the second participant if there is one. Since such a participant scheme is found in combination with three different process types – verbal, daily-material and BEHAVIOURAL – the pattern of Classroom Event is classified into three sub-types.

7.2.1.1 Verbal Event

The pattern of Verbal Event is identified through the choice of [**on-spot: person**] combined with the choice of **verbal** process:

t-m	text	first participant	process
Example 7–21 [from Text 7]			
36-T/5	This time, **one of you** will **be** the mother,	on-spot: person	identifying
	and **another one** [of you] will **be** Jim,	on-spot: person	identifying
	and **you make similar dialogues** about all these things, ern, that Jim's mother is worrying about,	on-spot: person	verbal
	and of course, **one of you** has to **give an answer**, if you are Jim – for example, "what would you do if you get food poisoning?" and **you say** "don't worry,	on-spot: person	verbal
	Mum, I'll . . ." – **you** just **say** something so that your mother won't worry about you.	on-spot: person	verbal

Example 7–22 [from Text 1]			
162-T/3	All right, all right, just now **we talked** about the people, the animals.	on-spot: person	verbal

In these examples, the choice of [on-spot: person:] as the first participant (*you, we*) is combined with the choice of verbal process (*make dialogues, give an answer, say, talked*). Where the move is realized by a long clause complex, the combination is nonetheless dominant across the clauses. Interpersonally, Example 7–21 displays the logogenetic pattern of Direction, which in this case is used to give directions for a role play between a mother and son (hence the two paratactic identifying clauses in the beginning); while Example 7–22 displays the pattern of Recapitulation. Ideationally, the logogenetic pattern thus formed serves to construe verbal events that take place right on the spot in the EFL classroom. In terms of the contextual value of the field of discourse, the pattern realizes an announcement of an oral activity, which gives the students an opportunity to practise speaking the target language, which is highly valued and encouraged in EFL learning.

7.2.1.2 Daily Event

The pattern of Daily Event is identified through the choice of [**on-spot: person**] as the first participant, combined with the process choice of [**material: daily**]. Whenever there is a second participant involved, the choice is also **on-spot**, either **textbook** or **language**. For example:

t-m	text	first participant	process	second participant
Example 7–23 [from Text 8]				
1-T/2	OK, **open** your **book** at page 540.	(on-spot: person)	material: daily	on-spot: textbook
Example 7–24 [from Text 5]				
95-T/13	Now, **let's come** to some of the words.	on-spot: person	material: daily	
Example 7–25 [from Text 2]				
87-T/10	**Let's go on** to the second paragraph.	on-spot: person	material: daily	

In the three examples above, the choice of the first participant involved in the daily-material process is [on-spot: person], either explicit or implicit; and the choice of the second participant is also on-spot. Even in Examples 7–24 and 7–25, where there is no second participant, the circumstantial element (*to some of the words*, *to the second paragraph*) involves an inside participant that is nonetheless [on-spot: language / textbook]. Interpersonally, the three moves form logogenetic patterns of Direction (*open your book*) or Orientation (*let's come to . . .*, *let's go on to . . .*). Ideationally, they all involve not only the subject but also the object and medium in everyday classroom teaching and learning, serving well to construe events of a daily kind taking place on the spot in the classroom, hence the term **Daily Event**. In terms of the contextual value of the field of discourse, the pattern of Daily Event realizes an announcement of daily classroom procedures.

7.2.1.3 *Behavioural Event*

The pattern of Behavioural Event is identified through the choice of [**on-spot: person**], combined with the choice of the **BEHAVIOURAL** process. Where a second participant is involved, the choice is [**on-spot: textbook**]. For example:

t-m	text	first participant	process	second participant
Example 7–26 [from Text 5]: recoding of Example 7–19				
87-T/7	Xxx, would **you** like to **read** [**aloud**] the first **paragraph**?	on-spot: person	BEHAVIOURAL (near material)	on-spot: textbook
Example 7–27 [from Text 5]				
40-T/2	Well, **go over** the whole **sentence** again.	(on-spot: person)	BEHAVIOURAL (near verbal)	on-spot: textbook
Example 7–28 [from Text 3]				
41-T/6	Well, if **the text** does not **tell you** directly, I think **you** can **infer** from what he said.	on-spot: textbook on-spot: person	verbal BEHAVIOURAL (near mental)	on-spot: person

In the three examples above, the choice of the first participant is again [on-spot: person], either explicit or implicit, and the choice of process is BEHAVIOURAL. Where a second participant is involved (*paragraph, sentence*), it is [on-spot: textbook]. In Example 7–28, it is the same choices of participant that appear in the secondary clause though the first and second are switched; and in the primary clause, though the process does not involve a second participant, the circumstance (*from what he said*) has an inside participant that is again [on-spot: textbook] (compare *what he said* with *the text* in the secondary clause). Interpersonally, the first two examples constitute an 'order' (*would you like to read, go over*) in the pattern of Action Exchange, while the last is in the pattern of Direction (*you can infer*). But ideationally, they all serve to construe a classroom event that is much focused on the physiological or psychological state of a conscious being, and thus called Behavioural Event. In terms of the field of discourse, the pattern of Behavioural Event realizes an invitation for conscious participation in classroom activities.

7.2.1.4 Summary

All in all, the pattern of Classroom Event construes the picture of a person who is present in the classroom and is currently involved in an event taking place on the spot. This is why the pattern, as can be seen from the above examples, tends to resonate with those proposal-based interpersonal logogenetic patterns, that is, patterns concerned with action rather than information, such as Direction (*make similar dialogues, open your book*), Orientation (*let's look at page 71, let's go on to the second paragraph*), and Action Exchange in which 'order' is a free move (*go over the whole sentence, would you like to read the first paragraph*); with Recapitulation (*just now we talked about the people*) as an exception since it is concerned with information instead. As a whole, the pattern of Classroom Event realizes the teacher's **management of the classroom process**. Table 7.4 is a multi-stratal representation of all sub-types of this ideational logogenetic pattern.

7.2.2 Life Experience

Another type of ideational logogenetic pattern discovered during the analysis of the data is here referred to as Life Experience, which construes events

Table 7.4 A summary of the ideational logogenetic patterns of Classroom Event

Classroom Event	lexicogrammatical UNIVARIATE			ideational function	value of field
	first participant	process	second participant		
Verbal Event	on-spot: person	verbal		construe verbal events taking place on the spot	announcement of oral activities
Daily Event	on-spot: person	material: daily	on-spot: textbook	construe daily events taking place on the spot	announcement of daily procedures
Behavioural Event	on-spot: person	BEHAVI- OURAL	on-spot: textbook	construe behavioural events taking place on the spot	invitation for conscious participation in activities

personally experienced by the students or the teacher elsewhere rather than in the classroom. Lexicogrammatically, the pattern is identified through the choice of, again, [**on-spot: person**] as either the first participant (*I experienced a small earthquake*) or the second participant (*did your parents give **you** any advice*). If there is another participant involved, first (*your parents*) or second (*a small earthquake*), it is usually a **relocated** participant – either [**thing: concrete**] or **person**. Such a participant scheme is consistently combined with one single process type sometimes, and a mixture of several different process types at other times, leading to a contrast between two sub-types of Life Experience: simple and complex.

7.2.2.1 Simple Experience

The pattern of Simple Experience is identified through the choice of a single process type combined with the choice of [**on-spot: person**]. In most cases, the process is **material** (here without distinguishing 'daily' from 'elevated') or **mental**. For example:

Example 7–29 [from Text 1]

t-m	text	first participant	process	second participant
42-T	Oh, how did **you** manage to **survive**?	on-spot: person	material	
43-S	坐在小船上 [sitting on a boat] (laugh).	(on-spot: person)	material	
44-T	And – so what did **you** do to **fight** against the flood?	on-spot: person	material	
45-S	Ern, **we** use, **used** some . . .	on-spot: person	material	
46-T	**used** some **basins**		material	thing: concrete
47-S	en, some basins to **pull** the **water** out,		material	thing: concrete
48-T	to **pull** out the **water**		material	thing: concrete
49-S	and to **put sand** on the door.		material	thing: concrete
50-T	to **put sand bags**		material	thing: concrete
51-S	Yes, **sand bags.**			thing: concrete
52-T	At the door to **keep** the **water** away?	(on-spot: person)	material	thing: concrete
53-S	Yeah . . .			

In this example, the choice of [on-spot: person] as the first participant (*you, we*) is consistently found in combination with the choice of material process (*survive, do, fight, use, put, keep*), and with the choice of a relocated concrete thing as the second participant where there is one (*some basins, the water, sand, sand bags*). Besides, such circumstantial elements as *against **the flood**, on/at **the door*** also involve a concrete thing as an inside participant. As such, the pattern construes events experienced in person by a human participant present in the classroom, i.e. a student or the teacher, but taking place in a world outside the classroom and having nothing to do with either the object or the medium of teaching and learning, i.e. language or textbook.

In other words, the events construed by such a logogenetic pattern constitute an individual's life experiences. As the pattern generally involves one type of process, it is viewed as the **simple** version of Life Experience. In terms of the contextual value of the field, this version realizes an account of a single aspect of an experience that the teacher or a student once had in his/her life. In Example 7–29, it is the material aspect of a student's past experience and hence overlaps with the interpersonal logogenetic pattern of Personal Story. It may also be something that a student or teacher is currently experiencing in his/her life, thus overlapping with the interpersonal pattern of Personal Detail. See a brief stretch of this kind in Example 7–30 below, where the pattern construes the feelings of a student, hence realizing an account of the mental aspect of an experience (note that within such circumstantial elements as *about my study*, *about anything* and *about my job*, the inside participants are all concrete things).

Example 7–30 [from Text 6]

t-m	text	first participant	process
92-T	OK, do **you have worries?**	on-spot: person	mental
93-S	Yes, recently **I'm worried** about, about my study.	on-spot: person	mental
94-T	And **you're worried** about anything in the future?	on-spot: person	mental
95-S	In the future **I worry** about my job.	on-spot: person	mental
96-T/1	**Worry** about your job.	(on-spot: person)	mental

In either case, the pattern is more related to the students than to the subject matter of the lesson. It enables the students' own life experiences to become part of the content of classroom discourse, which in turn is likely to make the students feel that the lesson is somehow relevant to their own life.

7.2.2.2 Complex Experience

Unlike the Simple Experience pattern, the Complex Experience pattern is not restricted to one type of process. Various process types – but most often, **material**, **mental**, **attributive** and **verbal** – can be mixed within a certain stretch of discourse, in which the first participant choice is predominantly [**on-spot: person**] and occasionally **generalized**, while the second participant (if there is one) is predominantly [**relocated: person / thing**]. From time to time within the same stretch of discourse, the two participant types may switch. This is because a complex human experience clearly involves not only the hero, but also other people, things, or even the society. See an example where Life Experience again resonates with the interpersonal pattern of Personal Story:

Example 7–31 [from Text 2]

t-m	text	first participant	process	second participant
1-T/4	Now, what about the rest of you – did **you come across**, en, an interesting **history teacher?**	on-spot: person	material	relocated: person
2-S	Yes, when **I was** in primary school, ern, I –	on-spot: person	attributive	
3-T	primary school			
4-S	**I have[had] a math teacher** who is a drawing teacher.	on-spot: person	attributive	relocated: person
5-T	**You mean**, ern, **drawing?**	on-spot: person	mental	thing: concrete
6-S	**Fine arts**.	(on-spot: person)	(mental)	thing: concrete
7-T/1	A teacher of fine art, okay, a teacher of fine art, okay.			
7-T/2	OK, and did **you think** he is interesting then?	on-spot: person	mental	
8-S	Yes, **he taught us** very well.	relocated: person	material	on-spot: person
9-T	So **you enjoyed** his **teaching?**	on-spot: person	mental	thing: concrete
10-S	But – **I** didn't **like him** very much,	on-spot: person	mental	relocated: person
	but **he** really **taught us** very well.	relocated: person	material	on-spot: person
11-T	OK, if you say **he taught** well,	relocated: person	material	
	how, how can that be **you** didn't quite **like him?**	on-spot: person	mental	relocated: person
12-S	Oh, I, because when **I saw him**, I, I would **feel** very sick, disgusted.	on-spot: person	mental	relocated: person

In this example, the choice of [on-spot: person] as the first participant (*you, I*) is dominant across the entire stretch of discourse, though occasionally switching to [relocated: person] (*he*). Thus the stretch is about events experienced by someone in the classroom. However, when there is a second participant (*history teacher, math teacher, him, drawing, us, his teaching, him*), it is relocated, either a person or a concrete thing. This indicates that the events have to do with the world outside the classroom. As to the process types chosen, they represent not only 'doing' (*come across, taught*) but also 'being' (*was, had*) and 'sensing' (cognitive: *mean, think*; emotive: *enjoy, like*; perceptive: *saw, feel*).

In other words, such a logogenetic pattern construes a more colourful as well as more comprehensive picture of an experience – covering what one (and others) did, when and where one did it, what one thought, and how one felt. So the pattern is viewed as the **complex** version of Life Experience. In terms of the contextual value of the field, it realizes an account of different aspects of a life experience of a student and/or the teacher. This is why it overlaps with the interpersonal pattern of not only Personal Story (in Example 7–31) but also Judgement (*if you were badly in need of help, what **would** you do [from Text 5]*; see also Example 6–33: *you **have to** memorize . . ., anyone **could** have his own opinion*) and Knowledge (*because **the society is** very complex . . . there **are** also good people [from Text 5]*). Like Simple Experience, it brings a student's or teacher's life experiences into the classroom, linking their own life with the subject matter of the lesson. The difference between the two versions lies mainly in the way a life experience is represented – from either a single or a multiple point of view.

7.2.2.3 Summary

In sum, the pattern of Life Experience construes the picture of a person who is present in the classroom world but involved in events that have to do with the person's life experiences rather than classroom activities. This is evident in the choice of a relocated or a generalized person or thing as one of the participants, as well as in the choices of varied process types. As such, the pattern realizes an **account of an individual's life experiences.** As a summary, Table 7.5 offers a multi-stratal representation of the pattern of Life Experience.

7.2.3 Text

Unlike the above two types of pattern, the pattern of Text construes events involving neither the teacher nor the students, but the subject matter of the text that is currently being taught and learnt in class, hence the name Text. Lexicogrammatically, it is identified negatively through the absence of, rather than positively through the presence of, the participant choice of [on-spot: person / language]. According to the specific kinds of combination of the ideational choices as identified during the analysis of the data, four sub-types of the Text pattern are distinguished as follows.

Table 7.5   A summary of the ideational logogenetic patterns of Life Experience

Life Experience	lexicogrammatical UNIVARIATE			ideational function	value of field
	process	first participant	second participant		
Simple Experience	material/ mental	on-spot (relocated): person	relocated (on-spot): person; relocated: thing: concrete	construe a single aspect of a life experience	account of life experiences
Complex Experience	material; attributive; mental; verbal			construe multiple aspects of a life experience	

7.2.3.1 In-Text

The pattern of In-Text construes events told in the text that is currently being taught and learnt in class. It is identified through a participant choice of [**relocated: person / animal / thing**] combined with the choice of a **material**, **mental** or **relational** process:

Example 7–32 [from Text 5]

t-m	text	first participant	process
81-T/2	OK, so er, well, was **he** ever **rejected** – I mean when he wanted to get a ride, was he ever rejected?	relocated: person	material
82-Sn	Yes.	(relocated: person)	(material)
83-T/1	Yes, yes, sometimes, sometimes yes.	(relocated: person)	(material)
83-T/2	**He** was **rejected** once, for instance – when?	relocated: person	material
84-S	One day, in the rain, en, **he** can't **get** a ride,	relocated: person	material
	so **he** was **left** stand out in the rain,	relocated: person	material
85-T	yeah		
86-S	until **a truck driver arrived**.	relocated: person	material
87-T/1	That's right, yes, until **a truck driver arrived**.	relocated: person	material
87-T/2	That is to say, well, several **cars or trucks passed**	relocated: thing	material
	by and nobody, no **driver picked** him up, so **he**	relocated: person	material
	had to **stand** in the rain, for some time until **a**	relocated: person	material
	truck driver came along.	relocated: person	material

Here, throughout the entire stretch of discourse, the choice of [relocated: person] as the first participant (*he, truck driver*) is consistently in combination with the choice of a material process. Where there is a second participant (*a ride* in 84-S) or a shift of first participant from person to thing (*cars and trucks* in 87-T/2), it is nonetheless a relocated participant. The same is true in a stretch of discourse featuring an **animal** participant:

Example 7–33 [from Text 1]

t-m	text	first participant	process
148-T/2	First of all, rats – so what did **rats do**?	relocated: animal	material
149-S(n)	**Sailing** down on soap boxes.	(relocated: animal)	material
150-T/1	Yes, **they sailed** down on soap boxes, very small	relocated: animal	material
	soap boxes, but **soap boxes were** not large	relocated: thing:	attributive
	enough to hold the rats, just like sailors.		
150-T/2	All right, and also, another kind of **animals**	relocated: animal	
	mentioned here?		
151-Sn	**Horses**.	relocated: animal	
152-T/1	**Horse**.	relocated: animal	
152-T/2	OK, what about the **horses**?	relocated: animal	
153-Sn	**Drifting**.	(relocated: animal)	material
154-T/1	All right, **they drifted** in the water and made a	relocated: animal	material
	very queer noise.		

In this way, the pattern of In-Text serves to construe events that take place in a world (real or fictional) other than the classroom, but are relocated into the classroom by means of the text currently being taught and learnt in class. This is why the pattern usually overlaps with the interpersonal pattern of Story. In terms of the contextual value of the field, it realizes a retelling of the story that is told in the text, which is found to be a fairly common activity in an EFL class.

7.2.3.2 Above-Text

The pattern of Above-Text construes abstract relationships that exist above actual details given in the text that is currently being taught and learnt. It is identified through a participant choice of [**relocated: thing: abstract**] combined with the choice of a **relational** process, either attributive or identifying:

Example 7–34 [from Text 5]

t-m	text	first participant	process
41-T/2	OK, now, next question: what do you think, what do you think, **was** the biggest **problem** during the journey?	thing: abstract	identifying
41-T/3	Anyone?		
	[for more than 6 seconds, no response]		
41-T/4	Well, you think chiefly the **problems were**, ern, whether he could get rides, whether the drivers would stop to pick him up, whether he can get food, and whether he can get shelter to pass the night – he can't sleep in the open, especially in some places.	thing: abstract	identifying
41-T/5	So, what do you think, what do you think **was** the biggest **problem**?	thing: abstract	identifying
	[for more than 6 seconds, no response]		
41-T/6	Well, if the **text** does not **tell** you directly, I think **you** can **infer** from what he said.	textbook on-spot: person	verbal BEHAVIOURAL
41-T/7	You remember what kind of journey was **he** going to **make**?	relocated: person	material
42-Sn	From coast to coast.		
43-T/1	Yeah, **he** was going to **make** a coast to coast journey.	relocated: person	material
43-T/2	Well, **it's** a large area in United States, from the Pacific to the Atlantic, from coast to coast.	thing: special	attributive
43-T/3	So you can imagine what, what **was** the biggest **problem**?	thing: abstract	identifying
44-S	[confusion]		
45-T	Yes, **speak** louder.		BEHAVIOURAL
56-S	**Rides.**	(thing: abstract)	(identifying)

Here, a combination of the choice of [relocated: thing: abstract] as the first participant (*problem*) with the choice of identifying process (*was*) is found to run through the entire stretch of discourse despite interruptions caused by exchange failures. The pattern construes an abstract relationship of identity that is currently being explored – *what was the biggest problem?* The question is asked three times (in 41-T/2, 41-T/5 and 43-T/3) by the teacher, but twice it fails to get a response from the students. After the first failure, the teacher follows the same pattern, offering a number of relationships of identity for the students to choose from, only to fail again. Inserted into the pattern are a few different choices in both participant type and process type, whose combination conforms to the patterns of Behavioural Event (*you can infer . . .*) that serves to invite conscious participation, and In-Text (*he was going to make . . .*) that serves to retell relevant details in the text. When the pattern is resumed (after 43-T/3), *the biggest problem* is eventually identified with *rides.*

In terms of the contextual value of the field of discourse, Above-Text realizes an analysis or synthesis of the text, which concerns but rises above the text. Thus it requires more efforts in thinking than In-Text; although, like the latter, it overlaps with the interpersonal pattern of Story. In other words, Above-Text is ideationally more demanding than In-Text. That is perhaps why it also overlaps with Knowledge (*the main idea is that . . . [from Text 10]*). In theory, efforts in thinking are facilitative to both text comprehension and speech production; but in reality such efforts seem to be somehow lacking in EFL classrooms, as reflected by the data.

7.2.3.3 Behind-Text

The pattern of Behind-Text construes necessary background behind things or persons mentioned in the text. It is identified through the choice of [**relocated: thing: concrete**] or [**relocated: person**] as the first participant, combined with a number of process types – mainly **relational** and **existential**. And in the case of a concrete thing, it is more often a **special** than a general thing. For example:

Example 7–35 [from Text 9]

t-m	text	first participant	process
29-T/12	OK, "Philips Interactive, for example, has dozens of titles, among them *A Tour of Smithsonian*" – you know where the **Smithsonian is**?	thing: concrete: special	attributive
30-S	[confusion]		
31-T	Un-hun, Smithsonian, **Smithsonian refers** to –	concrete: special	identifying

32-S	– in Washington D.C.		
33-T/1	Yeah, **that's** the, [a] very grand spectacle there.	concrete: special	attributive
33-T/2	OK, the **Smithsonian is** a group of museums.	concrete: special	attributive
33-T/3	And so far as I know, **there is** – when I visited Smithsonian in nineteen, er, nineteen-ninety-five – **there are** 17 **museums**, 17 museums, all situated around, the Loop.	concrete: general	existential
33-T/4	You know, the Loop – (drawing on the blackboard) OK, **this is** a loop.	concrete: special	attributive
33-T/5	OK, here **is the Capitol**, er, here should **be Lincoln Memorial**, and in the middle **is the Monument** of Liberation there.	concrete: special	attributive
33-T/6	And **that's** the, the whole Loop.	concrete: special	identifying
33-T/7	And, **Smithsonian, is** just situated around here.	concrete: special	attributive
33-T/8	And the wonderful thing, the most wonderful thing is that **Smithsonian, these museums**, they **are** all free – it's all free.	concrete: special concrete: general	attributive

Throughout this stretch of discourse can be seen a consistent combination of the choice of [relocated: thing: concrete: special] as the first participant (*Smithsonian, Loop, Capitol, Lincoln Memorial, Monument of Liberation*), with the choice of relational process – including both the attributive and identifying modes. In 33-T/3, though, there appears a participant choice of [concrete: general] (*museums*) combined with an existential process (*there are*). While the main line of the pattern construes various kinds of relationships that serve to either characterize or define a concrete, special entity, i.e. *the Smithsonian*, the side line construes an existing detail that adds to the description of a general entity (note that the choices of 'special' and 'general' actually co-exist in 33-T/8).

In terms of the contextual value of the field, Behind-Text realizes a description of the background to a person or thing mentioned in the text – such as *the Smithsonian* here in Example 7–35. This is why it is found to resonate with the interpersonal pattern of Knowledge. This kind of background knowledge is necessary in an EFL class, since learning a foreign language always implies learning about a foreign culture as well.

7.2.3.4 Beyond-Text

The pattern of Beyond-Text construes what is meant beyond the words in the text. It is identified through the choice of [on-spot: textbook] as the first participant, combined with the choice of a **verbal**, **mental** or **attributive** process. Commonly found examples include *why does the writer want to . . ., the text answers*

the question whether . . ., the first paragraph tells us . . ., the writer is being sarcastic, etc.
However, if part of a text from the textbook is directly quoted in a verbal clause
(e.g. **The writer says "with gangs".** *That means 'because of gangs'. [from Text 5]*), the
entire verbal clause is viewed as a textual Theme (see Chapter 8 for details).
See an example of Beyond-Text as follows.

Example 7–36 [from Text 5]

t-m	text	first participant	process
21-T/2	So ern, now, the next question is, what did he, what did the **writer** – what does the writer **want to say** to the reader through his experience described in the passage, what do you think, the writer **wants to tell** the reader?	on-spot: textbook	mental verbal
21-T/3	Anyone?		
21-T/4	Yes.		
22-S	Now you can still depend on the kindness of stranger.	(on-spot: textbook)	(mental verbal)
23-T/1	So the **writer wants to convince** the reader that you can still depend on the kindness of strangers, in spite of the increasing crime.	on-spot: textbook	mental verbal

As can be seen, the pattern here represents the text (writer) as wanting to say
something to the reader. Yet, in this hypotactic verbal group complex (for more
see Halliday 1994: 290), i.e. *want to say / tell / convince,* the verbal process (*say /
tell / convince*) is projected by the mental process (*want*); that is, nothing has
actually been said by the text writer. Even the desire (*want*) of the writer is
imagined rather than real (note the change from past tense to present tense
in 22-T/2). So, both the wording and the meaning are implied rather than
actually expressed in the text. This is why the pattern resonates with the
interpersonal pattern of Knowledge rather than Story. In terms of the contextual
value of the field, the pattern realizes an interpretation rather than a retelling
of the text.

7.2.3.5 Summary

In sum, the Text pattern construes events involving neither the subjects (i.e. the
teacher and/or students) nor the object (i.e. language) of teaching and learning
in the EFL classroom, but the subject matter of the text by means of which
language is taught and learned. That is, it realizes the **study of a text** from
various perspectives, as can be seen from the sub-types of the pattern presented
above. See Table 7.6 for a summary.

Table 7.6   A summary of the ideational logogenetic patterns of Text

Text	lexicogrammatical UNIVARIATE		ideational function	value of field
	first participant	process		
In-Text	relocated: person/ thing/animal	material/mental/ relational	construe events told in the text	retelling of the text
Above -Text	relocated: thing: abstract	identifying/ attributive	construe abstract relationships	analysis/synthesis of the text
Behind -Text	relocated: person/ thing: concrete: special	identifying/ attributive/ existential	construe defin tion or characteristic of special entities	description of background to the text
Beyond -Text	on-spot: textbook	verbal/mental/ attributive	construe meanings implied in the text	interpretation of meanings of the text

7.2.4 Linguistic Item

The pattern of Linguistic Item, the last ideational logogenetic pattern described here, is actually the most commonly found in EFL classroom discourse as reflected in the data. It construes various defining features of a linguistic item that is currently being presented in class, overlapping with the interpersonal pattern of Knowledge. The pattern is identified essentially through the participant choice of [**on-spot: language**], which can be combined with different process types, and with different participant types when another participant is involved. So the pattern is further classified into the following three sub-types.

7.2.4.1 Usage

The pattern of Usage construes the way a linguistic item is used. It is identified through the choice of **generalized** as the first participant, and the choice of [**on-spot: language: point**] as the second – or as the first in the case of a passive clause (e.g. *'ferocious' is used to* . . ., where the active participant is usually absent). Such a participant scheme is combined with the choice of a **verbal** or **material** process, realized specifically by the verbs *say / call* and *use / put (to use)*. In fact, *say* and *use* do not seem to make much difference when occurring in this pattern: *we seldom use 'kilograms'* is very similar to *we seldom say 'kilograms'*; so they are often used interchangeably (see Example 7–37). Thus the material process in this pattern is tentatively defined

as a **verbalized-material** process – in the sense that a material process is
verbalized by its linguistic Goal.[6]

Example 7–37 [from Text 3]

t-m	text	first participant	process	second participant
99-T/6	Another thing is, in spoken English, **we** seldom **use** **'kilograms'**.	generalized	verbalized -material	on-spot: language: point
99-T/7	**You** never hear **people talk about 'kilograms'**, right?	generalized	verbal	on-spot: language: point
99-T/8	For instance, in a shop, when **you get something, you** always **say** three **'kilos'** of apples, not three **'kilograms'** of apples,	generalized generalized	material verbal	relocated: thing on-spot: language: point
	as **it's** very bookish, it's not idiomatic.	on-spot: language: point	attributive	
99-T/9	So **we use** the **abbreviated form, 'kilos'**, all right?	generalized	verbalized -material	on-spot: language: label / point
99-T/10	So **we say 'seven hundred and fifty kilos of pork'**, rather than **'kilograms of pork'**.	generalized	verbal	on-spot: language: point

In this stretch of discourse, there is a consistent choice of verbal or verbalized-
material process (*say, use*), combined with the choice of a generalized first
participant (*we, you, people*) and [on-spot: language: point] as the second
participant (*'kilograms', 'kilos', 'seven hundred and fifty kilos of pork'*). The pattern
serves to construe verbal (or verbalized) events that involve, on the one hand,
all speakers of a language including people both outside and inside the present
classroom; and on the other hand, a specific item of that language. In terms of
the contextual value of the field, the pattern realizes an explanation of the
usage of a specific item in the target language. To the EFL learners, who are
trying to get as close as possible to the native speaker's competence, this kind of
explanation is helpful.

7.2.4.2 *Meaning*

The Meaning pattern, on the other hand, construes the definition of a
linguistic item. It is identified through a participant choice of [**on-spot:
language: point**] combined with the choice of an **identifying** process.
Sometimes, the pattern is found to contain, or even be gradually replaced by,
a side pattern, i.e. a **generalized** participant involved in a **material** process.
As this side pattern usually occurs together with the Meaning pattern and
performs the same ideational function, it is viewed as a supplement to Meaning,

called Side Meaning. For example:

Example 7–38 [from Text 4]

t-m	text	first participant	process
27-T/5	And "in its efficiency", what does the word **suggest, 'efficiency'**?	language: point	identifying
	[for more than 6 seconds, no response]		
27-T/6	What does **this word suggest**?	language: point	identifying
27-T/7	Say, if **you do your work** with great 'efficiency', what does **this mean**, you do your work with great 'efficiency'?	generalized / language: point	material / identifying
27-T/8	**You** can **do a lot of work** in a very short time.	generalized	material
27-T/9	So here when **'efficiency'** talks about the behavior of Nazi Germany, what does **this imply**?	language: point	identifying

Here, a consistent combination can be observed between the choice of [on-spot: language: point] as the first participant (*'efficiency'*) and the choice of identifying process (*suggest, mean, imply*), which construes a relationship between a linguistic item and its meaning. Meanwhile, embedded within this pattern is a side pattern: a generalized participant (*you*) involved in a material process (*do your work, do a lot of work*), which helps to materialize the meaning of the linguistic item (*'efficiency'*) and hence makes it easier to understand. In terms of the contextual value of the field, the Meaning (and Side Meaning) pattern realizes an explanation of the meaning of a linguistic item that is currently the object of teaching and learning in class.

7.2.4.3 Label

The pattern of Label focuses on the label given to a linguistic item instead of its meaning. It is also identified through the choice of an **identifying** process, which however is found in combination with the participant choice of [**on-spot: language: label**]. When a second participant is involved, it can be either a **point** or again a **label**. For example:

Example 7–39 [from Text 2]

t-m	text	first participant	process	second participant
101-T/1	Ern, OK, "To state that all are right when they say different things seems irrational" – what is here in this sentence, what **is the subject**, in this sentence?	language: label	identifying	
101T/2	And what **is the predicate**, or the **predicative** – predicate, the **verb**?	language: label	identifying	

101-T/3	What **is** the **subject**, first of all?	language: label	identifying	
102-S	**'that all . . .'**	(language: label)	(identifying)	language: point
103-T/1	No, I don't think so.	(language: label)	(identifying)	language: point)
103-T/2	The **subject is** the whole sentence then?	language: label	identifying	language: label
104-S	(after more than 6 seconds) En, **'different things'**.	(language: label)	(identifying)	language: point

As can be seen here, such label choices as *subject, predicate, predicative, verb* consistently co-occur with an identifying process (*be*). Where a second participant is involved, it is again a linguistic item, i.e. a point (*'that all . . .'*, *'different things'*; the word *so* in 103-T/1 is taken as a substitution of *the subject is 'that all . . .'*). In this way, the pattern construes a relationship between a linguistic item and its label. In terms of the contextual value of the field, it realizes an explanation of the grammatical role of a linguistic element.

However, it should be pointed out that while Label, Usage and Meaning are here described as distinct sub-types of Linguistic Item, they may also combine within the same stretch of discourse, as shown in Example 7–40 below (which actually precedes the stretch given in Example 7–38). When this happens, the pattern does not have to be defined as a sub-type, but simply as Linguistic Item (the same is true with the pattern of Text).

Example 7–40 [from Text 4]

t-m	text	first participant	process	second participant
25-T/4	And "in its cruelty and ferocious aggression", er, 'ferocious', and what, what **are** the **synonyms** for the word 'ferocious'?	language: label	identifying	
26-S	**'Fear'**.	(language: label)	(identifying)	language: point
27-T/1	**'Fearsome'**, that's right, **'fearsome'**.	(language: label)	(identifying)	language: point
27-T/2	And **'ferocious'** is often **used** to talk about wild animals, and very cruel people.	language: point	verbalized material	
27-T/3	So 'ferocious', the **synonyms** of the word **is 'fearsome'**, or **'savage'**, or **'very very cruel'**, **'violently cruel'**.	language: label	identifying	language: point
27-T/4	So here, **'ferocious aggression'** here **means**, **'savage attack on other countries'**, or, **'very cruel attack on other countries'**.	language: point	identifying	language: point
27-T/5	And ". . . in its efficiency", what does the word **suggest**, **'efficiency'**?	language: point	identifying	

7.2.4.4 Summary

In sum, the pattern of Linguistic Item construes a relationship of identity between a linguistic item and its defining features, or a verbal event involving all speakers of the language. In this way, it realizes an **explanation of the target language**, which is very common in the EFL classroom as found in the data. Table 7.7 offers a summary of all sub-types of the Linguistic Item pattern.

7.3 TEXT TYPE network: CONTENT

In the previous part of this chapter, first, the ideational systems in the REGISTER network of EFL classroom discourse – PROCESS TYPE and PARTICIPANT TYPE – were presented; then, the ideational logogenetic patterns identified as a result of coding the data according to the REGISTER systems were described and illustrated with examples taken from the data. In both cases, the description was given multi-stratally in spite of a focus on the ideational metafunction. In this section, all of the above-described ideational logogenetic patterns will be brought together into the ideational TEXT TYPE network of EFL classroom discourse, referred to as CONTENT. The section includes (1) a representation of the CONTENT network, and (2) an illustration of how CONTENT can be used to analyse and describe the ideational process of EFL classroom discourse.

7.3.1 Representation

In Section 7.2 above, the ideational logogenetic patterns identified in EFL classroom discourse are classified into four types according to the

Table 7.7 A summary of the ideational logogenetic patterns of Linguistic Item

Linguistic Item	lexicogrammatical UNIVARIATE			ideational function	value of field
	first participant	process	second participant		
Usage	generalized/ on-spot: language: point	verbal/ verbalized -material	on-spot: language: point	construe verbal events involving all language speakers	explanation of usage of a linguistic item
(Side) Meaning	on-spot: language: point/ generalized	identifying/ material	(on-spot: language: point)	construe an item-meaning relationship	explanation of meaning of a linguistic item
Label	on-spot: language: label	identifying	(on-spot: language: point)	construe an item-label relationship	explanation of gram. role of a linguistic item

different kinds of experiential content they construe. This is why the ideational TEXT TYPE network of EFL classroom discourse is referred to as CONTENT.

As described above, Classroom Event is a pattern that construes events involving both the subject and the medium of teaching and learning in the classroom, i.e. the teacher / students and the textbook, realizing the teachers' various ways of managing the classroom process. Life Experience construes events experienced by the teacher or a student but taking place outside rather than inside the classroom, realizing experiences in the person's life. Text construes events and relationships that do not involve the teacher or the students but are relocated into the classroom by means of the text, realizing the study of a text from a number of different perspectives. Linguistic Item construes events and relationships involving linguistic items currently being dealt with in class, realizing an explanation of the usage or other defining features of a linguistic item. See Figure 7.2 for a representation of the CONTENT system.

As pointed out repeatedly in Section 7.2, all of the ideational logogenetic patterns identified so far have been found resonating with one or more of the interpersonal logogenetic patterns described in Chapter 6. And the interpersonal pattern that is found to resonate most often with an ideational pattern is Knowledge. See Table 7.8 for a summary of how the logogenetic patterns described so far resonate across the two metafunctions. The Table does not include the interpersonal distinction between an Information Exchange and Information Chunk, because neither is found to resonate exclusively with a single ideational pattern (e.g. In-Text may overlap with both a story exchange and a story statement series), despite a

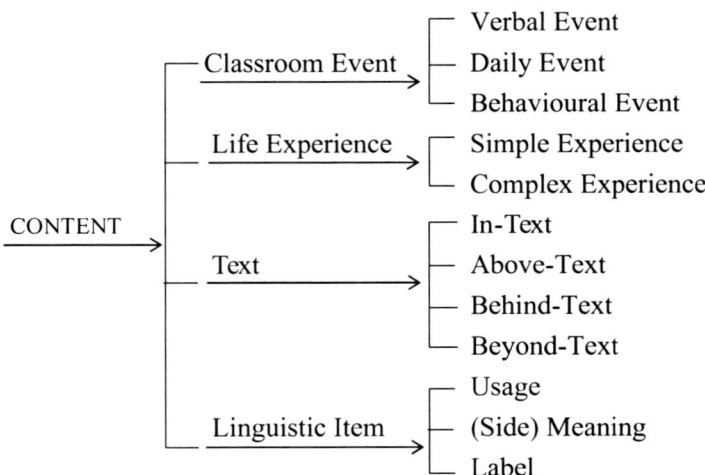

FIGURE 7.2   The CONTENT system in the TEXT TYPE network of EFL classroom discourse

Table 7.8 Resonation of ideational and interpersonal logogenetic patterns in EFL classroom discourse

interpersonal logogenetic patterns	ideational logogenetic patterns						
	Classroom Event	Life Experience	In-	Ab-	Bh-	By-	Linguistic Item
			Text				
Direction	√						
Orientation	√						
Recapitulation	√						
Action Exchange (Order)	√						
Personal Story		√					
Personal Detail		√					
Judgement		√			√		
Story			√	√			
Knowledge		√		√	√	√	√

tendency or Life Experience to resonate with an exchange, and for Behind-Text to overlap with a knowledge chunk.

7.3.2 Illustration

The CONTENT system has been applied to an analysis of the same text as analysed interpersonally in 6.3.2, i.e. Text 5. This section presents the analysis in order to illustrate how the CONTENT system can be used to analyse and describe the ideational process of an EFL classroom text.

Again, Text 5 was first coded according to the ideational systems in the REGISTER network of EFL classroom discourse (see Appendix II). As the ideational logogenetic patterns were found emerging out of successive lexicogrammatical UNIVARIATEs, the text was further coded according to the CONTENT system in the TEXT TYPE network of EFL classroom discourse (see the 'ideational' column in Appendix IV). Again, a limited number of choices other than the defining UNIVARIATEs embedded within a logogenetic pattern were ignored in the coding, while a local pattern embedded in a global one was coded.

As a result, a number of ideational phases in Text 5 can be seen as emerging out of the ideational logogenetic patterns thus identified. Here, the patterns of Classroom Event – which resonate with the pattern of Orientation (which serves as a boundary line between interpersonal phases) – function very well to announce the beginning of a certain kind of classroom activity. While an Orientation only orientates the speakers towards a new course of discourse, a Classroom Event specifies the content of the forthcoming discourse. Thus the patterns of Classroom Event, together with other, different types of ideational patterns, serve to distinguish five ideational phases in Text 5, as described below (their match or mismatch with the interpersonal phases will be pointed out wherever they occur).

Phase 1 [from 1-T/1 to 15-T/4]

This phase covers the first interpersonal phase (Classroom Conversation) as well as the first half of the second (Teacher Monologue). Ideationally, the phase begins with Daily Event (*I'm not going to give you a written check on preview*), which is immediately followed by Verbal Event (*let me ask you a few questions*). The former announces a daily classroom activity, i.e. preview of the text, while the latter specifies it as an oral instead of a written activity. However, this phase features not the pattern of Text, but rather the complex version of Life Experience, which construes from multiple points of view the students' experiences in their life outside the classroom, allowing the content of classroom discourse to become relevant to the students personally. The phase, therefore, is called **Warm-Up**.

Phase 2 [from 15-T/5 to 87-T/5]

This phase features the pattern of Text globally. It begins with Beyond-Text, which overlaps with the second half of the interpersonal phase of Teacher Monologue, construing a general interpretation of the text and constituting a switch from the students' life experiences to the text they are now learning. Then comes Verbal Event again (*let me ask you some questions about the text*) which resonates with (interpersonal) Orientation, re-orientating the current oral activity towards *preview* (which is specified in the very beginning of *Phase 1*). In fact, the ideational pattern that runs through the rest of the entire phase (overlapping with the third interpersonal phase, i.e. Teacher-Led Discussion) is In-Text, which realizes a retelling of the text. Embedded within this mainstream pattern are other sub-types of Text – including Behind-Text, Above-Text, and Beyond-Text – which are all concerned with the subject matter of the text in one way or another, lasting long or short depending on the degree of students' comprehension. Also embedded, occasionally, is the pattern of Meaning, which in time explains to the students a linguistic item they fail to use appropriately. But on the whole, this phase is focused on the story that is told in the textbook, hence called **Retelling**.

What deserves special attention is that the phase ends with Verbal Event (*I think you can all answer [all answered] the questions very well*) followed by Daily Event (*you did a very good job in previewing the lesson*), which resonate with the interpersonal pattern of Recapitulation (marking the end of an interpersonal phase). Besides, this Daily Event clearly refers back to the Daily Event in the very beginning of *Phase 1* concerning *preview*. In this way, they form a pair functioning as the boundaries of the *preview* activity that is carried out orally, thus linking Phases 1 and 2 into a higher-level phase that can be called **Oral Preview**.

Phase 3 [from 87-T/6 to 94-S]

This phase overlaps with the fourth interpersonal phase (Student Action). Ideationally, it begins with Daily Event (*let's open our book*), which announces the beginning of a new activity having to do with the textbook. Then appears Behavioural Event – *Xxx, would you like to read the first paragraph?* – followed by the actual behaviour of reading aloud produced by the student selected. The phase, therefore, is called **Reading Aloud**.

Phase 4 [from 95-T/1 to 95-T/12]

This phase switches from a student's reading aloud of the text to the text itself. It overlaps with the first part of the fifth interpersonal phase (Teacher Talk). Interpersonally, this part and its following part are separated by Orientation, but the two parts are taken as one phase because they both feature Knowledge Chunk (see 6.3.2). Ideationally, however, they are seen as two phases because they carry different types of content. The present phase features the pattern of Behind-Text that introduces the background behind some of the things mentioned in the text, though briefly embedding Usage that indicates the way a certain item in the text should be used. The phase ends with Beyond-Text that interprets the purpose of the paragraph. As such, the phase constitutes a distant study of the text rather than a close study of specific linguistic items, and hence is called **Text Study**.

Phase 5 [from 95-T/13 to 109-T/8]

This phase overlaps with the second part of the fifth interpersonal phase. It begins with Daily Event (*let's come to some of the words*), which announces the beginning of an activity having to do with linguistic items. In fact, the phase features globally the pattern of Meaning, which serves to define linguistic items selected from the text; although it sometimes embeds Behind-Text or Beyond-Text, which helps to broaden the meaning of the linguistic items being defined. So this phase is called **Language Study**.

However, it is worth noting that this phase ends with Daily Event again (*let's come to the next paragraph*), which announces another round of Phases 3, 4 and 5. Besides, the Daily Event at the beginning of Phase 3 – *let's open our book* – also functions to join these three phases together, since none of them can do without the textbook. So, the three phases are seen as together forming another higher-level phase: **Textbook Study**.

With the above ideational phases being identified, the ideational process of Text 5 can now be described – in terms of the **ideational structure** of the text, as represented in Figure 7.3 (following the same formula as describedin 6.3.2).

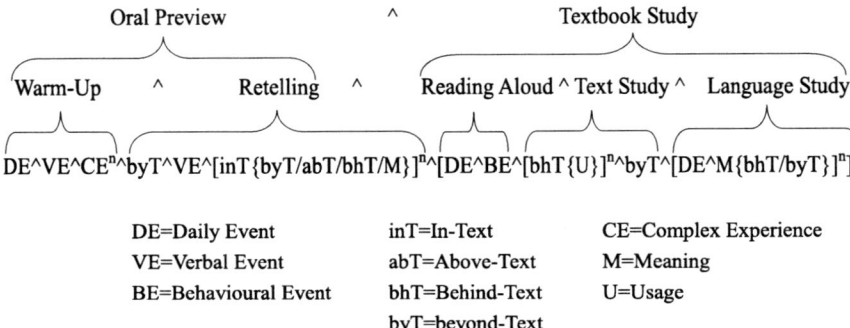

FIGURE 7.3   The ideational structure of Text 5

Clearly, the dynamic ideational process of an EFL class can be analysed by reference to the CONTENT system. As Figure 7.3 shows, being an Intensive Reading class that is much focused on a specific text and on linguistic knowledge, Text 5 is no exception in being text-centred and language-centred. First, the various patterns of Text are found in all phases except the first one (Warm-Up), though they are given different degrees of emphasis in different phases. Second, not only is the last phase (Language Study) entirely devoted to Meaning, but such phases as Retelling and Text Study also readily embed the pattern of either Meaning or Usage whenever necessary. Of course, it can also be seen that Life Experience manages to occupy a place in this class – in the phase of Warm-Up – so as to make the subject matter of the text somehow relevant to the students' own life. But further study is necessary to prove the effect of any ideational strategies the teacher may be found applying in classroom teaching.

Meanwhile, the ideational structure of Text 5 can be compared with its interpersonal structure to highlight where and how they resonate. See Figure 7.4 for an illustration.

Classroom Conversation	Teacher Monologue	Teacher-Led Discussion	Student Action	Teacher Talk	
OR^PS{J}ex^n	Kss3	OR^[S{K}ex{ss3}]^n	OR^Aex	[Kss2]^n^OR[Kex/ss/pex2/3]^n	
DE^VE^CE^n	byT^VE^[inT{byT/abT/bhT/M}]^n		DE^BE	[bhT{U}]^n^byT	[DE^M{bhT/byT}]^n
Warm-Up	Retelling		Reading Aloud	Text Study	Language Study
Oral Preview			Textbook study		

FIGURE 7.4   A comparison between the interpersonal and ideational structures of Text 5

While the interpersonal phases realize different kinds of interaction taking place in the classroom, the ideational phases realize the different kinds of content of classroom interaction. In Figure 7.4, it can be seen how logogenetic patterns resonate across the interpersonal and ideational metafunctions. In the following, such resonating relationships (indicated by ~) are further represented from the **ideational** point of view.

Oral Preview: Warm-Up
  Daily Event / Verbal Event ~ Orientation
  Complex (Life) Experience ~ Personal Story / Judgement / Knowledge
Oral Preview: Retelling
  Beyond-Text ~ Knowledge
  Verbal Event ~ Orientation
  In-Text / Above-Text ~ Story
  Beyond-Text / Meaning / Behind-Text ~ Knowledge
Textbook Study: Reading Aloud
  Daily Event ~ Orientation
  Behavioural Event ~ Order (in Action Exchange)
Textbook Study: Text Study
  Behind-Text / Usage / Beyond-Text ~ Knowledge
Textbook Study: Language Study
  Daily Event ~ Orientation
  Meaning / Behind-Text / Beyond-Text ~ Knowledge

From the **interpersonal** point of view, on the other hand, it can be briefly said that the Classroom Conversation engaged at the very beginning of the class is about the life experiences of several students represented from a multiply point of view; the Teacher Monologue that closes the conversation is a transition from the students' life experiences in the outside world to the subject matter of the text; the Teacher-Led Discussion that follows constitutes a retelling of the story told in the text; then the Student Action, as the first step in dealing with the text, is reading aloud the text; and finally the Teacher Talk that dominates the rest of this class is first about the text and then about linguistic items selected from the text.

Thus it is proved that the logogenetic patterns identified in EFL classroom discourse not only combine with one another within the same metafunction to co-articulate semantic phases in a text, but also combine across metafunctions to enable a multi-functional interpretation of the semantic phases.

7.3.3 Summary

In this section, all those ideational logogenetic patterns as described in the previous section are brought together into the ideational TEXT TYPE system of EFL classroom discourse, referred to as CONTENT. In order to illustrate how the CONTENT system can be used to analyse and describe the process of EFL classroom discourse, the section also presents an application of the CONTENT system in an actual analysis, again, of Text 5, and gives a description of the ideational structure of Text 5. It can be seen that the ideational and interpersonal flows of meaning in a text may resonate, which proves that the semantic structure of a text can be described both multi-stratally and multi-functionally – by applying the newly proposed TEXT TYPE model. The next chapter will be devoted to the textual analysis of EFL classroom discourse.

Chapter 8

Textual Analysis
of EFL Classroom Discourse

This chapter is devoted to the textual analysis of EFL classroom discourse. Again, the chapter is divided into three parts: (1) a description of the textual systems in the REGISTER network of EFL classroom discourse, (2) a description of the textual logogenetic patterns identified when applying the textual REGISTER systems to the analysis of the data, and (3) a representation of the textual TEXT TYPE network of EFL classroom discourse, along with an illustration of the network. Since the textual metafunction is an 'enabling' function that enacts the interpersonal and ideational metafunctions, this chapter will necessarily make frequent mention of a number of features described in the previous two chapters.

8.1 REGISTER network: textual

When observations were made of textual choices in each of the ten texts, it was found that the Thematic structure and Information structure, which operate at clause level, did not reveal as much about EFL classroom discourse as the cohesive ties, which operate at text level. So the Cohesion system in Functional Grammar was then applied to a detailed analysis of the ten texts. As the system did not always prove adequate in accounting for the facts about EFL classroom discourse, it was revised and extended. Thus the textual systems in the REGISTER network of EFL classroom discourse have been set up based on both Halliday's Cohesion system and its actual realizational forms as found in the data. The network is made up of three systems: (1) ELLIPTICAL CLAUSE, (2) REPETITION, and (3) TEXTUAL THEME.

8.1.1 The ELLIPTICAL CLAUSE system

In Functional Grammar, ellipsis is seen as a form of anaphoric cohesion realizing textual meaning. It sets up a relationship between two clauses by giving them the same grammatical structure, but leaving out certain elements in the second clause so as to give prominence to those present (e.g. – *What did you see?* – *I saw A kite.*). The ellipsed elements are viewed as **continuous** in terms of information flow, and those non-ellipsed as **contrastive**. To supply the missing words in the second clause and to insert them in place, the addressee must go back to the preceding text to look for a clause in the same grammatical structure. This is how ellipsis serves as a cohesive tie, and why Halliday (2004: 562) views ellipsis as 'a relationship in the wording rather than directly in the meaning'.

Halliday classifies ellipsis into three types: nominal, verbal and clausal. But only clausal ellipsis is recognized in the ELLIPTICAL CLAUSE system of EFL classroom discourse as set up here, because it is clausal ellipsis alone that is found prominent in the data, though it sometimes entails verbal ellipsis. Besides, in EFL classroom discourse, which is mostly dialogue, clause is found to be the basic functional unit, and an elliptical clause is found in an initiating as well as a responding move, an action as well as an information move. Thus the ELLIPTICAL CLAUSE system is composed of the following three options, and it is described in terms of the contrastive rather than continuous elements.

Elliptical clause as response

An elliptical clause found in a responding move has two realizational forms:

(1) It is realized by a declarative clause that Halliday considers as yes/no ellipsis of the whole clause, where the contrastive element is a **mood Adjunct of polarity** (*yes, no*) that either affirms or negates the proposition set out in the preceding question. For example (bold type indicates contrastive element, whereas underlining indicates continuous element):

Example 8–1: [from Text 5]
81-T/2:   OK, so er, well, was he ever rejected – I mean when he wanted to get
            a ride, **was** <u>he ever rejected</u>?
82-S: **Yes**.

Example 8–2: [from Text 6]
1-T/4:   Right, what do you think of the information provided by the text – **is**
            <u>there enough information</u>?
2-S: **No**.

(2) It is realized by a declarative clause in which all is continuous but the element in response to the **WH- element**, which gives the information as demanded in the preceding question, thus joining the question in generating one complete proposition:

Example 8–3: [from Text 9]
49-T/3:   **What**<u>'s the Chinese for 'cyberpunk'</u> then?
50-S: '电脑朋克'.

Example 8–4: [from Text 1]
199-T/2:   So **when** <u>did it start</u>?
200-S: Maybe, er **Monday**.

Both forms of the elliptical clause as response require that the addressee retrieve the missing words from the preceding clause in the initiating move, hence helping[1] to sequence the two moves into an adjacency pair. In the EFL classroom context, they are generally found in the students' speech.

Elliptical clause as question

In contrast, an elliptical clause as question is generally found in the teacher's speech initiating an exchange. Lexicogrammatically, it has three realizational forms:

(1) It is realized by an interrogative clause in which the contrastive element is the **Complement**. For example (some of the intermediate turns are omitted to save space, indicated by [......]):

Example 8–5: [from Text 1]
19-T/2: All right, <u>have you ever experienced</u> **any disaster in your life**?
. . . . . .
52-T: OK, **any other disasters**?
. . . . . .
64-T/2: OK, flood, earthquake, **anything else**?

Example 8–6: [from Text 3]
54-T/3: And can we say 'publications' – what is 'publications', <u>'publication'</u>
         <u>refers to</u> **what**?
. . . . . .
56-T/2: **What else**?

It should be noted that, whether the contrastive nominal group contains a lexical noun (e.g. *disasters*) or not (e.g. *anything, what*), it usually contains a comparative reference item (*other, else*, etc.), which sets up a relation of contrast and hence works jointly with ellipsis in marking a different member of Complement in the elliptical clause. In order to retrieve the continuous element, the addressee needs to reach back a number of moves. In this sense, the cohesive tie thus set up goes far beyond a single exchange.

(2) It is realized by an interrogative clause in which the continuous element is a question previously asked while the contrastive element is an **interpersonal projection**, which serves to make explicit the subjective orientation of the question:

Example 8–7: [from Text 5]
47-T/2: Now, was it so important – <u>why was it the biggest problem</u>, **have you**
         got any idea?
47-T/3: **Anyone**? [More than 6 seconds, no response]
47-T/4: Xxx, **have you got any idea**?
48-S: No.

The question (*why was it the biggest problem*) is presupposed so that its subjective orientation is given prominence. In this sense, the clause is not used as a question, but rather as an invitation to answer a question. So the move is called 'invite' as opposed to 'ask', though the former is dependent upon the latter.

Two things need to be further pointed out regarding the 'invite' move. First, apart from a complete projecting clause such as *have you got any idea*, an 'invite' has two other variant forms. One can be referred to as **Participant-present**. That is, everything else in the projecting clause can also be ellipsed except the Participant, such as *anyone (of you has got any idea why it was the biggest problem)* in 47-T/3. The other variant can be referred to as **Range-present**. That is, the only element present in the projecting clause is the mental or verbal process which, however, is nominalized to function as the Range of the process (see Halliday 1994: 146), and is again combined with a comparative reference item, e.g. *Any other suggestions? [Text 7: 48-T/2]* meaning *what else do you suggest that one should do when one gets food poisoning?* Second, since the only element present in an 'invite' is interpersonal projection, the move may vary in function according to the type of move in which its continuous element is found. If it is found in an 'ask', just as in Example 8–7, it is an 'invite-answer' move, which may function in place of 'ask' in an information exchange. If it is found in an 'order', e.g. *anyone (would like to translate the sentence)?* or *do you have any idea (how to translate it in a different way)?*, it would be an 'invite-comply' move, which may function in place of 'order' in an action exchange. Both sub-types of the 'invite' move help to link successive exchanges together (see 8.2 for more).

(3) It is realized by a clause in declarative mood but spoken with rising intonation, where the contrastive element is either an **Adjunct (circumstantial)** or the **Subject**:

Example 8–8: [from Text 6]
15-T/2:   OK, can anyone tell me, say, at the time AD 1, how many people there were in the world – say, <u>what's the population</u> **in AD 1**, remember?
. . . . . .
17-T/2:   But **by the time 1650**?

Example 8–9: [from Text 9]
25-T/4:   Ok, 'text', <u>what's</u> a **'text'**?
. . . . . .
27-T/2:   And **'video'**?

This kind of elliptical clause (except where the Adjunct is a WH-element, e.g. *but why?*) tends to blur the line between a question and statement, more or less reducing the demanding force upon the students (which deserves further study). That is perhaps why it is often found in the data, even in a single move (e.g. *Now, the northern part was called Union, and the southern part? [Text 8: 27-T/5]*).

Elliptical clause as order

An elliptical clause as order is also found in the teacher's speech initiating an exchange. It is realized by an imperative clause where the continuous element is the Predicator, which can be retrieved from another action move previously produced, either an 'orientate' or a 'direct', but not an 'order'. For example:

Example 8–10: [from Text 1]
167-T/3:   Now, **let's** do **the exercises**.
167-T/4:   Now, **the first one**, **Xxx**, please.
. . . . . .
169-T/3:   All right, **Number 2**.

The contrastive elements include (1) a **vocative** (*Xxx*), which replaces *let's* to address the person responsible for carrying out the action; (2) the **Complement** (*the first one, Number 2*), which replaces *exercises* to specify the object of the action; (3) the **Mood** in a metaphor of order (e.g. *Next one, Lyn, **would you** please? [Text 10: 34-T/2]*), which makes it easier for the addressee to refuse to comply; and (4) the **interjection** *please*, which mitigates the order. These four types of elements may all occur in an 'order'; or else each may be left out, with only one of them being left in. An elliptical clause as order presupposes the action being demanded, while specifying the object as well as the subject of the action.

It should be pointed out that, as found in the data, a vocative may occur either within an elliptical clause, or more than six seconds after an 'ask', 'order' or 'invite'. In the latter case, it is taken as a distinct move functioning to select the next speaker, and hence called 'nominate' – which can be realized by a mere *Xxx* (a student's name), or by *yes Xxx, ok you,* or just *yes*.

All in all, although Halliday (2004: 569) says 'ellipsis is largely limited to the immediately preceding clause', the elliptical clauses in the data turn out to extend their cohesive tie over a stretch of discourse, though they sometimes need to join hands with other cohesive devices such as comparative reference. Figure 8.1 is a representation of the ELLIPTICAL CLAUSE system, where the more delicate options are elements left in rather than out of the elliptical clause (CR = a comparative reference item).

8.1.2 The REPETITION system

In Functional Grammar, repetition is viewed as a kind of lexical cohesion, i.e. a textual resource that 'operates within the lexical zone of lexicogrammar' (Halliday 2004: 570); and lexis is viewed as a resource for making experiential meaning. However, as EFL classroom discourse is spoken language and mainly

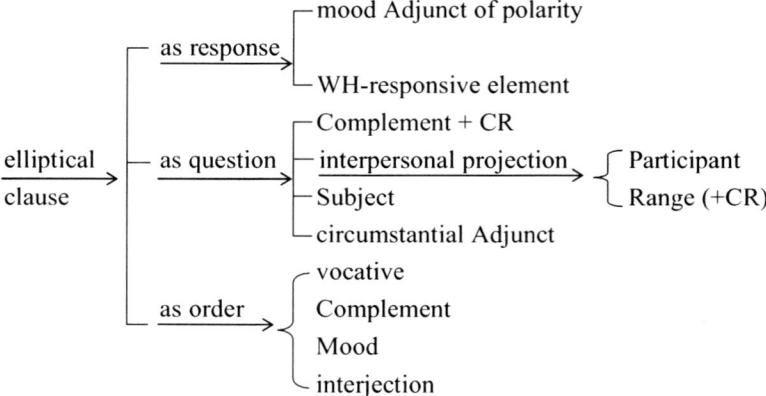

FIGURE 8.1   The ELLIPTICAL CLAUSE system of EFL classroom discourse

dialogue, repetition is by no means restricted to lexis (e.g. – *I stayed in the bus.* – *You stayed in the bus?*), nor is the function of repetition limited to the organization of experiential meanings. Actually, with 'turn' and 'move' being the basic units of analysis (see 5.2), it is hardly possible to examine repetition without looking at the moves that contain it; otherwise, repetition would be a feature of the texts in the students' textbook instead of a feature of EFL classroom discourse.

Thus the REPETITION system set up here is based on, but quite different from, Halliday's Repetition system, in that it is defined **within moves**. Specifically, it is concerned with repetition that occurs in a new move, without strict restriction in grammatical form. The repetition may involve a word, group or clause. It may be a word-for-word repetition or a paraphrase, an over- or under-repetition. Being in a new move, it serves not only to relate back ideationally to the preceding move, but also to push an interpersonal exchange forward in one way or another. It is a resource employed mostly in a teacher's move that follows a student's responding move, reflecting teachers' pedagogic strategies as well as textual features of classroom interaction. The system is made up of the following four options.

Repetition+

Here repetition+ refers to the repetition of an element in the preceding move with something added to it. It is found in four types of teachers' moves.

First, it is found in the follow-up move in the simple version of an information/ action exchange, i.e. 'acknowledge' or 'evaluate', helping to define the move as bound to the exchange (see also 6.2.3). Here repetition+ is realized in two ways:

(1) The repeated and added parts are related through 'expansion' (for more see Halliday 2004: Ch. 7), so that repetition+ serves both to link the responding and follow-up moves, and to give further information – either to improve the

response when it is genuinely incomplete in meaning, or just because the teacher is used to the role of an information-giver:

Example 8–12: [from Text 1]: repetition + variation
189-T/2:   So, what is a 'dummy', a 'clothes dummy'?
190-S: A 'model'.
191-T/1:   A 'model', but not alive, living model, yeah, something made of – usually in our stores.

Example 8–13: [from Text 8]: repetition + exposition
9-T/3:   Who was the President during that time?
10-S: Lincoln.
11-T/1:   Lincoln, Abraham Lincoln, the sixteenth President of the US.

(2) The repeated item is re-structuralized into a grammatically correct form, so that repetition+ serves both as a link with the responding move, and as an improvement of the response – by making it complete in both form and meaning:

Example 8–14: [from Text 9]
15-T/6:   OK, "the technological great grandchildren", that should be, which generation then?
16-S: Fourth.
17-T/1:   Yeah, the fourth generation, right.

Example 8–15: [from Text 8]
74-T/5:   Now, you see, "His extended right hand loosely grasped his rifle" – why not tightly?
75-S: Sleep.
76-T/1:   Yeah, he was sleeping.

Second, repetition+ is found also in a move following the responding move, but it is not a follow-up move as it is realized in an interrogative clause. It takes over an element in the preceding response, wraps it up in a new structure, and then turns it over to the previous speaker through the interrogative mood:

Example 8–16: [from Text 3]
50-T/2:   So, say the whole thing once again.
51-S: Every day, there are four point one five millions publications published, are published.
52-T: Oh, can we say 'millions publications' – is it possible?
53-S: Million.

Example 8–17: [from Text 6]
5-T/2:   And then why, why does the writer want to write this text, why?
6-S: Maybe to <u>warn people</u>.
7-T: <u>Warn people, of what</u>?
8-S: Ern, in your life, there is a serious <u>problem</u>.
9-T: <u>Problem of what</u>?
10-S: En, population is increasing.

In this way, the move offers a hint to the student that part of the response is either incorrect in form or incomplete in meaning, so that the move is always followed by another student move containing some kind of repair. Thus the teacher's move is called 'hint' and the student's move 'repair'. The two reciprocal moves, being added to the exchange through repetition+, are clearly dependent upon the preceding response instead of forming an independent pair. And repetition+, as applied here, serves both to link the responding and hinting move, and to encourage a student to self-repair and to increase output.

Third, repetition+ is again found in a new structure in the interrogative mood. But here, the repeated element is represented either as Phenomenon in a mental clause or as a mentally projected idea, with the Sensor being the addressee, i.e. the previous speaker:

Example 8–18: [from Text 1]
82-S: rushed down, er, er, and a bus is filled with people, <u>fell, went down to the</u> bottom of the hill.
83-T: Alright, <u>you mean fell down to the</u> . . . ?
84-S: Yes, fell down.

Example 8–19: [from Text 2]
77-S: The paper has the <u>trend</u> to encourage students to have their own opinion.
78-T: So <u>you think there is a trend, or a reform</u>?
79-S: Yeah.

This kind of repetition+ indicates uncertainty about the meaning of the preceding move or part of it, offering an interpretation of it for confirmation; so the move is always followed by another move that resolves the uncertainty. While the former move can be called 'request', the latter can be called 'resolve'. In the EFL classroom, repetition+ as applied here not only helps to identify another pair of dependent moves, but also serves to promote negotiation of meaning – which is believed to facilitate the production of comprehensible input and output.

Fourth, repetition+ can be found in the middle of a student's responding move that has clearly run into trouble. It takes over the half-finished item from the student's move and adds to it the right expression, form, or pronunciation;

and the student, in turn, will always take over what is suggested, resuming the response:

Example 8–20: [from Text 7]
71-S/b: Don't worry, Mum, I'll, I'll get some . . . er, <u>cream</u>.
72-T: <u>sun cream</u>
73-S/b: <u>sun cream</u>

Example 8–21: [from Text 2]
88-S: [reading aloud] ". . . different sets of facts in describing an event and this <u>lead them</u> –"
89-T: <u>leads them</u>
90-S: "<u>leads them</u> to different conclusions. At other times . . ."

Example 8–22: [from Text 9]
2-S: [reading aloud] ". . . and Escape from Cyber City, an . . . <u>animated [eni'meitid]</u>"
3-T: <u>animated ['ænimeitid]</u>
4-S: "an <u>animated ['ænimeitid]</u> adventure game."

Thus the teacher's move is called 'prompt'[2] and the student's move 'resume'. The former can be described in terms of repetition+, and the latter in terms of repetition (see discussion below). In the EFL classroom context, repetition+ as applied here serves both to sequence successive moves and to sustain students' speech.

Repetition–

Repetition– refers to a partial repetition of an element in the preceding move – partial in the sense of being incomplete in structure as compared with the original. It is found in the 'hint' move as described above. But here, instead of adding anything to the element taken from the preceding response, repetition– takes over the element and deletes part of it:

Example 8–23: [from Text 7]
22-S/a: En, what will, what will they have to do <u>if she accept the job</u>?
23-T: <u>if she –</u>
24-S/a: accepts

Example 8–24: [from Text 5]
30-S: I think <u>you wave your hands</u>.
31-T: <u>you wave your –</u>
32-S: And in this text, the stranger has his thumb up.

The element taken over from the previous move is usually a clause. With the clause structure being repeated,[3] that part of the clause being intentionally deleted – which is usually either incorrect in form or imprecise in meaning – becomes highlighted. In this way, repetition– becomes a variant realization of a 'hint' move, always followed by another student move containing some kind of repair. And repetition– as applied here, again, serves both to link a dependent move and to encourage a student to self-improve the response.

Repetition

Repetition refers to the repetition of an element taken from the preceding move, with nothing added to it or deleted from it. It is found in five types of moves. Apart from the 'resume' move produced by a student, as mentioned above, it can be found in a 'repeated question', i.e. a move that puts the same question (or a slightly paraphrased one) to another student, thus linking successive exchanges as well as offering students more practice opportunities:

Example 8–25: [from Text 6]
88-T: OK, do you have worries?
. . . . . .
92-T: OK, do you have worries?
. . . . . .
96-T/2:   Do you have worries?

Thirdly, it is found in an 'evaluate' or 'acknowledge' move – when the teacher is either satisfied with the response and would happily close the exchange, or not satisfied and would rather start a new exchange:

Example 8–26: [from Text 7]
19-T/2:   Er, the Republican party was founded in?
20-S: <u>Eighteen fifty-four</u>.
21-T/1:   Good, <u>eighteen fifty-four</u>.

Example 8–27: [from Text 1]
1-T/4:   What is a 'disaster'?
2-S: <u>'Damage'</u>.
3-T/1:   <u>'Damage'</u>, un-hun, okay, <u>'damage'</u>.
3-T/2:   What we – what's worse than damage?

Fourthly, it is found in the middle of the speech produced by another speaker, to indicate comprehension of the information just given, so that the other speaker will just go on speaking:

Example 8–28: [from Text 1]
88-S: [All people on my bus] got down the bus, <u>to see what was wrong</u>.
89-T: <u>to see what was wrong</u>
90-S: Yes, I, I, I stayed in the bus.

Thus the move can be called 'backchannel' (see also Martin 1992: 67), and its following move 'continue'. As found in the data, a 'backchannel'[4] may also be realized by paralinguistic items (*oh, un-hun*) or continuatives (*yes, right, really*; see 8.1.3); but when realized as repetition, it not only serves to extend an exchange, but also helps to ensure that everyone else in the classroom can hear what is said.

Fifthly, it is found to follow either a student's responding move or a teacher's initiating move, taking over an element from the preceding move and turning it back to the other speaker in an interrogative clause:

Example 8–29: [from Text 1]
53-S: I experienced <u>a small earthquake</u>.
54-T: <u>Earthquake, a small earthquake</u>?
55-S: Yeah, below three. (laugh)

Example 8–30: [from Text-5]
15-T/9:   Now, where did he – ern, I think you have read the notes – <u>where did the writer get the title from</u>?
15-T/10:   Xxx.
16-S: En, <u>where he get the title</u>?
17-T/1:   Yeah, the title *The Kindness of Strangers*, do you know where the writer, you know, got the title from?

Here, repetition also functions as a request for confirmation, so the move is taken as a 'request'.[5] It differs from the 'request' move as described above only in that it offers more or less a word-for-word repetition, while the former offers the speaker's own interpretation. In either case, the move does not fail to bring about a further move that resolves the uncertainty. So, repetition as applied here again serves to link a dependent move, as well as to promote comprehension and speech production in an EFL class.

Paraphrase

Paraphrase refers to a restatement of what is said in the preceding move, found in two types of moves. First, it is found in an 'acknowledge' or 'evaluate'. When the preceding response is given in the student's first language (i.e. Chinese),

the paraphrase is in fact inter-lingual, offering the meaning of the item in the
target language:

Example 8–31: [from Text 9]
27-T/2:   And 'video'?
28-S(n):   视频.
29-T/1:   Something that you can see, right? un-hun, and sound, something
           you can listen.

Where the response seems quite acceptable, the paraphrase merely serves to
offer a different way of expression, as well as to reinforce the response:

Example 8–32: [from Text 5]
23-T/2:   Why – well, how did he come to this conclusion, how did he come to
           this conclusion?
24-S: Because he traveled fourteen states through America with no money,
           just by the help of strangers.
25-T/1:   Ern yes, okay, he came to the conclusion after traveling across
           fourteen states of the United States, wholly depending on the
           kindness of strangers.

   Second, paraphrase is found in an information chunk, and more specifically,
in Variant 1 where the initial, central proposition comes from the textbook:

Example 8–33: [from Text 9]
29-T/8:   "Users pick and choose information that interests them."
29-T/9:   Ok, you only choose what you are interested in.
29-T/10:   Ok, something you are not interested in, you can, actually eliminate,
           ok, cast them away.

Here paraphrase not only offers different ways of expression, but also functions
similarly to such 'expository' relations as *that means, in other words* (see 8.1.3 for
more). Thus the move is called 'restate', and paraphrase as applied here is
viewed both as a cohesive device that ties up an information chunk, and as a
strategy of explaining a text in an EFL class.
   In sum, the REPETITION system is a resource for textualizing EFL classroom
interaction. As seen above, all options in the system operate within moves; and
by re-expressing the experiential meaning represented by the preceding move,
they serve well to tie up an exchange, a chunk, or even exchanges. Meanwhile,
they contribute to the description of the follow-up moves in an exchange that
were not fully described in Chapter 6, as well as a number of newly identified
dependent moves or pairs of moves.[6] Table 8.1 presents a summary of all moves
identified and described through REPETITION.

Table 8.1 A summary of the moves identified and described through REPETITION

move	realization	meaning	pedagogic role
acknowledge/ evaluate	repetition	acknowledge the response	
	repetition + expansion	acknowledge the response and give further information	improve the response towards completeness in meaning
	repetition + structure	acknowledge and structuralize the response	improve the response towards completeness in structure/meaning
	paraphrase (inter-lingual)	translate (part of) the response	teach the meaning of a linguistic item
	paraphrase	restate the response	teach different ways of expression
hint (^repair)	repetition + structure in interrogative mood	hint that the response is incomplete in meaning or incorrect in form	encourage students to improve the response and to produce more output
	repetition – part of an element	highlight the incorrect/imprecise part in an element	
request (^resolve)	repetition + mental clause/ projection in interrogative mood	provide an interpretation of (part of) preceding move and request for confirmation	enable negotiation of meaning; promote comprehensible input/output
	repetition in interrogative mood	request for clarification/confirmation	
prompt (^resume)	repetition + expression/form/ pronunciation	suggest the right expression/form/ pronunciation that should be used	sustain students' speech
resume	repetition	take over the item/pronunciation suggested	
backchannel (^continue)	repetition	indicate comprehension of the response	ensure everyone else can hear
repeated question	repetition	raise the same question again	give practice opportunities to more students
restate	paraphrase	restate the information given in the preceding statement	elaborates on the text; teach different ways of expression

8.1.3 The TEXTUAL THEME system

In Functional Grammar, Theme refers to an element placed at the initial position of the clause serving as the point of departure of the message. To be anchored in the realm of experience, the clause must have a topical Theme, i.e. an experiential element such as Participant, Process or Circumstance. Meanwhile, it may also have interpersonal Themes such as vocative, modal Adjunct and Finite operator, as well as textual Themes such as external conjunction (linking clauses in a clause complex), internal conjunction (linking spans of text), and continuity (marking a new turn or move in dialogue).

In the data used here, continuity and internal conjunction are found to be prominent and revealing about the textualization of EFL classroom discourse, even more so than the progression of topical Themes (which tends to reveal more about the texts in the students' textbook). So they have become the two major options in the TEXTUAL THEME system of EFL classroom discourse, a system set up based partly on Functional Grammar and partly on the facts found in the data.

Continuity

Halliday describes continuity in terms of continuatives, i.e. 'a small set of words which signal a move in the discourse: a response, in dialogue, or a new move to the next point if the same speaker is continuing' (2004: 81), such as *yes, no, well, oh, now*, etc. However, as found in the data, continuity not only serves to introduce a new turn or a new move, but also performs other textual functions of various kinds – and accordingly four types of continuity have been distinguished.[7]

The first type is realized by *all right*[8] and *now*. It is named 'boundive', because it occurs in (1) an action move such as 'orientate' and 'direct' that begins a semantic phase, (2) the first 'ask' or 'order' move that follows an 'orientate' or 'direct', and (3) the 'recap' move that closes a semantic phase. These moves are all found at the boundaries between semantic phases. For example:

Example 8–34: [from Text 1]
169-T/9:   All right, so much for my questions. [recap]
169-T/10:   Now, let's do the exercises. [orientate]
169-T/11:   Now, the first one, Xxx, please. [order]

Example 8–35: [from Text 2]
1-T/1:   All right, let's resume our class, okay? [orientate]
1-T/2:   And, so, a university student can comment on how history should be taught, and now, we'll comment on it. [orientate]
1-T/3:   Now, what about the rest of you – did you come across, en, an interesting history teacher? [ask]

In fact, a 'boundive' helps both to draw and to maintain a boundary, for it is also found in a move that resumes the mainstream logogenetic pattern of a semantic phase after the pattern has been interrupted by an embedded, different pattern:

Example 8–36: [from Text 7]
(action Exchange)
1-T/2: OK, ern, Xxx, you two, the first one. [order]
2-S/a: How will she feel if she's late for the interview? [comply]
3-S/b: She'll be furious with herself.[comply]
(knowledge Exchange)
4-T: OK, so 'furious' – this is the word I'd like you to pay attention to – can we say 'I feel furious', 'I feel furious'? [ask]
. . . . . .
(action Exchange)
8-T/3   OK, <u>now</u>, second one, Xxx, you two, please. [order]

The second type is realized typically by *OK*[9] and, with some teachers, by *well, right, so, er* and *oh*.[10] It is named 'initiative', because it is used to signal a new initiating move. The move generally occurs in the middle of a semantic phase, such as 4-T in Example 8–36 which involves a switch between the mainstream and embedded patterns. It may also occur at boundaries, such as 1-T/2 in Example 8–36. See some more examples:

(1) <u>OK</u>, what's your reaction – what did you do? [ask] [Text 1: 60-T/2]
(2) <u>OK</u>, next one: 'get sunburnt', you two. [ask] [Text 7: 69-T/2]
(3) <u>OK</u>, so the war started and the father and son held different opinions. [state] [Text 8: 42-T/4]

However, sometimes the teachers seem to be so used to their role as an initiator that they apply an 'initiative' even when making a dependent move such as 'resolve' and 'request', or an 'answer' move in a pseudo or genuine exchange:

(1) <u>OK</u>, 'epidemic disease', just now I said 'epidemic disease', en, e-p-i-d-e-m-i-c, 传染病. [resolve] [Text 1: 17-T/1]
(2) <u>OK</u>, if you say he taught well, how, how can that be you didn't quite like him? [request] [Text 2: 11-T]
(3) <u>OK</u>, 'sheer', straight up or down, that means, the cliff were very steep – er, you know that word 'steep' – very steep: straight up and down. [answer in pseudo-exchange] [Text 8: 98-T/2]

While the above two types of continuity are found in a new move in the same turn, the third type is found in a new turn, realized by *yes, yeah, right* or *oh*. It is called 'continuative', because it occurs in a move that helps to continue the current exchange, including such dependent moves as 'continue', 'resume' and 'backchannel', as well as a follow-up move. For example:

Example 8–37: [from Text 7]
41-S: 'Robbed'. [prompt]
11-T: <u>Yeah</u>, 'rob', okay, 'be robbed'. [resume]

Example 8–38: [from Text 1]
31-S: <u>Yeah</u>, because it rained about half a month, no, one month. [continue]
32-T: <u>Yeah</u>, because it rained too much and for a long time. [ackn]

Example 8–39: [from Text 5]
78-S: some people shared food and shelter with him, [continue]
79-T: <u>yes</u> [backchannel]
80-S: and some even gave him gift. [continue]
81-T/1:   <u>Yes</u>, gave him gift, that's right. [evaluate]

The fourth type has a unique textual meaning in EFL classroom discourse. It is named 'locative', realized by a quotation from a text in the students' textbook, which comes in the initial position of either Variant 2 of an information chunk (see 6.2.3), or an 'ask' move. For example:

Example 8–41: [from Text 4]
31-T/9:   <u>"No one has been a more consistent opponent of communism than I have for the last twenty-five years"</u>, "No one has . . ." here, 'no', a negative word is put at the beginning of the sentence for emphasis.
31-T/10: So "No one has been a more consistent opponent", this sentence is more emphatic than, let's say, 'I have always been a consistent opponent of communism'.

Example 8–42: [from Text 5]
95-T/14: Er, <u>"I came upon</u> . . ." What is the meaning of 'came upon'?
95-S: It means 'to find someone by chance'.

The quotation is not restricted in either length or form, ranging from a sentence to a word, from a complete to a broken sentence; hence not a proposition for the following clauses to hang onto. Nor does it represent the same experiential world as its following clauses – such as human world (*no one, I*) vs. linguistic world (*word, sentence, meaning of 'came upon'*). However, ideationally the quotation functions somewhat like a circumstance in the transitivity structure, since it can be referred to as *here in this sentence* or *here*, as shown below:

(1) Ern, OK, "To state that all are right when they say different things seems irrational" – what is <u>here in this sentence</u>, what is the subject, <u>in this sentence</u>? [Text 2: 101-T/1]

(2) So, "The angle where the soldier lay was on the same cliff. Had he been awake . . ." Now, what is omitted <u>here</u>? [Text 8: 98-T/8]

Thus the quotation is taken as a textual Theme, in the semantic function of (1) locating a new move in the ongoing dialogue, and (2) locating the move in the experiential world as represented by the textbook. And due to its two-fold function, a 'locative' may also be realized by – in place of a direct quotation – a verbal or existential clause such as **The writer says "with gangs".** *That means 'because of gangs'. [Text 5: 99-T/8];* **in our text, [there are] two phrases: one is "might well", another one "may well".** *'May well' suggests there is a reason why you may well say so. [Text 8: 104-T/2].*

Conjunction

Here 'conjunction' is used as a short form for 'internal conjunction'. It refers to the same resources for setting up logical relations between clauses within a clause complex, realized by adverbial groups or prepositional phrases (see Halliday 2004: 9.3.2). But the resources are now applied as cohesive ties between text spans – moves, exchanges or chunks in EFL classroom discourse – rather than between figures of experience; hence textual rather than ideational resources. Halliday (2004) points out that the most elaborated cohesive conjunctions are relatively rare in conversation. This is proved true by the data used here. The data-driven conjunction system established here is much simpler than that in Functional Grammar, though the major options remain (1) elaboration, (2) extension and (3) enhancement.

Elaboration refers to a re-presentation of the preceding text from another point of view, or a re-statement of it in different words. As found in the data, it is realized by three types of elaborating conjunctions: expository, exemplifying and clarifying. For example:

(1) <u>In other words</u>, if the cartridge box had not moved at regular intervals, he might have been thought to be dead, right? [expository] [Text 8: 78-T/5]

(2) <u>For example</u>: A excels B, in ern, let's say, in singing, A excels B in singing – the sentence means that A sings better than B. [exemplifying] [Text 4: 22-T/3]

(3) Do you know, <u>actually</u>, what we call this – the number of magazines published each day – do you know the special word for it? [clarifying] [Text 3: 65-T/2]

Extension, on the other hand, refers to an addition of something new to the preceding text. Here in the data, it is most commonly realized by additive and adversative conjunctions. For example (see also Examples 8–8 and 8–9):

(1) <u>But</u> if you were badly in need of help, what would you do, suppose you are badly wounded? [adversative] [Text 5: 7-T/2]

(2) <u>And</u> ". . . racial domination" – one of Nazi's devices, it's racism, racism. [additive] [Text 4: 20-T/2]

(3) <u>And</u> do you share the same idea with the writer, do you? [additive] [Text 6: 11-T]

Enhancement refers to an embellishment of the preceding text span with some circumstantial features. In the data used here, enhancing conjunctions are relatively fewer than the other two types, falling into two types – temporal and causal. It should be noted that the causal type, being internal rather than external, generally does not express cause-effect relation, but is 'a statement about the speaker's reasoning processes: I conclude from what you say (or other evidence)' (Halliday and Hasan 1976: 257). For example:

(1) Now, <u>the next question</u>: how was he received by the people, in the 14 states, generally speaking, well, how was he received? [temporal] [Text 5: 71-T/4]

(2) <u>So</u>, 'send for some bread' means 'ask somebody to get, er, ask somebody to get some bread', alright? [causal] [Text 1: 117-T/2]

(3) <u>So</u> the American Civil War broke out in 1861, ended in 1865, it lasted four years. [causal] [Text 8: 11-T/2]

As can be seen from all the examples above, a textual Theme realized by a choice of either continuity or conjunction can be found in a 'state' move as well as an 'ask'/'order' move. This suggests that such textual Themes serve to link not only one move with another within an information chunk or within an exchange, but also one exchange with another, or an exchange with a chunk (and vice versa) within an even larger span of text. That is to say, although a textual Theme is an element within the clause, its function extends far beyond the clause (for more, see Section 8.2 below).

8.1.4 Summary

In this section, a description is given of the textual systems in the REGISTER network of EFL classroom discourse (see Figure 8.2 for a summary). Driven by the facts as identified in the analysis of the data, the textual function of these systems is described in relation to moves, exchanges, chunks, or even larger spans of text. The next section will present various spans of text in terms of textual logogenetic patterns.

8.2 Logogenetic patterns: textual

Following the steps of analysis described in 4.2.4, the above-described three systems in the textual REGISTER network of EFL classroom discourse were used to code the ten texts. It is found that choices from the textual systems work both jointly and individually to signal transitions between moves, exchanges and chunks, as well as to tie up an exchange, a chunk, or an even larger span of text. Actually, the textual choices create textual logogenetic patterns of varying extent that form a compositional scale, as illustrated in Figure 8.3.

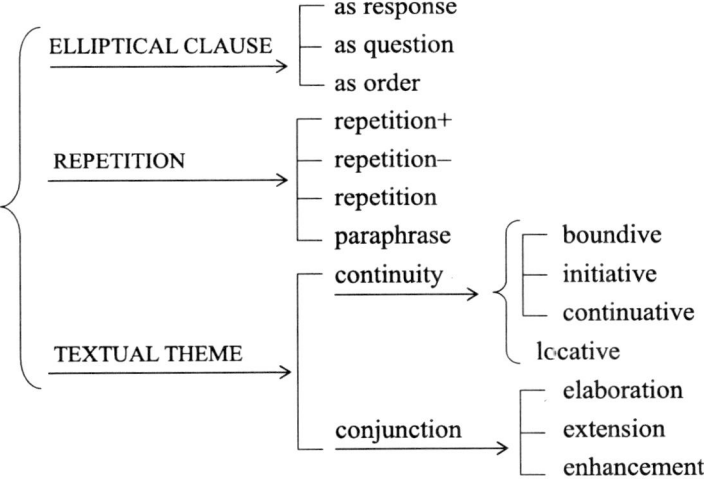

FIGURE 8.2   The textual REGISTER network of EFL classroom discourse

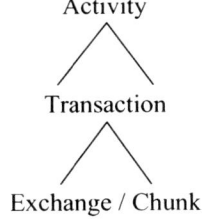

FIGURE 8.3   The compositional scale of textual logogenetic patterns in EFL classroom discourse

At the lowest rank are the patterns of **Exchange** and **Chunk**. They are described in Chapter 6 interpersonally, in terms of mood choices that define a sequence of moves as either an information or an action exchange, either an exchange or a chunk. Here they will be further described in terms of textual choices that define the specific ways in which moves sequence into an exchange or a chunk. At a higher rank is the pattern called **Transaction**, a term borrowed from Sinclair and Coulthard (1975). Whereas they only specify the structure of a transaction as [Boundary ^ Teaching ^{n} ^ (Boundary)] without describing how an unlimited number of teaching exchanges unfold one after another, the description of transaction given here will show how textual resources serve to sequence the exchanges and/or chunks within a transaction. At the highest rank is the pattern called **Activity**, defined as a span of text composed of transactions, somewhat similar to Sinclair and Coulthard's concept of transaction.

In this section, the textual logogenetic patterns at all ranks will be described multi-stratally and illustrated with examples taken from the data. It should be stressed, though, that the textual logogenetic patterns, in their 'enabling' function of organizing text spans, always overlap with logogenetic patterns within the other two metafunctions; therefore this section will make frequent mention of both the interpersonal and the ideational patterns discussed above.

8.2.1 Exchange

In fact, the relevant interpersonal logogenetic pattern presented in Chapter 6 is called **Information Exchange** or **Action Exchange**, distinguished according to mood choices. Here, the textual logogenetic pattern is called **Exchange** – without making a distinction between information and action – to indicate a focus on the textual rather than interpersonal aspect of the pattern. But a new distinction is made here, based on textual choices found in an exchange, between simple and complex exchange.

8.2.1.1 Simple Exchange

The simple version of an exchange, as described in 6.2.3, is composed of three basic moves: (1) ask / order, (2) answer / comply, and (3) acknowledge / evaluate. Interpersonally, the moves all hang onto the same proposition / proposal as specified in the initial move, hence viewed as forming one unit, i.e. an exchange. Here, the pattern of Simple Exchange is identified textually through the choice of **elliptical clause as response** in the second move, and in the third move the various choices of **repetition** plus an optional **continuative** as textual Theme. In other words, it is the textual choices that further explain how the three moves sequence into an exchange. Here are Examples 6–36 and 6–38 again, respectively numbered (1) and (2) and recoded for textual choice as well as move type:

	t-m	text	textual choice	move type
(1)	34-T/2	Next one, Lyn, would you please?		order
	35-S	true	elliptical	comply
	36-T/1	Yes, it's true.	continuative rep + structure	acknowledge
(2)	31-T/8	"No one has been a more consistent opponent of communism", and 'consistent opponent', what does this mean, 'consistent opponent'?		ask
	32-S	'Often compete'.	elliptical	answer
	33-T/1	'Often compete', and 'always compete'.	rep + expansion	acknowledge

Functionally, the choice of elliptical clause in the responding move – *(it is) true,* *('consistent opponent' means) 'often compete'* – requires reaching back to the initiating move for the continuous element, thus tying up the two moves; the choice of [repetition + structure / expansion] in the feedback move relates back ideationally to the responding move, thus linking these two moves; and the choice of continuity (e.g. *yes, it's true*) in the feedback signals a new move that follows up the completed proposal or proposition. In terms of the contextual value of the mode of discourse, the pattern realizes the most typical version of classroom dialogue: [T-Initiation ^ S-Response ^ T-Feedback]. But it should be noted that the students may get so used to producing an elliptical clause that they do not care enough about grammar in their speech. A case in point is Example (2) above, where a verbal group is wrongly produced by the student in place of a nominal group: *('consistent opponent' means) 'often compete'*. Besides, choices in the teacher's follow-up move – repetition or repetition+ or paraphrase – may have different effects on classroom teaching and deserve further study.

8.2.1.2 Complex Exchange

The complex version of an exchange is composed of the three basic moves plus an unlimited number of dependent moves, which form pairs dependent upon one of the basic moves. According to the kind of basic move that is being depended upon, the pattern of Complex Exchange is classified into the following two sub-types.

Response-dependent

A response-dependent complex exchange is brought about by a teacher. Following the student's response, the teacher tends to produce such dependent moves as 'hint' (^ 'repair'), 'request' (^ 'resolve'), 'prompt' (^ 'resume'), 'backchannel' (^ 'continue') – which are identified through various choices of **repetition** and/or **continuity**:

Example 8–43 [from Text 2]

t-m	text	textual choice	move type
17-T/3	So, in what way should history be taught?	initiative	ask[judgement]
18-S	Very high level, professional, specific.	elliptical	answer
19-T	ern, right	continuative	backchannel
20-S	Of course, he must major in history.		continue
21-T	He should be a history major.	paraphrase	backchannel
22-S	And they must know ways to learn better.	additive	continue
23-T	un-hun	(paralinguistic)	backchannel
24-S	And then they can think, as a teacher, how to teach.	additive	continue
25-T	un-hun	(paralinguistic)	backchannel
26-S	I have a former classmate – when I, when I was in junior middle school, my hometown, my history teacher was a teacher of Chinese.		continue [personal story]
27-T	yes	continuative	backchannel
28-S	So he asked the students to read the paragraphs, and then come to the main idea.	causal	continue
29-T	OK, so you, you actually read the texts?	initiative/rep	request
30-S	We get [got] the main idea, and then, he told us to, ern, to even, he told us to draw, en, en . . .		resolve
31-T	draw the topic sentence	rep + expression	prompt
32-S	features, of, ern, of the style.		continue
33-T	The style, okay.	repetition	backchannel
34-S	Yes, he is abnormal.	continuative	continue
35-T/1	Okay, you think he isn't right – NOT abnormal – you don't think he is right (laugh), you don't think he is right, okay, yes.	paraphrase	acknowledge

In this example, the choices of repetition and continuity – found in every teacher's move except the first and last – have brought about eight dependent pairs: six initiated by 'backchannel' (including two realized by paralinguistic items), one by 'request', and one by 'prompt'. Functionally, these dependent moves all relate back to the preceding response while eliciting a further move, and they together create an exchange of up to 19 moves in length (one of the longest found in the data). In terms of the contextual value of the mode, the pattern of Complex Exchange stretches the typical three-move classroom exchange towards a lengthy dialogue that sounds much more natural and closer to a daily conversation (note a shift in 26-S from the interpersonal pattern of Judgement to that of Personal Story, with the latter resonating with the ideational pattern of Life Experience). In other words, despite the fact that the exchange is initiated by the teacher, the pattern enables classroom dialogue to progress in a conversation-like manner. Such variation in the mode of classroom discourse is certainly useful in sustaining student speech and in creating a good atmosphere (apart from portraying the teacher as much more supportive than in a simple exchange).

Initiation-dependent

An initiation-dependent complex exchange can be brought about by a teacher or a student. With a teacher, it features such dependent moves as 'invite' and 'nominate', which are identified through the choice of **elliptical clause as question** and come after either an 'ask' move (see Example 8–7, where it is an 'invite-answer'), or an 'order' move (see Example 8–44 below, where it is an 'invite-comply').

Example 8–44 [from Text 8]

t-m	text	textual choice	move type
80-T/5	OK, another example – how do you say 要不是有你的帮助, 他不可能按时完成那项工作. 要不是有你的帮助, 他不可能按时地完成那项工作?		order
80-T/6	Anyone?	elliptical	invite-comply
81-S	But for your help, he will not, he will not have finished his homework on time.		comply
82-T/1	In time, un-hun, in time, but for your help, he could not have finished his work in time.	rep + structure	acknowledge

Here, the 'invite-comply' move is identified through the choice of elliptical clause (as question) in which only the subjective orientation is present. This allows the move to relate back to the teacher's own initiation while pointing at all those supposed to produce the action. To some extent, the initiation-dependent pattern of Complex Exchange brought about by a teacher reflects the teacher's precaution against an exchange failure (though it sometimes still occurs, such as in Example 8–7). This is perhaps why the pattern is often found where an exchange failure is more likely, i.e. in action exchanges, or exchanges of such information types as story and knowledge. In terms of the contextual value of the mode, the pattern adds to the classroom dialogue an effort on the part of the teacher to ensure that the dialogue will progress as expected.

With a student, an initiation-dependent complex exchange (though not very common) features such dependent moves as 'request', 'hint' and 'backchannel', which are identified through various choices of **repetition**. It should be noted that these moves, when used by a teacher, are dependent upon a student's responding move; but when used by a student, they are dependent upon the teacher's initiating move – either an 'ask' (see Example 8–30) or a 'state':

Example 8–45 [from Text 1]

t-m	text	textual choice	move type
119-T/2	And 'carts', it's like a wagon, it's like a wagon, 像个马车, and usually it has got two wheels – a two-wheel vehicle.	additive	state
120-S	老师 [teacher]，那 [well] "there were some bread carts up the hills from us" – the carts, carts are also by us, you mean?	rep + mental projection	request
121-T	'The hills from us', 离我们比较远的一些山上.		resolve
122-S	'The hill from'?	repetition	request
123-T	'From' means, 'hills from us' here refers to the distance.		resolve
124-S	'Away, away from'?	repetition	request
125-T	Yes, 'away from us'.	repetition	resolve
126-S	But is it away from us?	rep + structure	request
127-T/1	I mean – yes, you can understand in this way – 'away from us', yes.		resolve

Here, the choices of repetition mark off altogether four dependent pairs initiated by the 'request' move – all produced by a student. The 'request' move serves to relate back to a preceding 'state' or 'resolve' move while eliciting another 'resolve'. In terms of the contextual value of the mode, the initiation-dependent pattern of Complex Exchange brought about by a student unexpectedly prolongs an ongoing chunk; or rather, it turns what starts as a monologue into a dialogue, entirely for the benefit of the student's comprehension. In this sense, the pattern not only reflects active participation on the part of the student, but also functions to shift, temporarily, the essential mode of classroom discourse – i.e. teacher-initiated dialogue or teacher monologue – towards student-led dialogue. And through repeated negotiation of meaning, it generates both comprehensible input and output that are facilitative to language learning.

Finally, it should be pointed out that a teacher may combine response-dependent and initiation-dependent moves in the same complex exchange:

Example 8–46 [from Text 5]

t-m	text	textual choice	move type
15-T/9	Now, where did he – ern, I think you have read the notes – where did the writer get the title from?		ask [story]
15-T/10	Xxx		nominate
16-S	En, where he get the title?	repetition	request

17-T	Yeah, the title *The Kindness of Strangers*, do you know where the writer, you know, got the title from?	repetition	resolve
18-S	From a movie.	elliptical	answer
19-T	yes	continuative	backchannel
20-S	En, from a movie called *A Streetcar Named Desire*.		continue
21-T/1	Yes, *A Streetcar Named Desire*, that's from a movie, that is, at the end of this play or the movie, yes, a character said: "You can still depend on – I can still depend on the kindness of strangers", and so on, okay, that's right.	rep + expansion	evaluate

This can be viewed as a mixed version of the Complex Exchange pattern, which extends an exchange at every possible place, reflecting every effort made by the teacher to guarantee successful completion of an exchange. When story or knowledge exchanges are unavoidable in classroom teaching but are likely to meet with difficulty, such a mixed pattern seems particularly helpful, for it treats the 'testees' in such a patient and supportive manner as to give them confidence, and it is therefore more likely to make the exchange a success.

8.2.1.3 Summary

The pattern of Exchange is actually created out of both interpersonal and textual resources. In Chapter 6, it is described in interpersonal terms under the name of Information Exchange or Action Exchange. Here in this section, it is described in textual terms under the name of Exchange. As a textual logogenetic pattern, Exchange is identified through textual choices, which help to define the bound moves in a simple exchange, and the dependent moves in a complex exchange, and hence display how moves are textualized in an exchange. In relation to the mode of discourse, the pattern of Exchange is a realization of **classroom dialogue**. See Table 8.2 for a summary of the pattern.

8.2.2 Chunk

Like Exchange, the pattern of Chunk is described in interpersonal terms in Chapter 6 under the name of **Information Chunk**, and here it is called **Chunk** and described in textual terms instead. In the pattern of Exchange, which is identified in dialogue, textual resources serve mainly to textualize interpersonal meanings; whereas in the pattern of Chunk, which is identified in monologue, they serve mainly to textualize ideational meanings. Actually, the Chunk pattern is here described in terms of specific types of logical relations that are realized by conjunction choices and function as links between moves within a chunk. The pattern is classified into the following two sub-types. [1]

Table 8.2   A summary of the textual logogenetic patterns of Exchange

Exchange			textual choice	textual function	mode value
Simple Exchange	ask/order				
	answer/comply		elliptical clause as response	require reaching back to ask/order for the continuous element	typical classroom dialogue
	evaluate/ acknowledge		repetition/repetition+ /paraphrase (continuative)	relate back to answer/comply	
Complex Exchange	initiation-dependent	T's invite/ nominate	elliptical clause as question (interpersonal projection: Subject-present)	require reaching back to the initiation while pointing at those supposed to give information or action	classroom dialogue: ensured
		S's request/ hint/backch	repetition/repetition+	relate back to the (teacher's) initiation while eliciting a further move	classroom dialogue: student-led
	response-dependent: hint/request/ prompt/backch		repetition/repetition+; continuative	relate back to the response while eliciting a further move	classroom dialogue: conversation -like

8.2.2.1 Exposition Chunk

The pattern of Exposition Chunk is identified through textual choices in the 'restate' move in a chunk, including the choice of **expository conjunction** as the textual Theme of the clause, and/or the choice of **paraphrase**. See Example 8–33 and also the following examples:

t-m	text	textual choice	move type
Example 8–47 [from Text 2]			
88-T/3	Er, then, "Historians often disagree sharply."	initiative/temporal	state
88-T/4	They differ entirely.	paraphrase	restate
88-T/5	Their ideas are entirely different.	paraphrase	restate
Example 8–48 [from Text 8]			
78-T/4	OK, "But for a slight rhythmic movement, of the cartridge box, at the back of his belt, he might have been thought to be dead."	initiative	state
78-T/5	**That means,** he lay there motionless and asleep, but his breath caused the cartridge box at the back of his belt, to move regularly, rhythmically.	expository paraphrase	restate
78-T/6	**In other words,** if the cartridge box had not moved at regular intervals, he might have been thought to be dead, right?	expository paraphrase	restate

In Example 8–47, the choice of paraphrase serves to relate both of the bound moves back to the initial 'state' move by re-expressing the experiential meaning represented in the initial move (note the synonyms and repeated words as well). In Example 8–48, an expository conjunction is added to the paraphrase, making the elaboration relationship more explicit. Such textual choices in the 'restate' move help both to define the bound moves in a chunk, and to explain how they are bound to the initial 'state' move. In this way, the pattern of Exposition Chunk displays the internal organization of a chunk. In terms of the contextual value of the mode, the pattern realizes the teacher's monologue.

This kind of teacher's monologue can also be further defined. As found in the data, the initial proposition in almost all chunks of this pattern comes from the textbook (enclosed by quotation marks), so the chunks are in fact equal to Variant 1 – which is defined in Chapter 6 as a series of 'state' moves. Now that it is clear how the following 'state' (now called 'restate') moves are bound to the initial 'state' move, Variant 1 – when realized in the Exposition Chunk pattern – can be further defined as 'text exposition'. Chunks of this kind are found to be fairly common in EFL classroom discourse, especially in the Intensive Reading class. They not only constitute input but also facilitate comprehension of other input. In this sense, the teacher's monologue also has a positive role to play in EFL learning.

8.2.2.2 Exemplification Chunk

The pattern of Exemplification Chunk is identified through the choice of **exemplifying conjunction** as the textual Theme of the clause in a bound move here referred to as 'exemplify'. Besides, the chunk tends to be concluded by a further 'restate' move introduced by a **causal conjunction** as the textual Theme of the clause. For example:

Example 8–49 [from Text 8]

t-m	text	textual choice	move type
104-T/2	Now, in our text, [there are] two phrases: one is "might well", another one, "may well", "might well" and "may well". 'May well' suggests there is a reason why you may well say so, 你可以这样说.	boundive locative	state
104-T/3	**Say**, he may well be praised – 他值得表扬.	exemplifying	exemplify
104-T/4	**So**, 'may well', you see, suggests a reason, there is a reason for doing something or for something.	causal paraphrase	restate
104-T/5	'Might well', 'might well', another story, [means] 'be likely to'.		state
104-T/6	**Say**, had I had time – if I had had time – I might well have visited the Big Ben; had I had another chance, I might well have watched the Grand Canyon.	exemplifying	exemplify
104-T/7	**So**, 'might well', 可能会, ern, 可能会怎么怎么样.	causal/paraphrase	restate

Here, the first chunk is introduced by a 'locative' (*in our text [there are] two phrases* . . .), as well as a 'boundive' (*now*) that resumes the ideational pattern of Meaning just now interrupted (by an action exchange), so that the central proposition (*'may well' suggests* . . .) comes pretty late. Following the initial 'state' move is an 'exemplify' move introduced by *say*, which develops the meaning of *may well* by giving an example (*may well be praised*). Then a 'restate' move is introduced by *so*, which paraphrases the meaning given in the initial 'state' move – maintaining the Meaning pattern (*'may well' suggests* . . . .). The second chunk follows the same pattern. In this pattern of Exemplification Chunk the textual choices, again, both help to define the 'exemplify' and 'restate' moves, and explain how they are bound to the initial 'state' move. The pattern functions to tie up successive moves into a chunk; contextually it is the realization of the teacher's monologue.

Again, this kind of teacher's monologue can be further defined. As the first move in a chunk of this pattern always contains a 'locative', the chunk is clearly Variant 2 as described in Chapter 6. Since a 'locative' both signals a new move and locates the move in the experiential world as represented by the textbook, Variant 2 – when realized in the pattern of Exemplification Chunk – can be further defined as 'text-bound explanation'.

8.2.2.3 Summary

In sum, while the pattern of Chunk is described interpersonally in terms of mood choices in Chapter 6 under the name of Information Chunk, here it is described in terms of textual choices. Again, it is those textual choices that help to define bound moves in a chunk and serve to textualize successive moves in the same chunk. In terms of the mode of discourse, the Chunk pattern is a realization of **the teacher's monologue**. See Table 8.3 for a summary of the pattern.

Table 8.3 A summary of the textual logogenetic patterns of Chunk

Chunk		textual choice	textual function	mode value
Exposition Chunk	state	[quotation from textbook]		teacher's monologue: text exposition [Variant 1]
	restate	paraphrase; expository conjunction	relate back to the initial statement	
Exemplification Chunk	state	[locative]		teacher's monologue: text-bound explanation [Variant 2]
	exemplify	exemplifying conjunction	relate back to the initial statement	
	restate	causal conjunction; paraphrase	relate back to the initial statement	

8.2.3 Transaction

Both Exchange and Chunk, as described above, are at the lowest rank in the compositional scale of the textual logogenetic patterns as identified in the data. That is why the two patterns are described in terms of how they are internally textualized, and their internal textual features only serve to distinguish different types of exchanges and chunks. Meanwhile, such patterns are units that combine in one way or another to form a higher-rank textual pattern, i.e. Transaction. So, they are here examined again – regardless of whether an exchange is simple or complex and whether a chunk is an exposition or exemplification – just in terms of how exchanges and chunks sequence into a transaction, that is, how transactions are internally textualized. Accordingly the pattern of Transaction is classified into the following three types.

8.2.3.1 Continuation

A transaction taken as continuation is composed of at least one exchange or chunk – [exchange ^{n}] or [chunk ^{n}]. It is identified through the choice of **initiative** and/or **locative** as the textual Theme of the clause in the initial move of either the exchange or chunk, be it an 'ask'/'order' or 'state'.[12] Where the mainstream pattern has been interrupted, a continuation comes with a **boundive** instead. The pattern is further classified into two sub-types, as illustrated below.

Exchange Continuation

Example 8–50 [from Text 4]

t-m	text	textual choice	exchange
1-T/2	"In this broadcast, I said the Nazi regime is indistinguishable from the worst features of communism", 'Nazi regime', and what does 'regime' mean?	locative	continuation simple exchange
2-S	A 'system'.	elliptical	
3-T/1	That's right, a 'system', and a 'system of government', or 'political system'.	rep + structure	
3-T/2	**So,** "the Nazi regime is indistinguishable from the worst features", what does 'features' mean, 'features'?	initiative locative	continuation simple exchange
4-S	'Characteristics'.	elliptical	
5-T/1	'Characteristics', that's right, 'characteristics', and 'qualities'.	rep + expansion	
5-T/2	**Er, so,** ". . . indistinguishable from the worst features", 'indistinguishable', 'indistinguishable', what does it mean?	initiative locative	continuation complex exchange: I- /R- dependent
5-T/3	Xxx		
6-S	You can't, en . . .	elliptical	

7-T	you can't . . .	repetition
8-S	. . . tell them apart.	
9-T/1	tell them apart, that's right, so 'indistinguishable'	rep + expansion
	means 'you cannot tell them apart'.	

Here the initiating move in each of the three exchanges is introduced by a 'locative', and by an 'initiative' (*so*) as well in the second and third exchanges, so that they simply move on one after another, each being a new exchange. Actually, the pattern of Exchange Continuation tends to occur in succession, especially when the teacher is satisfied with the student's response in the previous exchange and decides to move on, or else when the response is not totally satisfactory but the teacher decides to improve it in the follow-up move rather than switch to a monologue (note the positive comment *that's right* as well as the choice of repetition+ in Moves 3-T/1, 5-T/1 and 9-T/1). In terms of the contextual value of the mode, the pattern enables classroom dialogue to progress in a clear-cut and efficient manner.

It should be noted that in the case of a simple (3-move) exchange (such as the first two exchanges in Example 8–50), the dialogue may sound just like an oral test. If a 'locative' is simultaneously chosen as the textual Theme of the clause in the initiating move, the dialogue becomes a 'text-bound oral test'. However, with complex exchanges, especially the response-dependent type, the dialogue would sound less test-like, or even conversation-like, as shown in the following recoding of Example 6–30:

Recoding of Example 6–30

t-m	text	textual choice	exchange
52-T	**OK**, any other disasters?	initiative	continuation
53-S	I experienced a small earthquake.		complex
54-T	Earthquake, a small earthquake?	repetition	exchange:
55-S	Yeah, below three. (laugh)	continuative	R-dependent
56-T	**Right**, what happened?	initiative	continuation
57-S	Oh, just I, I stayed on my bed, after work, and felt . . .		complex exchange:
58-T	. . . felt a bed shake?	rep+expression	R-dependent
59-S	Er, 特别小的一个 [a very small one].		
60-T/1	Yeah, a small bed shake. (laugh)	continuative paraphrase	
60-T/2	**OK**, what's your reaction – what did you do?	initiative	continuation
61-S	I just – I didn't know, on that day, en, news, the experts say there's an earthquake, en . . .		complex exchange:
62-T	So you didn't realize it was an earthquake?	rep+structure	R-dependent
63-S	Yeah –		

Chunk Continuation

Example 8–51 [from Text 9]

t-m	text	textual choice	chunk
43-T/2	**OK, and** "Other titles, like Jazz Giants . . ." If you enter, er this corridor, or, let's say, if you, er select or click, er this title Jazz Giants, and then possibly can listen, to all the masters who play jazz, right?	initiative locative additive	expansion chunk: text-bound explanation
43-T/3	**OK**, jazz began from the nineteen twenties, that's the musical history.	initiative	continuation chunk:
43-T/4	Actually jazz started from the 1920s, the American black people.	expository	presentation
43-T/5	**OK**, jazz is a kind of music which I like most, OK, because jazz actually, is quite er, quite melodious and also melancholy.	initiative	continuation chunk: presentation
43-T/6	And what I like most is the melancholy note of jazz.	additive	
43-T/7	**And also** another title here, "Escape from Cybercity", which is an animated, animated adventure game, ok, this is a kind of game just like a cartoon.	additive locative	expansion chunk: text-bound explanation

As can be seen, the outer two chunks are both introduced by a locative, constituting a text exposition; and they are linked by an additive, forming an expansion transaction (see relevant discussion below). The middle two chunks constitute an embedded transaction within the text exposition transaction. They are both introduced by an 'initiative' (*OK*), which indicates a step forward to something new – (from text exposition) first to the origin of jazz, and then to attributes of jazz (both in the ideational pattern of Behind-Text). The two chunks thus form the pattern of Chunk Continuation. In terms of the mode of discourse, the pattern enables monologue to progress or diverge whenever the teacher considers necessary.

The pattern is most often employed by the teacher to present additional information, such as in Example 8–51 where the pattern is used to add background information about jazz. In chunks of this kind, the initial proposition comes from the teacher; so they are in fact Variant 3 as described in Chapter 6. Now that it is clear that the chunks are organized so as to present something new, Variant 3 – when realized in the pattern of Chunk Continuation – can be more specifically named 'presentation'.

The pattern is also used by the teacher to explain a text that is currently being taught and learnt in class, in a monologue of either the 'text exposition' type (Variant 1) or the 'text-bound explanation' type (Variant 2). In these two cases, however, the pattern may easily leave the monologue with a note of monotony, as shown in the example below:

Example 8–52 [from Text 2]

t-m	text	textual choice	chunk
88-T/9	**OK**, en, OK, "… the more they remember, the higher their grades."	initiative	continuation chunk: text exposition
88-T/10	OK, if you remember the facts, then you get the high mark, or high grade.	paraphrase	
88-T/11	**Yes**, "From this experience a number of conclusions seem obvious …"	initiative	continuation chunk: text exposition
88-T/12	In other words, it seems quite natural students would reach these conclusions.	expository paraphrase	
88-T/13	**OK**, "… the study of history is the study of 'facts' about the past; the more 'facts' you know, the better you are as a student of history."	initiative	continuation chunk: text exposition
88-T/14	If they remember more these facts, then they are more experienced, they are more, en, they are better trained in history.	paraphrase	
88-T/15	Then – **OK**, "… the professional historian is simply one who brings together a very large number of 'facts'."	initiative	continuation chunk: text exposition
88-T/16	In other words, in our idea, historians, the professional, are the people who know more facts, than we, actually, yeah, than us students.	expository paraphrase	

8.2.3.2 Rotation

A transaction taken as rotation is composed of at least two and generally more than two exchanges – [exchange ^ exchange ^{n}]. The first exchange is usually a continuation, while the rest are related to it through choices of **repetition** or **elliptical clause as question**. It is basically the same question or invitation that is being addressed to different students. The pattern of Rotation falls into the following two categories.

Information Exchange Rotation

With information exchanges, the pattern is identified through the choice of **repeated question** (see Example 8–25), or an **elliptical clause as question** in which the contrastive element is either **Subject/Complement** (in an 'ask' move) or **interpersonal projection** (in an 'invite-answer' move).

For example:

Example 8–53 [from Text 6]

t-m	text	textual choice	exchange
55-T/2	**Now, right**, now people have lots of worries, but what are the things people are most worried, what are the things people are most worried about, do you know?	initiative [ask]	continuation information exchange
56-S/a	打仗 [war].	elliptical	
57-T	Ern, war.	paraphrase	
58-S/b	Medication.	elliptical	
59-T	Medication.	repetition	
60-S/c	Environment.	elliptical	
61-T/1	Environment, okay, environment.	repetition	
61-T/2	**What else?**	elliptical [ask]	rotation information exchange
62-Sn	[confusion]		
63-T/1	Resources, environmental resources.		
63-T/2	**What else?**	elliptical [ask]	rotation information exchange
64-S	Education.	elliptical	
65-T/1	Education, okay.	repetition	

Here, the two rotation information exchanges are both initiated by an 'ask' move realized by an elliptical clause, in which the contrastive element is Complement (*what*) accompanied by a comparative reference item (*else*)[13]. The elliptical question requires that the addressee go back to the preceding text for a question that contains the continuous element, thus linking the two successive exchanges into one transaction. No matter how many times the elliptical question occurs, it is equally related to the previous non-elliptical question; so that the transaction may extend over a pretty long span of text. In terms of the value of the mode, the pattern of Information Exchange Rotation enables classroom dialogue to progress in a more thoughtful and exhaustive manner than the pattern of Exchange Continuation, since it helps to make sure that a question gets fully answered and more students get a chance to speak. In this sense, the kind of classroom dialogue realized by this pattern can be more specifically called 'multiple-answer dialogue'.

Action Exchange Rotation

With action exchanges, the Rotation pattern is identified through the choice of an **elliptical clause as question** in which the contrastive element is **interpersonal projection**. The elliptical question functions as an invitation to comply with an order previously given, that is, as an 'invite-comply' that can replace an 'order' in an action exchange:

Example 8–54 [from Text 10]

t-m	text	textual choice	exchange
73-T/2	And Number 2, Emily, please.	elliptical [order]	action
74-S	I think the answer is B.		exchange
75-T/1	B.		
75-T/2	Anyone disagrees, any different idea, no different idea?	elliptical [invite-comply]	rotation action exchange
76-S	I choose D.		
77-T/1	D, okay.		

Here the rotation action exchange is initiated by an 'invite-comply' move, which is used to elicit a different version of a verbal action being demanded. Because the continuous element in the elliptical clause has to be retrieved from a previous action move (actually a much earlier one; for details see 8.2.4.1 below), the clause serves to relate the current action exchange back to the preceding exchange(s). In terms of the contextual value of the mode, the pattern of Action Exchange Rotation enables classroom dialogue to progress in a light-hearted manner when an error has occurred in a student's response – that is, when the action being demanded has not been properly performed. It encourages the students to perform the demanded action again and hence to correct their own errors. This kind of classroom dialogue can be more appropriately called 'multiple-comply dialogue'.

8.2.3.3 Expansion

If the exchanges or chunks in the Continuation pattern are relatively independent, and those in Rotation are equally dependent upon the very first information or action move that is realized by a complete clause, those in Expansion can be said to be inter-dependent. In other words, a transaction taken as expansion is composed of more than one exchange or chunk logically related through the choice of **conjunction**. The pattern of Expansion is classified into the following three types.

Exchange Expansion

The pattern of Exchange Expansion can be represented as either [exchange ^ exchange] or [chunk ^ exchange]. That is, an exchange may come after either an exchange or a chunk, but it always comes as an expansion – identified through the choice of **conjunction** as the textual Theme of the clause in the initial move. For example:

Example 8–55 [from Text 6]

t-m	text	textual choice	exchange
1-T/4	**Right**, what do you think of the information provided by the text – is there enough information?	initiative	initiation exchange
2-S	No.	elliptical	
3-T	Why, **but** why you think there isn't enough information?	adversative	expansion exchange
4-S	En, because we know, we know more about it.		
5-T/1	Okay, you know more about it, yes.	repetition	
5-T/2	**And then** why, why does the writer want to write this text, why?	causal	expansion exchange
6-S	Maybe to warn people.	elliptical	
7-T	Warn people, of what?	rep+structure	
8-S	Ern, in your life, there is a serious problem.		
9-T	Problem of what?	rep+structure	
10-S	En, population is increasing.		
11-T	**And** do you think you share the same idea with the writer, do you?	additive	expansion exchange
12-S	I think, there is quite enough information.		

This is a case of [exchange ^ exchange], where all exchanges except the first one are introduced by a conjunction (*but, and then, and*), which serves to link the successive exchanges into one transaction, with each exchange being a logical development of its preceding one. The conjunction may also go with an elliptical question in which the contrastive element is a circumstantial Adjunct (*But by the time 1650?* in Example 8–8) or a WH-element (*but why / why not / when / where / how?*). In the case of [chunk ^ exchange], the exchange would be a logical development of its preceding chunk (e.g. *Well, it's a large area in United States, from the Pacific to the Atlantic, from coast to coast. // So you can imagine what was the biggest problem? [from Text 5: 43-T/2 to T/3]*). In either case, the pattern of Exchange Expansion enables classroom dialogue to progress in a logical manner and enables the teacher to guide the students in their thinking and in producing the expected response.

Exchange-Chunk Expansion

The pattern of Exchange-Chunk Expansion can be represented as [exchange ^ chunk]. That is, a chunk following an exchange is related to the exchange through expansion – identified through the choice of a **causal, elaborating** or

extending conjunction as the textual Theme of the clause in the initial move of the chunk. For example:

Example 8–56 [from Text 3]

t-m	text	textual choice	exchange/chunk
32-T	**Yes**, '产量' 是什么 [what is '产量']?	initiative	continuation
33-S(n)	'Output'.	elliptical	exchange
34-T/1	Yes, 'output', alright.	repetition	
34-T/2	**But** 'product' 是什么 [what is 'product']?	adversative	expansion
35-S(n)	'产品'.	elliptical	exchange
36-T/1	'产品', alright.	repetition	
36-T/2	那'生产'是什么 [**then** what is '生产']?	causal	expansion
37-S	'Production'.	elliptical	exchange
38-T/1	'Production'.	repetition	
38-T/2	**So** 'product' 是产品, the same with 'produce', alright; 'production' is the process of producing, alright; and the result of production is 'output', alright.	causal paraphrase	expansion chunk

Here the first three exchanges are actually in the pattern of Exchange Expansion as described above, while the chunk that comes at the end is introduced by a causal conjunction (*so*), which indicates a conclusion the speaker has drawn from what is previously said, thus relating the chunk back to the preceding exchanges in a logical way. As such, the pattern of Exchange-Chunk Expansion realizes a mode of classroom discourse that is found to be fairly common in the classroom, i.e. dialogue followed up with monologue, which allows the teacher to reinforce or develop what the students have just said in the dialogue.

Meanwhile, it should be noted that the initial proposition in a chunk of this pattern comes from the teacher rather than from the textbook, so the chunk is a Variant 3 as described in Chapter 6. Now that it is clear that the chunk comes as a follow-up to the preceding exchange(s) rather than as a presentation of something new, Variant 3 – when realized in the pattern of Exchange-Chunk Expansion – can be futher defined as 'follow-up chunk'; and according to the specific type of conjunction actually chosen, it can be more specifically referred to as follow-up clarification, addition, conclusion, etc.

Chunk-Chunk Expansion

The pattern of Chunk-Chunk Expansion can be represented as [chunk ^ chunk "]. That is, it is simply a sequence of chunks, identified through an **extending conjunction** that links the successive chunks and is usually accompanied by a **locative**:

Example 8–57 [from Text 2]

t-m	text	textual choice	chunk
82-T/2	**OK**, "Most students . . ." – Chinese students have a sort of echo in their mind, because you have relatively the same sort of experience, don't you think so?	initiative locative	continuation chunk: text- bound explanation
82-T/3	**And** ". . . are usually introduced to the study of history by way of" – by means of – "a fat textbook" – a very thick, a thick or a big textbook – "and become quickly immersed in a vast sea of names, dates, events and statistics" – the hard facts, we call 'hard facts', er, like when this event took place, and who actually played the role, and when and where did it happen, right, and things like that.	addit ve locative	expansion chunk: text-bound explanation
82-T/4	**And then**, "become quickly immersed in a vast sea", usually we say, 'immersed in water', you see, in liquid, for 'immerse' here is used figuratively.	additive locati:e	expansion chunk: text-bound explanation
82-T/5	We also call it a sort of metaphor.	paraphrase	
82-T/6	It means 'in, involved in the sea'.	expository	

Here the latter two chunks are both introduced by an extending conjunction (*and, and then*), which ties up the successive chunks into one transaction. As all chunks are also introduced by a 'locative', the pattern of Chunk-Chunk Expansion in fact realizes, in terms of the mode, the teacher's monologue that again can be called 'text-bound explanation' (Variant 2). See also Example 8–51.

However, it should be pointed out that the logical relationship in this pattern seems less clear than in either [exchange ∧ chunk] or [chunk ∧ exchange]. In Example 8–57, as the words quoted in the three 'locatives' are actually taken from one and the same sentence in the students' textbook, the conjunctions used (*and, and then*) seem more like a device sequencing the chunks into a transaction focused on the same sentence (or paragraph) in the students' textbook, than a tie linking what is said in the successive chunks themselves. Further study is required in this regard.

8.2.3.4 Summary

In sum, a transaction is composed of at least one, and usually more exchanges and/or chunks in a series, so the patterns of Transaction are at a higher rank in the compositional scale of textual logogenetic patterns in EFL classroom discourse. The patterns are here described in terms of textual choices that sequence exchanges and/or chunks into various types of transaction. It should be noted that the different types of transaction can be embedded in or combined with one another in an EFL class.[14] But in any case, they can all be described by reference to the various patterns of Transaction. See Table 8.4 for a summary of the patterns (V = Variant).

8.2.4 Activity

The pattern of Activity is at the highest rank in the compositional scale of textual logogenetic patterns as identified in EFL classroom discourse. In other words, an activity is composed of transactions. The term **activity** is used because the text span under discussion tends to coincide with such classroom activities as doing an exercise, reading aloud part of a text, pre-/post-reading discussion, etc. But this does not mean that activity is a pedagogic unit. It is a semantic unit, defined textually and usually overlapping with a particular semantic phase (see 8.3.2 for more).

It is found in the data that an activity is always marked in the very beginning by a **boundive** that introduces an 'orientate' and/or 'direct' move announcing the beginning of a new classroom activity; and optionally marked at the end

Table 8.4   A summary of the textual logogenetic patterns of Transaction

Transaction		textual choice	textual function	mode value
Continuation	Exchange Continuation	initiative (locative) [in initial move]	signal a move-on exchange	classroom dialogue: test-like (text-bound)/ conversation-like
	Chunk Continuation	initiative (locative) [in initial move]	signal a move-on chunk	teacher's monologue: presentation [V3]/text exposition [V1]/text-bound explanation [V2]
Rotation	Information Exchange Rotation	elliptical clause as question; repeated question	relate to a previous question	classroom dialogue: multiple-answer
	Action Exchange Rotation	elliptical clause as question [in invite-comply]	relate to a previous action move	classroom dialogue: multiple-comply
Expansion	Exchange/Chunk -Exchange Expansion	conjunction (elliptical clause as question)	logically join an exchange with another/a chunk	classroom dialogue: logically guided
	Exchange -Chunk Expansion	causal/ extending/ elaborating conjunction	logically join a chunk with exchange(s)	dialogue followed up by monologue: follow-up elaboration/extension/ conclusion [V3]
	Chunk-Chunk Expansion	conjunction; locative	sequence chunks	teacher's monologue: text-bound explanation [V2]

again by a **boundive**, which introduces a 'recap' move announcing the end of an activity. Between the boundaries are an unlimited number of transactions, as continuation or rotation or expansion. The pattern can be represented as [boundary $\wedge$ transaction ^{n} ($\wedge$ boundary)], and it is viewed as the **general** version of the Activity pattern because it is shared by all activities. According to the specific ways in which textual resources help to organize the successive transactions between the two boundaries (which may not always be clear, though[15]), two **specific** versions of the pattern have been identified: orbital and serial.[16]

8.2.4.1 Orbital Activity

An activity taken as orbital is one in which a number of transactions are equally dependent on one pivot, forming a satellite-nucleus relationship. The pattern of Orbital Activity is identified through the choice of **elliptical clause as order** in the initiating move of each of the successive transactions. To retrieve the continuous element in each elliptical clause, the addressee must go back to the same, preceding action move that is realized by a complete imperative clause. For example (only the elliptical 'order' is given, to save space):

Example 8–58 [from Text 10]

t-m	text	textual choice	action move
16-T/2	Now, let's read the statements and decide it's true or false.	boundive	orientate
16-T/3	First you read the statement and then you tell they are true or false.		direct
16-T/4	Xxx, number one, please.	elliptical	order (1)
......	......		
18-T/2	And number two, Dianna, would you please?	elliptical	order (2)
......	......		
30-T/3	Next one, Annie, please.	elliptical	order (3)
......	......		
34-T/2	Next one, Lyn, would you please?	elliptical	order (4)
......	......		
36-T/2	Next one, Xxx, please.	elliptical	order (5)
......	......		
42-T/2	The next one, Mat, please.	elliptical	order (6)
......	......		
44-T/2	The next one, Jane, please.	elliptical	order (7)
......	......		
53-T/4	Now, the eighth statement, Xxx, please.	elliptical	order (8)
......	......		
55-T	Another one, Lina.	elliptical	order (9)
......	......		
61-T/6	And the last one, Effie, would you please?	elliptical	order (10)
......	......		

This activity begins with an 'orientate' move that is introduced by a 'boundive' (*now*) and realized by a complete clause. Next to this beginning boundary is a 'direct' move realized again by a complete clause. Then there is a succession of transactions composed of action exchange(s), each being initiated by an 'order' move. From the change of turn numbers, it can be seen that some transactions (i.e. 1, 3, 4, 6 and 8) last only a couple of turns, being a single action exchange; whereas others are longer, with expansions and/or continuations, and embedding knowledge exchanges. The seventh is the longest transaction, so that the eighth 'order' comes as resumption (note the 'boundive' *now* in Move 53-T/4). In spite of that, all of the 'order' moves have one thing in common: they are realized by an elliptical clause where the continuous element is the Predicator, i.e. the verb, which can only be retrieved from the 'direct' move (and here also the 'orientate' move) that comes at the very beginning. No matter how many elliptical orders are given, each of them is equally dependent on the 'direct' move. In this sense, the 'direct' move is the nucleus and all of the action transactions are the satellites. See Figure 8.4 for an illustration of the pattern of Orbital Activity in Example 8–58.

Functionally, the elliptical order presupposes the action being demanded (*read the statement and decide it's true or false*). Each time it appears, it specifies a new object (*Number 1, Number 2, next one, the eighth statement, the last one*) as well as a new subject (*Xxx, Dianna, Annie, Lyn, Mat, Effie*) of the action. To retrieve the action being demanded, i.e. the Predicator, the addressee must go back to the very first action move that is realized by a complete imperative clause. In this way, the pattern of Orbital Activity serves to tie up an entire action phase. In terms of the mode, the pattern enables classroom dialogue to extend for quite a considerable length without losing track. So it is mostly found in an exercise-oriented class, such as Extensive Reading, Oral Interpretation, or Comprehensive English.

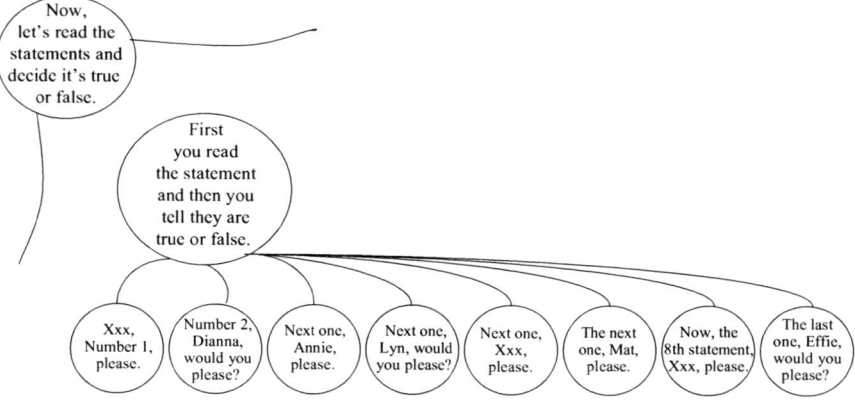

FIGURE 8.4   The pattern of Orbital Activity in Example 8–58

It should be noted that the Complement in the elliptical clause (i.e. *Number 1, next one, the eighth statement*, etc.), when occurring without a Predicator before it, may seem like a temporal conjunction. But this is not the case because, without the initial 'direct' move, it simply does not make sense; although expressions such as *the next question*, when used in an initiating 'ask' move, is taken as a temporal conjunction (see below).

8.2.4.2 Serial Activity

An activity taken as serial is one in which a number of transactions form such a sequence that each transaction is dependent on the immediately preceding one. The pattern of Serial Activity is identified through the choice of **temporal conjunction** as the textual Theme of the clause in the initiating move of the successive transactions. Here is an example (again, only the 'ask' move is given, to save space):

Example 8–59 [from Text 5]

t-m	text	textual choice	move
16-T/2	Well, **now, so now** let me ask you some questions about the text.	boundive	orientate
16-T/4	**First**, what do you know about the title, what do you know about the title – the title is *The Kindness of Strangers* – what does that mean?	temporal	ask (1)
. . . . . .	. . . . . .		
18-T/2	So en, **now, the next question** is, what did he, what did the writer – what does the writer want to say to the reader through his experience described in the passage, what do you think, the writer wants to tell the reader?	boundive temporal	ask (2)
. . . . . .	. . . . . .		
30-T/3	OK, **now, next question**: what do you think, what do you think, was the biggest problem during the journey?	boundive temporal	ask (3)
. . . . . .	. . . . . .		
34-T/2	**Now, the next question**: how was he received by the people, in the 14 states, generally speaking, well, how was he received?	boundive temporal	ask (4)
. . . . . .	. . . . . .		
36-T/2	**All right**, well, I think you can all answer [all answered] the questions very well, and you did a very good job, in previewing the lesson.	boundive	recap

This activity again has a clearly marked beginning boundary, i.e. an 'orientate' move introduced by a 'boundive' (*now*). Then there is a succession of transactions, each being initiated by an 'ask' move that is introduced by a temporal conjunction (*first, the next question*). Between the successive 'ask'

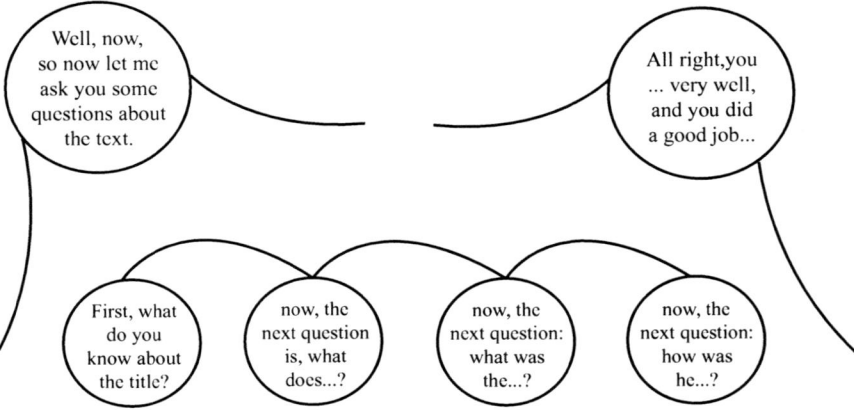

FIGURE 8.5   The pattern of Serial Activity in Example 8–59

moves, there are usually a large number of turns, which indicates that most transactions are lengthy, with multiple continuations, expansions or rotations, and inevitably with embeddedness. This is why each time the temporal conjunction re-occurs, it is accompanied by a 'boundive' – as a boundary-maintaining device that signals resumption of the activity after some kind of failure or digression. Finally comes a 'recap' move, again introduced by a 'boundive' (*all right*), which closes the activity. See Figure 8.5 for an illustration of the pattern of Serial Activity in Example 8–59.

Functionally, the choice of temporal conjunction, as the textual Theme of the clause in all of the 'ask' moves, serves to relate the successive transactions in such a way that each one is dependent on its preceding one. As such, the pattern of Serial Activity serves to textualize an activity in a logical way. In terms of the mode, the pattern enables classroom dialogue to progress in such an organized manner that it may again extend to an unlimited length without losing track. Furthermore, by constantly reminding the students what they have just done and what to do next, the pattern is useful in keeping the students alert to each coming question, especially when their answers are not likely to be spontaneous and have to be based on their comprehension of the text or on their memory. That is why the pattern often overlaps with the interpersonal pattern of Story instead of Personal Story, and with the ideational patterns of Text instead of Life Experience.

8.2.4.3 Summary

In sum, the pattern of Activity described here is at the highest rank in the compositional scale of textual logogenetic patterns as identified in EFL classroom discourse. As the activities found in the data are generally better

Table 8.5 A summary of the textual logogenetic patterns of Activity

Activity		textual choice	textual function	mode value
general		boundive [in an 'orientate'/ 'direct'/'recap' move]	signal the boundaries of an activity	classroom activity
specific	Orbital Activity	elliptical clause as order [in the initiating move of each successive transaction]	link all transactions with the initial 'direct' or 'orientate' move	classroom dialogue: lengthy
	Serial Activity	temporal conjunction [in the initiating move of each successive transaction]	relate successive transactions logically	classroom dialogue: lengthy and organized

textualized at the boundaries than in the middle part, the pattern is described as both a general and a specific version (see Table 8.5 for a summary). It should be pointed out that in the description of textual logogenetic patterns throughout this chapter, the term 'textual choice' is used in place of UNIVARIATE for the sake of consistency (textual choices do not recur within patterns at the lowest rank because they only serve to textualize the patterns internally; nor do they recur at the highest rank; only with patterns at the rank of transaction do they repeat themselves).

8.3 TEXT TYPE network: PROGRESSION

In this chapter, first, the textual systems in the REGISTER network of EFL classroom discourse are presented; then, the textual logogenetic patterns identified as a result of coding the data according to the REGISTER systems are described and illustrated with examples taken from the data. In both cases, the description is given multi-stratally in spite of a focus on the textual metafunction. What is more, a compositional scale of the textual logogenetic patterns has been identified. In this final section, the logogenetic patterns at all ranks will be brought together into the textual TEXT TYPE network of EFL classroom discourse, referred to as PROGRESSION. The section includes (1) a representation of the PROGRESSION network, and (2) an illustration of how the network can be applied to the analysis and description of the textual process of EFL classroom discourse.

8.3.1 Representation

The textual logogenetic patterns of EFL classroom discourse can be found at three ranks – exchange/chunk, transaction, and activity – which form a compositional scale. At the lowest rank, the patterns of Exchange and Chunk are described in terms of the specific ways in which an exchange or a chunk is textualized internally, thus classifying exchanges and chunks in EFL classroom discourse into several different types. At a higher rank, the patterns of Transaction are described in terms of the specific ways in which transactions are formed out of various types of exchanges and/or chunks, leading to the identification of different types of transaction. And at the highest rank, the patterns of Activity are described in terms of specific ways in which activities are formed out of various types of transaction, giving definitions of different types of activity. But the patterns at all ranks have one thing in common. That is, they each constitute a **progressive** text span: they both relate to a preceding text span and push discourse forward in one way or another, revealing various modes of progression of EFL classroom discourse. That is why the textual TEXT TYPE network of EFL classroom discourse is referred to as PROGRESSION. See Figure 8.6 for a representation of the network.

8.3.2 Illustration

This section presents an application of the PROGRESSION system to an analysis of the same text, i.e. Text 5, which was analysed interpersonally in 6.3.2 and ideationally in 7.3.2.

First, the text was coded according to the textual systems in the REGISTER network of EFL classroom discourse (see Appendix III). As the textual logogenetic patterns were found emerging out of successive textual choices, the text was further coded according to the PROGRESSION system in the TEXT TYPE network of EFL classroom discourse (see the 'textual' column in Appendix IV). In order to mark off textual patterns at different ranks of the compositional

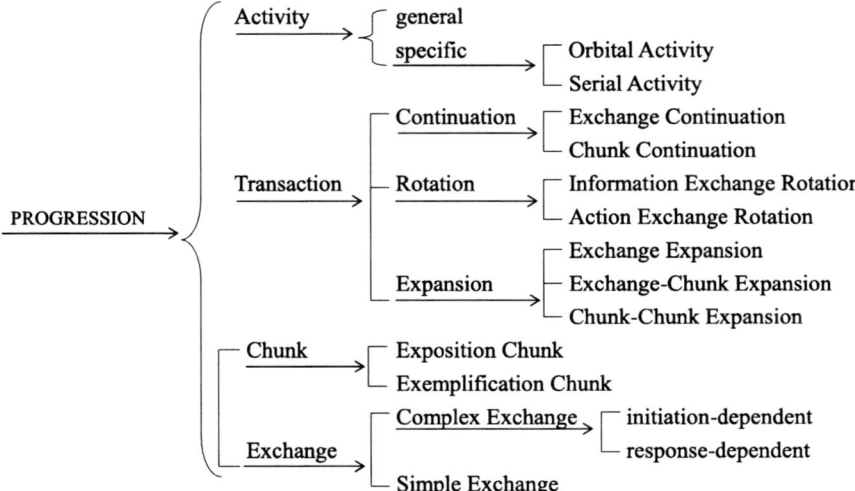

FIGURE 8.6   The PROGRESSION system in the TEXT TYPE network of EFL classroom discourse

scale, different kinds of horizontal rules are used in Appendix IV. The 3-point (1 point = 0.353 mm) shaded rule marks off an activity, the 2.25-point rule marks off a transaction, the 1.5-point rule marks off an exchange or chunk within a transaction, the dotted one marks off an expansion exchange or chunk within a transaction, the wavy one a rotation exchange within a transaction, and the 0.5-point one a bound move within an exchange or chunk.

Once the whole text is coded for PROGRESSION, different types of textual logogenetic patterns at different ranks can be clearly observed, and their relationships with the interpersonal and ideational patterns also become clear (read Appendix IV horizontally for patterns across metafunctions). Actually, the function of textual resources is to textualize interpersonal and ideational meanings in such a way as to enable a text to do its job in the given context of situation. So, first of all, see Figure 8.7 for an illustration of the resonation of the semantic phases in Text 5 across metafunctions (where the textual structure is only described at the activity rank), and then a detailed textual analysis of Text 5 (which specifies both the ways this text progresses in each activity, and the roles played by the textual patterns in textualizing interpersonal and ideational meanings).

Activity 1 [from 1-T/1 to 15-T/5]

The first activity displays the general pattern of Activity: it is composed of a beginning boundary plus two transactions that are not related in a specific way. But both transactions are rather involved and lengthy, containing initiation-/response-dependent exchanges. The first transaction is in the pattern of Exchange-Exchange Expansion, which embeds a rotation exchange. While rotation serves to put the same question to different students, expansion allows the question to go further and deeper. The second transaction is an Exchange-Chunk Expansion, which enables the teacher to wind up the activity with a follow-up addition. Thus the first activity is basically dialogue, though guided and further developed at the end by the teacher. This kind of mode fits the interpersonal phase of [Classroom Conversation ^ Teacher Monologue].

Meanwhile, specific features of the transactions reveal their role in textualizing the ideational meaning of the activity. First, the initial move in the first transaction

interpersonal	Classroom Conversation	Teacher Monologue	Teacher-Led Discussion	Student Action	Teacher Talk	
ideational	Warm-Up		Retelling	Reading Aloud	Text Study	Language Study
	Oral Preview			Textbook Study		
textual	Activity 1		Activity 2	Activity 3		Activity 4

FIGURE 8.7 Resonation of semantic phases in Text 5 across metafunctions

is introduced by an adversative conjunction (*but*), indicating a logical relation between the current transaction and what is said in the preceding 'orientate' move, a case seldom found in the data. But a re-examination of the experiential content of the two related parts reveals the truth: the daily event being announced in the 'orientate' move is a *preview of the text*, whereas the following transaction is concerned with the students' life experience. It is this contrast in content that requires the adversative *but*. Besides, the expansion relationship found in both transactions is realized by the same adversative conjunction *but*. The first time it is used to introduce the teacher's 'ask' move, and the second time the teacher's follow-up chunk (addition). This reveals the teacher's effort to lead the dialogue towards a pre-determined route. Again, a re-examination of the experiential content of the transactions shows that it is a route from the Warm-Up phase towards the Retelling phase (note that the activity begins with the ideational pattern of Complex (Life) Experience, and ends with Beyond-Text). The teacher is trying to make the students recognize that the subject-matter of the text they are learning is relevant to their own life. For the same reason, the exchanges are found to alternate between the complex and simple versions, between conversation-like and test-like, a mode of dialogue quite suitable for the Warm-Up phase.

So, it can be said that the way this activity is textualized is more or less motivated by the kinds of interpersonal and ideational meanings being made. The choice of rotation exchange serves to involve more students in classroom conversation; the choice of expansion exchange serves to lead the conversation in a way that prepares the students for the content of the text to be learnt; and the choice of both simple and complex exchanges, followed up with a chunk, makes classroom interaction appear very much teacher-controlled even with student participation.

Activity 2 [from 15-T/6 to 87-T/5]

The second activity displays the specific pattern of Serial Activity (see also Example 8–59). It is composed of both a beginning and ending boundary ('orientate' and 'recap'), plus four transactions in the middle that are related through temporal conjunctions. The pattern serves well to enable a flow from one ideational focus to another as it is going from one transaction to another. The first transaction resonates with In-Text (*where did the writer get the title*, a question that comes to replace *what do you know about the title* when the latter ends up a failure to get a response), the second transaction resonates with Beyond-Text (*what does the writer want to tell the reader*), the third with Above-Text (*what was the biggest problem during the journey*), and the fourth with In-Text again (*how was he received by the people in the 14 states*).[17] It is the textual choices that organize the successive transactions that are different in ideational meaning into one single activity.

At the transaction rank, the mainstream pattern throughout this activity is Exchange Continuation, which matches the interpersonal phase of bilateral interaction (Teacher-Led Discussion). A continuation exchange serves to signal a new step forward after an interruption caused by an embedded ideational or interpersonal pattern. In fact, it always occurs to indicate a switch between Beyond-Text and In-Text, between In-Text and Meaning, or between Knowledge and Story. In this way, it helps to keep the discussion progressing despite interruptions or digressions.

Other types of Transaction patterns are embedded where the progression of the discussion has met with genuine difficulty. A continuation chunk comes mainly as a rescue where there is an exchange failure. The teacher's presentation chunk comes in time to guide the students in their struggle for the right answer; that is why it is always followed by an exchange introduced by a causal conjunction, forming the pattern of Chunk-Exchange Expansion. Where an exchange has not failed but obviously has run into trouble (with a disclaimer), a rotation exchange appears so that the question eventually gets answered. In places where an answer is given but is not satisfactory, an expansion exchange comes along to dig into the question before it gets fully answered. Even when the answer is correct, an expansion chunk may nonetheless occur to offer a follow-up conclusion or exposition – as reinforcement.

At the lowest rank, the chunks found here generally come as either presentation or follow-up chunk. That is, they are not bound to the textbook, which suits the current interpersonal phase of Retelling. The exchanges are mostly the complex type, either initiation-dependent or response-dependent, or both; which ensures that the discussion not only progresses smoothly but also sounds conversation-like rather than test-like. This seems to be a useful choice when the information being exchanged is story rather than personal story, so that the dialogue going on is unlikely to be spontaneous.

So, again, the way this activity progresses is appropriate to the flow of both interpersonal and ideational meanings. The choice of Serial Activity serves to organize the Retelling phase in such a way that the story told in the textbook gets retold from various perspectives; the choice of Exchange Continuation both creates dialogue and keeps it moving forward, while the choice of Expansion or Rotation allows the teacher to lead the discussion towards its destination in spite of midway difficulties; and the choice of Complex Exchange, along with follow-up chunks or a presentation, makes the Retelling phase appear teacher-guided as well as conversation-like.

Activity 3 [from 87-T/6 to 95-T/12]

The third activity displays the general rather than specific version of the Activity pattern. It is composed of a beginning boundary plus two transactions. The first transaction is a continuation exchange, a complex one of the response-dependent kind. The transaction proves appropriate in the present interpersonal phase of Student Action that matches the ideational phase of Reading Aloud. It enables the teacher to provide assistance to the student who is clearly having difficulty with pronunciation while doing his reading aloud.

The second transaction is a Chunk-Chunk Expansion, made up altogether of four chunks. The first three are linked through an additive conjunction (*and*) plus a locative, forming a sequence focused on the very first sentence in the paragraph that has just been read aloud, giving a text-bound explanation about a few special things mentioned in that sentence (Behind-Text). The last chunk is introduced by a causal conjunction (*so*), bringing about an interpretation of the paragraph (Beyond-Text) that the teacher has reached based on the explanation just given. The transaction as a whole – which is textualized into a piece of teacher's monologue – enables a proper expression of its experiential content, i.e. the background knowledge and the general idea of the paragraph.

Additionally, the fact that these two transactions are textualized as one activity serves as further evidence for the ideational interpretation that they are independent lower-level phases (Reading Aloud and Text Study) but are parts of the same higher-level phase (Textbook Study).

Activity 4 [from 95-T/13 to 109-T/8]

This final activity also displays the general version of the Activity pattern. It is composed of a beginning boundary, plus a number of transactions that are found in a variety of Transaction patterns but are unrelated in any specific ways.

The mainstream pattern of Transaction found here is Chunk Continuation, with each chunk being a new step forward. As this activity actually overlaps with the ideational phase of Language Study (which features the pattern of Meaning), most of the continuation chunks here contain a locative. In other words, these chunks constitute a text-bound explanation, which serves well to enable a proper expression of the experiential content; though they do sound rather monotonous, especially when occurring in succession.

As if to reduce the effect of monotony, the teacher chooses to alternate Chunk Continuation with other patterns of Transaction. Among them, Exchange Continuation is most common, which temporarily shifts the burden of text-bound explanation partially onto the students. Where the student's answer is incomplete, the teacher applies a follow-up chunk to expand the answer. The teacher also employs the pattern of Chunk-Exchange Expansion once, which allows her to guide the students in their thinking before demanding a response from them.

At the lowest rank, the chunks are textualized in different ways so as to perform different textual functions, although interpersonally they are equally unilateral (as Knowledge Chunk). In this activity, they function not only as a text-bound explanation or a follow-up expansion as mentioned above, but also as a presentation, in which the teacher gives background information about a thing mentioned in the textbook. As for exchanges, they all belong to the simple type; and except for one expansion, they all function as continuation while containing a locative. As such, the exchanges sound very much test-like – which can be further shown by the fact that the students' answers to the questions are often given collectively and are very short elliptical clauses that often contain nothing but the mood Adjunct of polarity.

On the whole, this activity is textualized basically as monologue, with dialogue occurring now and then for a change. The mode of monologue seems to be called for by the ideational rather than the interpersonal meanings being made in the activity, that is, by a need to give an explanation of the linguistic items selected from the textbook.

Following the above textual analysis, the textual structure of Text 5 can now be represented in Figure 8.8. As can be seen, the textual process of Text 5 can be clearly analysed and described by reference to the PROGRESSION system. The reason why thetextual phases are merely listed as Activity 1, 2, etc. rather than given names (as in the description of the interpersonal or ideational structure of Text 5) is that the textual patterns do not independently express meanings – they merely **enable** the text to progress in such a way that both the interpersonal and ideational meanings can appropriately flow in the given context of situation. For the same reason, the above description of the textual structure of Text 5 necessarily entails how textual patterns textualize interpersonal and/or ideational patterns.

Actually, as illustrated earlier in Figure 8.7, the three structures of Text 5 – interpersonal, ideational and textual – all tend to resonate with one another,

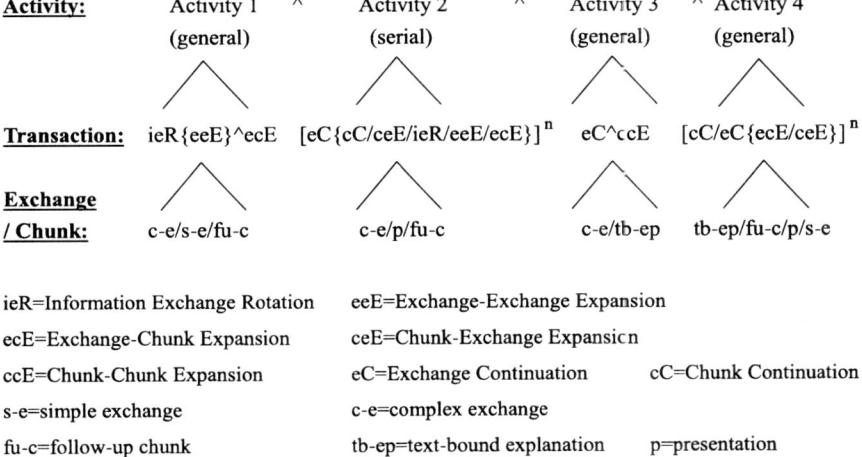

FIGURE 8.8   The textual structure of Text 5

though they do not match completely. Together, they provide a multi-functional description of the semantic structure of the text. Also, the descriptions of the three structures are multi-stratal, since they are all given in terms of multi-stratal logogenetic patterns. In other words, when applying the TEXT TYPE model in an analysis of the process of a text, the analyst is enabled to approach the global structure of the text in nearly every possible way: either uni-functionally or multi-functionally, either 'from above' or 'from below', and with a focus either on the linguistic system or on text as process.

8.3.3 Summary

In sum, while the interpersonal logogenetic patterns realize different types of interaction taking place in the classroom, and the ideational logogenetic patterns realize different types of content of classroom interaction; the textual logogenetic patterns textualize the various interaction types and content types. This section first brings all the textual patterns together into the textual TEXT TYPE system of EFL classroom discourse, referred to as PROGRESSION. Then, it presents an application of the PROGRESSION system to an actual analysis of the textual process of Text 5, which has led to a description of the textual structure of Text 5, thus demonstrating the applicability of the system.

The analysis of Text 5 also shows that the textual structure of a text can be described as a compositional scale. At the lowest rank there is no structure, although the different types of exchanges and chunks can reveal how classroom interaction, along with its content, is enacted in relation to the context of situation. However, exchange and chunk are the basic units in the textual analysis of a text, because not only do they form transactions at a higher rank, but the way they sequence and progress define transaction types. Indeed, it is the various types of transaction that seem more revealing about the textual process of a text, and about the teacher's management of the classroom process. The top rank, on the other hand, reveals how transactions sequence into an activity, which is clearly marked at the boundaries whereas the middle part is either logically related or left open. Together, the three ranks **enable** a text to progress step by step towards its completion.

Furthermore, the analysis shows that the textual logogenetic patterns at different ranks are usually called for by the interpersonal and/or ideational logogenetic patterns identified in the same span of text. In other words, the textual progression of a text has to be made appropriate to the interpersonal and ideational flows of meaning. It is the co-articulation of the three structures of the same text – interpersonal, ideational and textual – that offers a multi-stratal as well as multi-functional description of the process of a text.

Chapter 9

Conclusion

This final chapter will conclude the book by (1) giving a summary of the study presented in this book; (2) listing the contributions the study has made to the studies both in SFL and in EFL classroom discourse analysis; (3) pointing out the limitations of the study, while making suggestions for further research.

9.1 Summary

With a view to enhancing the applicability of SFL in discourse analysis, this book focuses on how to model text as an ongoing process rather than as a finished product, a question that is yet to be addressed fully and explicitly in SFL. In keeping with this focus, the book first explores the philosophical framework of SFL, i.e. the SFL architecture of language, in order to locate the concept of text in SFL and to contextualize the present study. As shown in the SFL architecture, the linguistic system is instantiated by register (subsystem) that is instantiated by text; and like the system and subsystem, text is inherently multi-stratal and multi-functional. Therefore, text cannot be properly modelled without reference to a register or the overall system, nor can it be modelled at a single stratum or within a single metafunction.

In the light of the SFL architecture of language, the book then presents a review of major models of text as process in the SFL school, giving special attention to models oriented towards spoken discourse in general and classroom discourse in particular. As the review indicates, while descriptions of text as process have been given in terms of various global or local structures of texts, offering insights into the issue; none of the structural descriptions is related simultaneously to all the metafunctions and strata of language, leaving quite a number of theoretical and methodological problems unsolved. It remains a question whether SFL, Functional Grammar in particular, is an adequate tool in analysing flows of meaning in text as an ongoing process, just as in analysing lexicogrammatical features in text as a finished product.

To address the question, the book goes on to make a number of theoretical assumptions based on the SFL philosophy, on insights drawn from existing models of text as process, and on a few concepts newly developed in SFL. It is assumed that text as process can be viewed as the **semantic structure of text** that can be described in terms of **a pattern of logogenetic patterns** that can be analysed lexicogrammatically in terms of **UNIVARIATE**, and that eventually the subsystem for text as process can be represented as a **system** of logogenetic patterns that is realized in the semantic **structure** of text.

Based on those assumptions, a new model of text as a process called TEXT TYPE is proposed. In this model, 'register' (as subsystem that engenders texts) is reinterpreted as two distinct but symbiotically interacting subsystems, referred to as respectively REGISTER and TEXT TYPE. While REGISTER is defined as a system network of lexicogrammatical options whose probabilities of occurrence are adjusted to the situation type in question, that is, as a synoptic system oriented towards text as product; TEXT TYPE is defined as a system network of logogenetic patterns formed by UNIVARIATEs (chosen from the REGISTER system) whose sequences of occurrence are adjusted to the given situation type, that is, as a dynamic system oriented towards text as process. In this sense, the description of text as process necessarily involves the establishment of both the synoptic and the dynamic system, and both systems are equally multi-stratal and multi-functional.

Following the presentation of the TEXT TYPE model, the book gives a description of a new method of using Functional Grammar in analysing text as process, as suggested by the new model. The method specifies seven steps of analysis from four different directions: (1) from below (i.e. bottom-up), (2) from above (i.e. top-down), (3) from specific, and (4) from generalized. Whichever direction is taken, the analyst is enabled to give a multi-stratal and multi-functional description of text as process.

In order to demonstrate the TEXT TYPE model and its method of analysis, the book moves on to present an application of the model to the analysis of authentic EFL classroom discourse. Actually, the application has achieved even more than expected, doing all of the following simultaneously:

1. it demonstrates how the TEXT TYPE model can be used in an analysis of text as process;
2. it shows the feasibility of the TEXT TYPE model;
3. it reveals the inadequacy of some of the systems in Functional Grammar when they are applied to EFL classroom discourse, and comes up with extensions and revisions;
4. it gives a multi-stratal and multi-functional description of the process of EFL classroom discourse in the Chinese context;
5. it offers a framework for analysing EFL classroom discourse – from a dynamic as well as a synoptic perspective;
6. it gives a description of various features of the EFL classroom situation, the process of EFL classroom teaching and learning, and the discourse strategies of EFL teachers and learners, all within the Chinese context.

9.2 Contributions

The present study has made a number of contributions to the studies both in SFL and in EFL classroom discourse analysis.

With respect to SFL studies, a major contribution made by the present study is the development of the TEXT TYPE model. Theoretically, the model is significant in that the reinterpretation of 'register' from both a static and an active perspective has added to our understanding of **subpotential** in the SFL architecture of language. It enables a view on **instantiation** not only as a process by which a choice is made from the network of meaning potential, but also as a process, or rather as processes, by which successive choices are made as a text unfolds; not only as a set of choices that have higher frequencies in a given text and hence reveal what and how the text means, but also as sequences of choices that form semantic phases in a text and hence reveal how meanings flow in a text; and therefore as a process leading to not only a synoptic subpotential that accounts for texts as a finished product, but also a dynamic subpotential that accounts for texts as an ongoing process. In this way, the model constitutes a step forward from clause-based grammar towards text-based semantics. Practically, the model has strengthened the applicability of SFL in discourse analysis by offering a new method of using Functional Grammar. The method enables the analyst to treat grammatical choices not only as constituents forming a clause structure, but also as semantic features linking successive clauses into an unfolding phase in the development of a text. In other words, the method allows the analyst to go beyond a synoptic analysis of text as product, and to move on to a dynamic analysis of text as a process. In addition, by suggesting seven rigorous steps and four directions of analysis, the method allows the analyst to focus either on the three metafunctions simultaneously or on one particular metafunction, and to approach texts either 'from below' or 'from above'.

Secondly, if the semantic stratum should be modelled as a compositional scale, just as the grammatical stratum is modelled (see Halliday 2004: Ch. 10), the present study constitutes an attempt at semantic modelling – based on research into the semantics of text. Actually, the study focuses on the intermediate rank(s) between text at the top rank and the smallest meaning features directly created by grammar at the bottom. Although at the present stage of the study it is not yet clear how many ranks can be distinguished in between, it is certain that the intermediate rank(s) can be identified and described in terms of logogenetic patterns, and that it is the units at these intermediate ranks that compose the semantic structure of text. Moreover, it can be seen in this study that the semantic compositional scale tends to be specific to text types. This is especially true with the ideational logogenetic patterns as identified in the data (Classroom Event, Linguistic Item, etc.), while the textual logogenetic patterns are already seen as forming a three-rank compositional scale of EFL classroom discourse. The interpersonal patterns (Boundary, Information Type, etc.), on the other hand, seem to apply to other types of spoken discourse as well. Of course, further study is needed before any solid claims can be made in this respect.

Thirdly, based on the analysis of textual as well as interpersonal choices found in the data, the study has led to the identification and/or description of a number of delicate categories of speech functions, i.e. move types, including:

1. bound moves in an exchange: answer, comply, acknowledge, evaluate;
2. bound moves in a chunk: restate, exemplify;
3. initiation-dependent moves: invite (both invite-answer and invite-comply), nominate, repeated question;
4. response-dependent moves: hint (^ repair), request (^ resolve), prompt (^ resume), backchannel (^ continue).

Fourthly, in the course of applying the systems of Functional Grammar in the analysis of the data, some of the systems were found to be inadequate in describing obvious facts about EFL classroom discourse. As driven by the data, these systems have been either extended or revised, while a few new systems have been set up, as listed below. Whether these systems are entirely specific to EFL classroom discourse or are also applicable to other types of discourse deserves further study.

1. **MOOD system** Additional realizational forms of mood metaphor are recognized, while a systemic contrast between explicit and implicit is newly subsumed in the Indicative system.
2. **SUBJECT PERSON system** A major systemic contrast between engaged and disengaged is added, and two new terms – interactant-involved and pseudo-interactant (between the two poles of interactant and non-interactant) – are newly identified and described.
3. **PROCESS TYPE system** The behavioural process is classified into two sub-types: behavioural (construing physiological or psychological behaviour) and BEHAVIOURIAL (overlapping with another process and hence may take on a second participant); and the material process is classified into daily-material and elevated-material.
4. **PARTICIPANT TYPE system** It is an experiential system newly set up, comprising three options – on-spot, relocated and generalized – which are realized by a noun or pronoun chosen as Thing in the nominal group functioning as Participant.
5. **ELLIPTICAL CLAUSE system** It is a textual system set up based on Halliday's Ellipsis system, but described in terms of elements left in rather than left out of the elliptical clause, covering semantic relations that extend beyond the immediately preceding clause.
6. **REPETITION system** It is a textual system newly set up, described in relation to the move that contains repetition and hence not restricted to lexis, composed of four options: repetition+, repetition–, repetition and paraphrase.

7. **TEXTUAL THEME system**   It is a textual system set up based on Halliday's Theme Type system, but extending 'continuity' into four newly identified options: boundive, initiative, continuative and locative.

In relation to EFL classroom discourse analysis, the present study constitutes a substantial effort to push it forward. The analysis done in the study is both linguistically-based and data-based. It has not only led to the establishment of an analytic framework applicable to future analyses of EFL classroom discourse, but also revealed features of EFL classroom discourse in the Chinese context. The achievements made in the analysis are summarized below, through answering those questions raised earlier in this book (see 5.1).

Answers to the theoretically-oriented questions

1. The lexicogrammatical systems that shift their probabilities in the EFL classroom situation and are therefore included in the REGISTER system network of EFL classroom discourse are as follows (see Figures 6.6, 7.1 and 8.2).
   Interpersonal: MOOD; SUBJECT PERSON; DEICTICITY; ASSESSMENT
   Ideational: PROCESS TYPE; PARTICIPANT TYPE
   Textual: ELLIPTICAL CLAUSE; REPETITION; TEXTUAL THEME
2. The lexicogrammatical logogenetic patterns that have been identified in EFL classroom discourse and are included in the TEXT TYPE system network of EFL classroom discourse are as follows (see Figures 6.7, 7.2 and 8.6).
   INTERACTION (interpersonal):
   (a) unilateral: Orientation; Direction; Recapitulation; Information Chunk
   (b) bilateral: Action Exchange; Information Exchange
   (c) Information Type: Knowledge; Story; Judgement; Personal Detail; Personal Story
   CONTENT (ideational):
   (a) Classroom Event: Verbal Event; Daily Event; Behavioural Event
   (b) Life Experience: Simple Experience; Complex Experience
   (c) Text: In-Text; Above-Text; Behind-Text; Beyond-Text
   (d) Linguistic Item: Usage; (Side) Meaning; Label
   PROGRESSION (textual):
   (a) Activity: General; Serial; Orbital
   (b) Transaction: Continuation; Rotation; Expansion
   (c) Exchange: Simple Exchange; Complex Exchange
   (d) Chunk: Exposition Chunk; Exemplification Chunk
   It should be noted that some of the patterns are formed by UNIVARIATEs from one single system, while many others are formed out of a combination of UNIVARIATEs from several different systems within the same metafunction.

3. The lexicogrammatical logogenetic patterns thus identified are found both articulating semantic phases in a text within one metafunction, and resonating across metafunctions so as to allow a multi-functional interpretation of the semantic phases.
4. The FTM values in the EFL classroom situation are found to vary and hence to form various contextual stages relatable to the different semantic phases in a text, so that the logogenetic patterns thus identified can be said to be multi-stratal (see Tables 6.3/4/5/6/7, 7.4/5/6/7, and 8.2/3/4/5).

Answers to the practically-oriented questions

1. The contextual values of EFL classroom discourse in the Chinese context display the following variations in terms of FTM.

   Tenor   teacher-student relationship: controller vs. controlled; commander vs. commanded; information giver vs. receiver; initiator vs. responder; tester vs. testee; guide vs. explorer; interlocutor vs. interlocutor

   Field   management of the classroom process: announcement of daily procedures / oral tasks; invitation for conscious participation; account of life experience [occasional]
   study of a text: retelling; analysis/synthesis; description of the background; interpretation of the meaning
   explanation of the target language: usage / meaning / grammatical role of a linguistic item

   Mode   classroom dialogue: typical (IRF); ensured; student-led; conversation-like; test-like; multiple-answer/comply; logically-guided; lengthy; lengthy and organized
   teacher's monologue: text exposition; text-bound explanation; presentation; follow-up elaboration / extension / conclusion

   Such FTM variations reveal features of the EFL classroom environment in the Chinese context. In terms of the tenor, the teacher is playing a dominant role while the students are passive followers. In terms of the field, apart from everyday management and an occasional account of personal life experiences, activities in the classroom are generally centred on the textbook or items of the target language. In terms of the mode, dialogue and monologue are both employed, often in an alternating manner. While dialogue is used in accounts of life experiences and in some part of text study, monologue occurs more often – not only in classroom management but also in linguistic explanation and in most part of text study.
2. The various kinds of meanings identified in EFL classroom discourse (in terms of multi-stratal logogenetic patterns) reveal features of the process of EFL classroom teaching and learning in the Chinese context. It is essentially

a process of exchanging or merely giving information (interpersonally), generally centred on linguistic knowledge or content of the textbook (ideationally). As for how the classroom process progresses (textually), the teachers seem to be more conscientious in organizing their dialogue with the students than in organizing their own monologue, more efficient than logical, and more ready to take the floor than to leave the next turn open to the same or another student.

3. With regard to how meanings are expressed lexicogrammatically by the Chinese EFL teachers and students, the following are particularly worth mentioning:

(a) The teachers' speech is generally grammatical and appropriate to the context of situation, while the students' speech is erroneous or incomplete from time to time.

(b) Some teachers (especially in Texts 5 and 10) frequently choose a metaphorical form in asking a question or giving an order (e.g. *can you imagine what was the biggest problem? Lyn, would you please?*), which can be more engaging and more polite than the congruent forms.

(c) Most teachers (especially in Texts 2, 4, 5, 8 and 9) prefer statement chunks to exchanges in a phase of text study, which can be very efficient but somehow monotonous.

(d) Sometimes a teacher may choose a generalized pronoun (*you, we*) and/ or a material (instead of relational) process in explaining the usage or meaning of a linguistic item, which brings the item closer to real life and hence makes it easier to understand.

(e) The teachers tend to apply such moves as 'backchannel' (*yes, un-hun*), 'hint' (*can we say that?*) and 'request' (*you mean . . .?*) while a student is relating a personal story, retelling a text, or doing an exercise; which proves to increase student output.

(f) Most teachers tend to choose 'continuity' (indicating a new turn or new move) more often than 'conjunction' (indicating logical relations) in organizing classroom discourse, in both dialogue and monologue. (Further study is needed to find out whether this is characteristic of discourse in language classrooms only, and what effect it has on learning.)

(g) A tendency can be identified in the students' speech to use an implicit – or rather, incomplete – clause in answering questions (e.g. T: *that should be which generation?* S: *fourth*), which indicates negligence of grammatical correctness that may eventually lead to unconsciousness of errors (e.g. T: *"His extended right hand loosely grasped his rifle" – why not tightly?* S: *Sleep.*).

9.3 Limitations and suggestions

Admittedly, the present study has several limitations, which also point to a number of directions for future research.

First, this study was initially driven by the presumption that SFL should be able to serve as an equally adequate model in analysing text as process just as in analysing text as product; that is why the author has made an attempt to describe text as process within the philosophical framework of SFL. In the course of doing so, however, the author may have focused on theories, methods and concepts within SFL at the cost of a wider range of other theories and methods that could have been helpful. For instance, those scholars who adopt a social perspective in discourse analysis have a lot to offer regarding the description of text as process, especially those analysing institutional discourse, professional discourse or situated discourse (see 1.1.2). In order to improve the TEXT TYPE model, it may be helpful to go beyond the SFL framework and be more open to influences from outside, and to take up other types of discourse as well.

Secondly, in order to establish the REGISTER network of EFL classroom discourse, the author has extended or revised a number of systems in Functional Grammar and has set up a few new systems. Although every effort is based on the actual analysis of the data, the author's own understanding of the systems unavoidably has a role to play; besides, manual instead of machine-aided analysis may incur occasional inconsistencies or even misinterpretations. To further verify the systems in the REGISTER network of EFL classroom discourse as set up here, it is advisable to set up a corpus of EFL classroom discourse and to design a computer program that can be applied in the analysis. Likewise, the TEXT TYPE network of EFL classroom discourse as set up here requires verification of the same kind, as well as revisions where necessary. Both are rich areas for further investigation.

Thirdly, as the data used here actually constitute a variety of English (see Kachru 2006), sometimes referred to as China English (Du and Jiang 2001; Jiang and Du 2003), the analysis of the data has raised a number of issues (already pointed out in the notes) that are worth further study. For example, Chinese EFL teachers often use an attributive-possessive clause combined with a generalized pronoun (i.e. *you have*) in places where no possessive relationship exists, e.g. *you have silverware* 银器, *and tinware – tin is another kind of metal; you have this word right below the word California;* etc. Here, the '*you have*-clause' functions like an existential clause (*there be*). This is most probably caused by a transfer from the Chinese word 有, which can be translated into both *have* and *there is/are*. Issues of this kind are not explored here as they are beyond the scope of the present study; and yet they deserve further exploration from the perspective of either World Englishes or second language learning.

Last but not least, before analysing the data it was assumed that the discourse behaviours of the ten "good" teachers should suggest strategies to be followed by average EFL teachers; and during the analysis of the data, it was found that these teachers' speech in class did suggest strategies in the light of current theories in applied linguistics (see 1.3). Some of these strategies are listed in the above answers to the practically-oriented questions, and many more are discussed in Chapters 6, 7 and 8 at the semantic stratum in functional terms, as well as at the contextual stratum in terms of field or tenor or mode. These discussions, however, are rather tentative due to a lack of empirical evidence. It is suggested that these strategies be further investigated, especially those in asking a question, giving feedback, lending support to a student who is giving a response, explaining a linguistic item, and managing the classroom process as a whole. In particular, the effect of the strategies on EFL learning needs to be demonstrated through either a quantitative study or action research.

All in all, both SFL and classroom discourse analysis are rich areas for exploration. A journey into these areas can be painstaking, but the journey is worth the pain.

Notes

Chapter 2

[1] In SFL, 'lexicogrammar' refers to both grammar and vocabulary, which are viewed as the two poles of a single continuum: a phrase is a contraction of a clause while a group is an expansion of a word. But this term is frequently replaced by 'grammar' for short because 'it becomes cumbersome to use this term all the time' (Halliday 1994: xiv).

[2] Actually language is expressed in both sounding and writing, i.e. both phonology and graphology. In this book, 'phonology' is often used in place of 'phonology/graphology' in order to save space.

[3] A 'whole text' refers to a text that is more than one sentence in length, usually with a beginning, middle and end. Although the term 'text' in SFL refers to any instance of the linguistic system, with no connotation of size or medium of expression, most texts in real life are longer than one sentence.

[4] As Halliday (1978: 114) says, 'a semantic description is the description of a register.'

Chapter 3

[1] Eggins and Slade (1997: 43) define this tradition as an approach that seeks to 'offer functional interpretations of discourse structure as the expression of dimensions of the social and cultural context.' See also Butler (2003).

[2] Round brackets indicate optionality of enclosed elements, the caret sign indicates sequence of elements, the dot between elements indicates more than one option in sequence, square brackets indicate the range of optionality of sequence, the leftward curved arrow indicates iteration, and braces indicate the range of elements whose degree of iteration is equal.

[3] What is called 'functional tenor' by Gregory is referred to as 'role' by Ure and Ellis (1977) and 'pragmatic purpose' by Fawcett (1980).

[4] Martin (1999: 29) explains that 'the term register was preferred to context of situation in part because of our concern to get away from the materialist (i.e. non-discursive) readings the term context invites . . . this difference is purely terminological'; whereas Halliday (in Thompson and Collins 2001) says 'on a purely terminological point, I think he [Martin] slightly misunderstood the notion of register as I originally meant to define it.' For a review of the concept of register, see Matthiessen (1993).

[5] The distinction between 'outside' and 'inside' derives from the way Martin represents his language-based theory of context – as three co-tangential circles. See figure illustrations in Martin (1992, 1999).

6 The distinction between 'expected' and 'discretionary' is comparable to that between 'preferred' and 'dispreferred' as proposed by Schegloff and Sacks (1973) in their theory of adjacency pairs.

7 Note that, while Halliday uses the term 'exchange' to refer to a clause in its interpersonal function (i.e. an interact), Martin uses it to refer to a sequence of moves, following Sinclair and Coulthard (1975; see 3.3.1 for more) as well as the convention in the analysis of spoken discourse.

8 The distinction between 'support' and 'confront' is comparable to Burton's (1978, 1980, 1981) distinction between 'supporting' and 'challenging' moves; and according to Burton challenging moves have a prolonging effect in conversation.

9 Some other well-known models are left out because their concerns and perspectives are more educational and/or sociological than linguistic. For instance, Flanders' (1960) model is educational, concerned with the improvement of classroom practices. Mehan's (1979) model is ethnographic, aimed at the routines that structure the behaviors of teachers and students in the classroom. Lemke's (1990) model is more sociological than socio-semiotic, specifically concerned with how the way science is 'talked' can shape attitudes and values that lead to the mystique of science and students' alienation from science.

10 It should be noted that at that time a complete theory of language as social semiotic (by Halliday) was not yet available.

Chapter 4

1 For how 'probabilities' can be attached to the terms (i.e. options) in a system, see Halliday and James (1993). For quantitative profiles of registers, see Matthiessen (2002b).

2 Actually, Halliday often associates 'probability' with the system, and 'frequency' with the text, and compares their relationship to that of climate and weather. See, for example, Halliday (1991).

3 At the present stage of the study, no statements can be made about the phonological/ graphological stratum.

4 Halliday does not seem to have specified any logogenetic patterns at the contextual stratum so far, but he believes logogenesis pertains to all the strata. Here, it is held that, since the context of situation and text realize each other, there is no reason why contextual meaning should remain static during the dynamic flow of a text. The values of FTM in the same situation type may also vary so as to form **contextual logogenetic patterns** that emerge along with the semantic and grammatical logogenetic patterns. For example, the field of EFL classroom discourse may switch from daily activity realized by verbal processes, to story retelling realized by material processes (for details, see Chapter 7).

Chapter 5

1 The research is supported by funds from the Chinese Ministry of Education under the title of Excellent Young Teachers Program (EYTP).

[2] These sounds reveal a transfer from the speaker's first language, i.e. Chinese.

[3] When coding the ten texts move by move, due to a limitation of time, energy and technical resources, the texts were slightly shortened by cutting out some parts that are hardly different from others in terms of logogenetic patterns. For example, in the same class, a teacher may consecutively lead the students to go over up to four to five paragraphs of the same text that is being taught, ask up to eight to ten comprehension questions about the same story told in the textbook, or ask the students to complete an exercise of up to ten sentences that all demonstrate the same grammatical feature (e.g. conditional clause). These similar parts, according to observations made in Steps 1 and 4, display very similar grammatical and semantic patterns and, usually, a clearly signaled boundary (e.g. *Now, let's move on to the next paragraph*). It is thus believed that deletion of those more or less repetitive parts will not affect the results of the analysis.

Chapter 6

[1] This system, in the third edition of *An Introduction to Functional Grammar* (Halliday 2004), is sometimes named 'deicticity' (pp. 158, 349) and sometimes called '(interpersonal) deixis' (pp. 116, 135). The two terms refer to the same thing. The former is chosen here, because the latter is easily associated with 'reference' (as a cohesive tie).

[2] The structural realizations as actually found in the data sometimes present a much diversified picture, and it has to be admitted that not all of them are fully dealt with in the systems set up here. Some deserve further study.

[3] Some of the instances seem to carry a transfer from the speakers' first language, i.e. Chinese. The Chinese variety of English is an interesting area of study, drawing increasing attention in China in recent years (see Du and Jiang 2001; Jiang and Du 2003).

[4] As found in the analysis of the data, an evaluative adjective is almost always accompanied – or 'amplified,' in Martin's terminology – by the intensifier *very*; therefore 'intensity' is not included in the ASSESSMENT system as a separate feature.

[5] Sometimes the clause containing assessment and coming after the responding move is interrogative rather than declarative, e.g. *Is it a good sentence? Can we say that?* In that case, it is not an evaluation, but a 'hint' at something wrong or inappropriate in the response just produced (see 8.1.2 for more).

[6] This is a text in the textbook called *Contemporary College English: Intensive Reading I*, edited by Yang Limin and published by Foreign Language Teaching and Research Press in Beijing in 2001.

Chapter 7

[1] This could be the result of a transfer from the speakers' first language, i.e. Chinese, which is typically paratactic rather than hypotactic. Further study needs to be done to prove this.

² Not coded for PROCESS TYPE are (a) mental and verbal processes in the function of interpersonal projection; (b) action exchanges used to complete an exercise in class, such as (1) completing a dialogue by using conditionals, (2) making a choice between 'true' and 'false', where the concern is with the completion of an action rather than the experiential content of the clause.

(1) T: C, you two please.   (2) T: OK, the next one, Jane, please.
     S/a: What will she do if   S: It's false.
           they offer her the job?   T: It's false.
     S/b: If they offer her
           the job, she'll accept it.

³ The issue, of course, is worth further exploration, especially from the perspective of pragmatics or studies of so-called 'China English'.

⁴ This is only a theoretical assumption, which requires further verification.

⁵ This could be a transfer from the speakers' first language, i.e. Chinese, since both *there be* and *have* are translated into 有 in Chinese. This issue, however, is again related to China English and deserves further study.

⁶ The concept of verbalized-material process is, to a great extent, a makeshift at the present stage of the study. Further efforts are needed to theorize the phenomenon that is noticed here, i.e., one process changing into another as a result of the influence of the participant(s) involved – comparable to the phonological phenomenon called 'assimilation'.

Chapter 8

¹ The word 'help' is used because an answer is tied to a question also through the common proposition the two moves generate together (see 6.2.3.2). After all, the textual metafunction is merely an 'enabling' function; a textual resource may have to work together with either another textual resource or a resource in a different metafunction. This is why the word 'help' is frequently used in this chapter.

² In fact 'prompt' is not realized by repetition+ alone, but also by an expression needed for the responding move to continue, as shown below [from Text 1]:
     80-S: and the earth on the top of the hill, er . . .
     81-T: rushed down
     82-S: rushed down . . .

³ Here the continuous elements are present whereas the contrastive one is ellipsed, so it is not seen as a case of ellipsis.

⁴ A 'backchannel' may sometimes appear just like an 'acknowledge', realized by repetition+ or paraphrase. The reason might be that, while the teacher intends to produce an 'acknowledge' so as to end the exchange, the student takes the move as 'backchannel' and continues to talk.

⁵ Again, repetition and repetition+ may not be the only realizational forms of a 'request' (it can be a mere *sorry?*), but they are certainly important resources for making a request.

[6] The second part in these pairs is mainly identified through the first part. Only 'resume' is here described by reference to repetition, and 'continue' by reference to continuity. Further study is needed in order to give a full description.

[7] Admittedly, the differences among the four types of continuity may occasionally blur due to an overuse of *OK* and *so* by some teachers (e.g. in Texts 2 and 9), most probably caused by their personal style or an influence from their first language. The issue is worth further exploration, especially in relation to World Englishes or China English.

[8] As continuity, it is spelt *all right* (pronounced with a rising intonation). When it is a lexical word meaning 'acceptable', it is spelt *alright* (pronounced slowly with falling intonation).

[9] Again, as continuity it is spelt *OK* (pronounced with a rising intonation). When used as a lexical word meaning 'acceptable', it is spelt *okay* (pronounced with falling intonation).

[10] For a detailed discussion of the specific functions of these Adjuncts, see Schiffrin (1987).

[11] Excluded from the description are chunks that simultaneously involve several different types of logical relations without displaying any distinct patterns. It deserves further study why the conjunction is freely employed by some of the teachers and whether this has an impact on teaching and learning.

[12] In the first exchange, especially when it immediately follows a 'direct' or an 'orientate' move, the initiating move may occur without a textual Theme, since the initiating force is largely expressed by the preceding 'direct' or 'orientate'. This exchange, however, is still treated as a continuation exchange.

[13] The elliptical question *what else* may appear like what Halliday and Hasan (1976: 215) take as a request for confirmation of an existing element in the preceding statement (e.g. – *John is coming to dinner.* – *And who else?*), but it is not, in EFL classroom discourse. Because it comes after a statement produced by the same speaker (i.e. the teacher's feedback), and it presupposes the non-elliptical question that is several moves apart and again produced by the same speaker.

[14] Embeddedness at the rank of transactions cannot be fully explained at the present stage of the study and deserves further investigation.

[15] One reason might be that they are in fact related through reference or lexical cohesion, which is not examined here. But a more likely reason is that most EFL classes – at least as indicated by the data – are skill-oriented rather than content-oriented, and thus there is less need to be logically organized.

[16] The two terms 'orbital' and 'serial' are borrowed from Martin (1997), Iedema (1997), and White (1997), who treat them as two different structuring principles: 'Orbital structure takes one segment as nuclear, and associates other segments with this nucleus as satellites; with serial structure, there is no nuclear segment on which others depend – the text unfolds step by step, with each step dependent on the immediately preceding [one]' (Martin 1997: 17). Here, the two terms are merely used to describe two different activity structures as identified through textual choices; their associations with other metafunctions require additional research.

[17] In-Text occurs more often than other patterns of Text because it offers evidence to support answers to questions raised in the Beyond/Above-Text patterns.

Appendices

Appendix I: Text 5 coded interpersonally

t	sp/m	mood	Sub per	deicticity	assessment	text
1.						Good morning, everybody.
	T/1	decl imp	sp	future present	subj prob	Er, you probably guess, I think, that I am not going to give you a written check on preview because I have written all the useful expressions I expect you to use when you answer my questions, so let me ask you a few questions.
	T/2	interr	addr addr-inv	past		But before I ask you – the first question is: before you came to Beijing, er, did your parents give you any advice, for instance, you see, when you are badly in need of help, who you can depend on?
	T/3	interr	(addr-inv)	(past)		Anyone?
	T/4	interr	addr-inv	past		Xxx, did your parents give you any advice?
2.	S	decl	(addr-inv)	(past)		Yes.
3.	T	interr	non-int	present		Yes, what is it like?
4.	S	decl	sp-inv	past		My mother told me that you can only depend on our, relatives in Beijing, and not strangers.

No.	Spk					Utterance
5.	T/1	decl				Not strangers, not to depend on strangers, ern, when you are in great difficulty, when you are in trouble, you have to turn to relatives – you have relatives in Beijing.
	T/2	interr	addr-inv	past		Now, what did your parents say to you?
6.	S	decl	sp-inv	past		My parents said that the only one you can depend on is yourself.
7.	T/1	decl				Depend on yourself, you can't depend, you know, you can't trust, you can't depend on anybody else, just yourself.
	T/2	interr	addr	modal		But if you were badly in need of help, what would you do, suppose you are badly wounded?
8.	S	decl	sp	modal		I'll call, call the police, or call the emergence agency. (laugh)
9.	T/1	decl			accep	Okay, okay, that's right.
	T/2	interr	addr-inv	past	subj prob	Now, why do you think they advised you not to trust strangers, why did, did your parents advise you not to trust strangers?
10.	S	decl				Yes, especially in a train.
11.	T	interr	sp-inv	present		especially in a train, why – my question is why?
12.	S	decl	(sp-inv)	(past)		... because the society is very complex,
13.	T					umm
14.	S	decl				and there are many bad person we don't know.
15.	T/1	decl	non-int	present	obj prob accep	Yes, there are a lot of bad persons, so you can't trust strangers, maybe this is right, maybe this is right.
	T/2	decl	non-int	present	obj prob	But at the same time, well, it seems that there are also good people.
	T/3	decl	non-int	present	eviden	But everywhere in the world, people say that they are losing their faith in the goodness of human nature.

(Continued)

t	sp/m	mood	Sub per	deicticity	assessment	text
	T/4	decl	non-int	present		So whether we can still depend on the help of strangers, this is the question that I think a lot of people have in mind.
	T/5	decl	non-int	present		And the text today, the text we are going to have today, answers the question whether we can still depend on the kindness of strangers, in other words, whether we can still depend on a kind stranger to help us when we are badly in need.
	T/6	imp	sp			Well, now, so now let me ask you some questions about the text.
	T/7	interr	non-int	present		First, what do you know about the title, what do you know about the title – the title is *The Kindness of Strangers* – what does that mean?
	T/8	interr	(non-int)	(present)		Anyone?
	[more than 6 seconds, no response]					
	T/9	interr	non-int	past		Now, where did he – erm, I think you have read the notes – where did the writer get the title from?
	T/10					Xxx.
16.	S	interr	non-int			En, where he get the title?
17.	T	interr	non-int	past		Yeah, the title *The Kindness of Strangers*, do you know where the writer, you know, got the title from?
18.	S	decl	(non-int)	(past)		From a movie,
19.	T					yes
20.	S		(non-int)	(past)		en, from a movie called *A Streetcar Named Desire.*
21.	T/1	decl	non-int	past	accep	Yes, *A Streetcar Named Desire*, that's from a movie, that is, at the end of this play or the movie, yes, a character said: "You can still depend on – I can still depend on the kindness of strangers", and so on, okay, that's right.

	T/2	interr	non-int	present	subj prob	So ern, now, the next question is, what did he, what did the writer – what does the writer want to say to the reader through his experience described in the passage, what do you think, the writer wants to tell the reader?
	T/3	interr	(non-int)	(present)		Anyone?
	T/4					Yes.
22.	S	decl	(non-int)	(present)		Now you can still depend on the kindness of stranger.
23.	T/1	decl	non-int	present		So the writer wants to convince the reader that you can still depend on the kindness of strangers, in spite of the increasing crime.
	T/2	interr	non-int	past		Why – well, how did he come to this conclusion, how did he come to this conclusion?
	T/3	decl	sp	modal		Well, maybe I will ask somebody – Xxx.
24.	S	decl	non-int	past	obj prob	Because he traveled fourteen states through America with no money, just by the help of strangers.
25.	T/1	decl	non-int	past		Ern yes, okay, he came to the conclusion after traveling across fourteen states of the United States, wholly depending on the kindness of strangers.
	T/2	interr	non-int	past		OK, so, what kind of journey did he have – did he, er, make the journey by trains, by bus, or by driving his own car, how?
	T/5					Xxx.
26.	S	decl	(non int)	(past)		By hitchhike.
27.	T/1	decl	(non-int)	(past)		By hitchhiking – you said 'by hitchhike'.
	T/2	imp	addr	modal		But how can you explain the word 'hitchhike'?
28.	S	decl	non-int	past		Yes, he didn't have a penny and he didn't drive a bike, so he had to, en, on other person's bike, to carry on his journey.

(Continued)

t	sp/m	mood	Sub per	deicticity	assessment	text
29.	T/1	decl	(non-int)	(past)		Not his bike, I think in the United States, people don't … (laugh).
	T/2	interr	pseudo-in	present		Now, if you want to 'get a ride' – that means to get a ride from somebody, from a driver, from a car or a truck passing by – what do you do?
	T/3					Anyone – Xxx.
30.	S	decl	pseudo-in	present	subj prob	I think you wave your hands.
31.	T					you wave your –
32.	S	decl	non-int	present		And in this text, the stranger has his thumb up.
33.	T/1	decl			accep	Un-hun, right.
	T/2	decl	pseudo-in	present		And also, sometimes, you also carry a sign, indicating or displaying where you are going.
	T/3	decl	pseudo-in	present		For instance, if you want to go to Chicago, you have this word 'Chicago'.
	T/4	decl	pseudo-in	present		So you hold a sign, displaying the destination and then you thumb out, you thumb out.
	T/5	decl	pseudo-in	present		That is to say, you, er, you stretch out your arm and wave your thumb, this way.
	T/6	decl	non-int	past	eviden	OK, now, well, I remember Xxx said he didn't have a penny with him, and, well, of course you can get a ride – he can get a ride by hitchhiking, but what about the food and shelter, where did he get food and shelter?
	T/7					Xxx.
34.	S	decl	non-int	past		He get [got] food from, strangers.
35.	T/1	decl			accep	Strangers, okay.
	T/2	interr	(non-int)	(past)		But what about the shelter?
36.	S	decl	(non-int)	(past)		In strangers' house.

37.	T	interr	non-int	past	subj prob	In what – in strangers' house – do you think he, he, he always passed the night in strangers' house?
38.	S	decl	non-int	present	subj prob	I think that depends.
39.	T					yes
40.	S	decl	non-int	past		He put up a tent.
41.	T/1	decl	non-int	past	accep subj prob	Yes, that's right, sometimes he put up a tent – so you can imagine that he had brought with him a tent.
	T/2	interr	non-int	past	subj prob desirab	OK, now, next question: what do you think, what do you think, was the biggest problem during the journey?
	T/3	interr	(non-int)	(past)		Anyone?
	[more than 6 seconds, no response]					
	T/4	decl	non-int	past	subj prob eviden	Well, you think chiefly the problems were, ern, whether he could get rides, whether the drivers would stop to pick him up, whether he can get food, and whether he can get shelter to pass the night – he can't sleep in the open, especially in some places.
	T/5	interr	non-int	past	subj prob desirab	So, what do you think, what do you think was the biggest problem?
	[more than 6 seconds, no response]					
42.	T/6	decl	addr	modal	subj prob	Well, if the text does not tell you directly, I think you can infer from what he said.
	T/7	interr	non-int	past		You remember what kind of journey was he going to make?
	Sn	decl	(non-int)	(past)		From coast to coast.
43.	T/1	decl	non-int	past		Yeah, he was going to make a coast to coast journey.
	T/2	decl	non-int	present		Well, it's a large area in United States, from the Pacific to the Atlantic, from coast to coast.
	T/3	interr	non-int	past	desirab	So you can imagine what, what was the biggest problem?

(Continued)

t	sp/m	mood	Sub per	deicticity	assessment	text
44.	S					[confusion]
45.	T	imp				Yes, speak louder.
46.	S	decl	(non-int)	(past)		Rides.
47.	T/1	decl	pseudo-in	present		You don't say 'rides', but 'getting rides', 'getting rides'.
	T/2	interr	non-int	past	desirab	Now, was it so important – why was it the biggest problem, have you got any idea?
	T/3	interr	(non-int)	(past)		Anyone?
	[more than 6 seconds, no response]					
	T/4	interr	(non-int)	(past)		Xxx, have you got any idea?
48.	S	decl	(non-int)	(past)		No.
49.	T					Ern, yes Xxx.
50.	S	decl	sp	past		I didn't hear clearly what she said.
51.	T	decl	non-int	past	desirab	Well, she said getting, getting rides was the biggest problem, during the journey.
52.	S	decl	(non-int)	(past)	subj prob	En, I think so.
53.	T	interr	(non-int)	(past)	subj prob	Why do you think so?
54.	S	decl	non-int	past modal	obj prob	Because if he didn't get a ride in time, perhaps some, some dangerous things will happen, like some robbers, some thieves may do some harm to him.
55.	T/1	decl	non-int	modal	obj prob	Yes, they may attack him.
	T/2	interr	non-int	present	subj prob desirab	Now, do you think it is easy to get a ride, is it easy to get a ride from strangers?
56.	Sn	decl	(non-int)	(present)	desirab	No.
57.	T	interr	non-int	present	desirab	Why not, do you think? Why isn't it so easy to get a ride?

58.	S	decl	non-int	present	subj prob desirab	I think it isn't easy to make people believe that you are innocent,
59.	T					yes, un-hun
60.	S	decl	pseudo-in	modal		you must, must make them believe that you are just a passer-by, you won't do any harm to them, so they will offer you a ride.
61.	T/1	decl	non-int	present	accep	Yes, okay.
	T/2	decl	non-int	present	eviden	Now, so we say, well, about food, Americans are always very generous: if you want food, they would like to offer food readily because if not, you know, I think it can be dangerous for them.
	T/3	decl	non-int	modal	eviden	Then also about shelter; well, Xxx said that he must have brought a tent with him; he could pitch his tent in any place.
	T/4	decl	non-int	past	subj prob eviden	Well, but actually in the text, somewhere I think, the writer mentions that he wanted to pitch a tent, sometimes.
	T/5	interr	non-int	past		OK, now, how come he wanted to make a trip like that – it was a very hard journey, I suppose – how come he came to make, to decide that he should make a trip like that?
	T/6					Xxx.
62.	S	decl	non-int	past		Because he used to pass by a hitch, hitch …
63.	T					hitchhiker
64.	S		non-int	past		hitchhiker, and this made him think a lot,
65.	T					un-hun
66.	S					whether people in the United States would still like to help a stranger.

(*Continued*)

t	sp/m	mood	Sub per	deicticity	assessment	text
67.	T/1	decl	non-int	past	accep	That's right, that's right, because he himself once drove past a hitchhiker, well, he didn't hesitate at that time, but later on, later on, he felt very bad; that is why he wanted to make a – such a trip, depending totally on the kindness of strangers.
	T/2	interr	non-int	past		OK, so why did he make, why did he decide to make a coast-to-coast journey – why didn't he concentrate, or why didn't he limit his journey in one area, for instance, the eastern part of United States, the central part, or the western part, why?
	T/3					Xxx.
68.	S	decl	non-int	past		Because different path roads in different parts of America – he wanted to experience the differences between different parts.
69.	T	interr				Different parts, and also?
70.	S					the whole country
71.	T/1					the whole country
	T/2	decl	non-int	past		So, he wanted to experience, he wanted to know how he would be treated in different parts of United States, whether people everywhere, er, would treat him in the same way.
	T/3	decl	non-int	modal		This way, he would make his conclusion more convincing, so that is why.
	T/4	interr	non-int	past		Now, the next question: how was he received by the people, in the 14 states, generally speaking, well, how was he received?
	T/5	interr	(non-int)	(past)		Anyone?
	T/6					Yes, Xxx.
72.	S	decl	non-int	past	subj prob	I think he was warmly received.
73.	T	interr	non-int	past		He was warmly – do you mean he was always, warmly received?
74.	S	decl	non-int	past		Not always, but generally speaking he was lucky.

75.	T/1	decl	non-int	past		He was lucky, he was warmly received.
	T/2	interr	non-int	past		Well, were people ready to give him a ride – erm how, if I ask you how he was warmly received, how would you answer the question?
76.	S	decl	non-int	past		En, a lot of people were so kind as to give him ride,
77.	T					yes
78.	S	decl	non-int	past		some people shared food and shelter with him,
79.	T					yes
80.	S	decl	non-int	past		and some even gave him gift.
81.	T/1	decl			accep	Yes, gave him gift, that's right.
	T/2	interr	non-int	past		OK, so er, well, was he ever rejected – I mean when he wanted to get a ride, was he ever rejected?
82.	Sn	decl	(non-int)	(past)		Yes.
83.	T/1	decl	(non-int)	(past)		Yes, yes, sometimes, sometimes yes.
	T/2	interr	non-int	past		He was rejected once, for instance – when?
84.	S	decl	non-int	past		One day, in the rain, en, he can't get a ride, so he was left stand out in the rain,
85.	T					yeah
86.	S					until a truck driver arrived.
87.	T/1	decl			accep	That's right, yes, until a truck driver arrived.
	T/2	decl	non-int	past		That is to say, well, several cars or trucks passed by and nobody, no driver picked him up, so he had to stand in the rain, for sometime until a truck driver came along.
	T/3	decl	non-int	past	obj prob	Well, maybe this was not the first time, this was not the only time he was rejected.

(*Continued*)

t	sp/m	mood	Sub per	deicticity	assessment	text
	T/4	decl	non-int	past		But generally speaking, he was warmly received.
	T/5	decl	addr	past	capab	All right, well, I think you can all answer [all answered] the questions very well, and you did a very good job, in previewing the lesson.
	T/6	imp / state	sp+ / sp+	future		Now, let's open our book and we'll ask someone to read the first paragraph.
	T/7	imp	addr	modal		Xxx, would you like to read the first paragraph?
88.	S					OK. "One summer I was driving from my hometown of Ta ..."
89.	T	decl				Well, it's 'Tahoe'.
90.	S					"Tahoe city, Cali ..."
91.	T					California
92.	S					"California, to New ..."
93.	T					New Orleans
94.	S					"New Orleans. In the middle of the desert, I came upon a young man standing by the roadside. He had his thumb out and held a gas can in his other hand. I drove right by him. There was a time in the country when you'd be considered a jerk if you passed by somebody in need. Now you are fool for helping. With gangs, drug addicts, murderers, rapists, and thieves lurking everywhere, 'I don't want to get involved' has become a national motto."
95.	T/1	decl	non-int	present	eviden	OK, now, here you have this: "I was driving from my hometown of Tahoe city ..." Now I asked someone where Tahoe city is located, and they say it's somewhere in California, it's somewhere, you know [points at a map], in the northern part of the mountains.
	T/2	decl	non-int	present		You see, here are the mountains.
	T/3	decl	non-int	present		It's somewhere here.

No.	Turn					Text
	T/4	decl	non-int	present		You have this word, 'California', right below the word California, that is where Tahoe city is located.
	T/5	decl	non-int	present		So that's his hometown.
	T/6	decl	pseudo-int	present		And "was driving from my hometown of Tahoe city, California", now, if you mention 'Tahoe', a small town in the United States, you usually also mention where, in which state, this place is located.
	T/7	decl	non-int	present	subj prob	And I think this is a very good thing, because maybe sometimes, sometimes you know, in different states, they have towns with the same name.
	T/8	decl	non-int	present	subj prob	For instance, in China, there are more than one 'Linxia', but one is in Henan; the other may be in other places.
	T/9	decl	non-int	present	subj prob	So, and "California ..." – each state has a short form – er, so, " ... California to New Orleans", well, I think that's a long trip, it's a long trip.
	T/10	decl	non-int	present		So, the first paragraph tells us an incident that actually made the writer decide to take this long, cross-country journey.
	T/11	interr	non-int	present		Well, what is it, what is the incident that's talked about?
	T/12	decl	(non-int)	(present)		OK, he did not stop for a hitchhiker.
	T/13	imp	sp+			Now, let's come to some of the words
	T/14	interr	non-int	present		Er, "I came upon ..." What is the meaning of 'came upon'?
96.	S	decl	non-int	present		It means 'to find someone by chance'.
97.	T/1	decl	non-int	present		Yes, 'to find someone or something by chance', so he happened to find a man standing by the roadside.
	T/2	decl	non-int	present		Now, "He had his thumb out..." This means if you want to get a ride – I think we talked about this – if you want to get a ride, then you stretch your arm, and wave your thumb like this.
	T/3	decl	non-int	present		This means that you want to get a ride.

(Continued)

t	sp/m	mood	Sub per	deicticity	assessment	text
	T/4	interr	non-int	present		OK, so this person, erm, "had his thumb out and held a gas can in his other hand", now, why does he hold a gas can – what does that mean?
	T/5	decl	non-int	present	eviden subj prob	Some people think that this means that he, erm, he ran out of gas, and he couldn't drive on, but I don't think so, I don't think he had a car, en, this person.
	T/6	interr	non-int	present		So, what does that mean, holding a gas can?
	T/7	imp	addr	modal		Well, I'm not quite sure but you can guess, you can guess why.
98.	S	decl			obj prob	Maybe the petrol.
99.	T/1	decl	non-int	present		Yes, yes, so this shows that, probably, he would share the gas – Americans call it gas; petrol is a British word – or he was ready to share, I think, the money the driver would have to pay, for gas.
	T/2	decl	sp+	modal	obj prob	But maybe we have to ask some Americans, since maybe in different states, people, you know, have different ways we don't know.
	T/3	decl	non-int	present		But this is only a guess.
	T/4	interr	non-int	present		Then, well, in the next sentence, the writer mentions what – did people usually pass by hitchhikers, well, did people, in the past, usually pass by hitchhikers?
	T/5	decl	non-int	present		No, so the writer says "there was a time in the country when you'd be considered a jerk" – a very stupid person, well, a very unkind person – "if you did that, in the past." So that means in the past people were ready to picky up hitchhikers, but now, no.
	T/6	decl	non-int	present		Now, the writer says "now you are a fool for helping." It means things have changed a great deal.
	T/7	decl	non-int	present		The writer says "with gangs". That means 'because of gangs'.
	T/8	interr	non-int	present		"... drug addicts, murderers, rapists, thieves lurking everywhere", what is the meaning of 'lurking everywhere'?
100.	S	decl	(non-int)	(present)		'Hiding'.

101.	T/1	decl	(non-int)	(present)		'Hiding somewhere, waiting to do something very bad', so, 'lurking'.
	T/2	interr	non-int	present		So, "I don't want to get involved has become a national motto", but, now, what is, er, what is a 'motto'?
102.	T/3	interr	non-int	present		Xxx, do you know what a 'motto' is?
	S	decl	non-int	present		En, it means a short sentence or phrase chosen and used as a guide or rule of behavior, or as an expression of the aims or ideas of a family, a country, an institution.
103.	T/1	decl	non-int	present		Yeah, that's a very short sentence or phrase, you know, er, in which people express their purpose in life, and maybe it tells us the guiding principle of a certain group, or a certain school.
	T/2	interr	non-int	present		So, "... a national motto..." you know the national motto, of United States, do you know, there is a national motto of the US?
104.	Sn					Yeah.
105.	T/1	interr	non-int	present		But what is it?
	T/2	decl	non-int	present		It's not of course "I don't want to get involved", of course this is not their national motto, but there is one.
	T/3	interr				OK, do you know anything about this?
	T/4	decl	pseudo-int	present		Well, *In God We Trust* – this is the 'national motto' of the United States – this, you find this motto, their motto, national motto, in their currency – money, the coins, also paper money – er; *In God We Trust*.
	T/5	decl	non-int	present		Of course, it is taken, I think it is derived, it derives from a song, a battle song, which later became the national anthem of the United States.
	T/6	decl	non-int	present		Well, there is another motto.
	T/7	decl	non-int	present		That is called the United States motto.
	T/8	decl	sp+	present	subj prob	But I think we don't have time.
	T/9	interr	non-int	present	subj prob	Now, do you think, er, "I don't want to get involved" has been made officially the national motto of the United States?

(Continued)

t	sp/m	mood	Sub per	deicticity	assessment	text
106.	Sn	decl	(non-int)	(present)		No.
107.	T	interr	non-int	present	subj prob	Now, why do you think does the writer say this, if it is, er, it's not a really a national motto, why does the writer say this?
108.	S	decl				Humorous.
109.	T/1	decl	non-int	present	subj prob	Well, I don't think it's humorous, but it's sarcastic, bitter, sarcastic, the tone's sarcastic.
	T/2	decl	non-int	present		Actually, nobody say this is the national motto, as *In God We Trust* actually was made official, was adopted by Congress in 1956.
	T/3	decl	non-int	present		But, well, I think the writer is being very sarcastic, saying that "I don't want to get involved" – that I don't want to help a stranger, for fear – well, I don't want to help a stranger, because I don't want to get attacked, because he or she might be a murderer, and so on.
	T/4	decl	non-int	present		So this shows, the writer thinks, you know, er, the moral of the nation is declining: instead of helping other people, they say 'I don't want to get involved, I have to protect myself.'
	T/5	decl	non-int	present		Well, about 'mottos', you know, it also embodies the principle.
	T/6	decl	non-int	present		For instance, now, some schools have mottos, such as Unity, Honor and so on.
	T/7	decl	addr	modal	subj prob obj prob	So I think you may want to create a motto for your class, maybe you can think about that.
	T/8	imp	sp+			Now let's come to the next paragraph, the next paragraph.
	T/9	imp	addr	modal		Well, let's see, Xxx, would you like to read?
110.	S					"Several states later, I was still thinking about the hitchhiker, leaving him stranded in the desert did not bother me too much. What bothered me was how easily I had reached the decision. I never even lifted my foot off the accelerator …"

Appendix II: Text 5 coded ideationally

t	sp/m	1st participant	process	2nd participant	text
1.					Good morning, everybody.
	T/1	on-s: person	material material verbal	textbook lang; label on-s: person	Er, you probably guess, I think, that I am not going to give you a written check on preview because I have written all the useful expressions I expect you to use when you answer my questions, so let me ask you a few questions.
	T/2	on-s: person relo: person	material ver/attri mental	relo: person on-s: person	But before I ask you – the first question is: before you came to Beijing, er, did your parents give you any advice, for instance, you see, when you are badly in need of help, who you can depend on?
	T/3				Anyone?
	T/4	relo: person	verbal	on-s: person	Xxx, did your parents give you any advice?
2.	S				Yes.
3.	T		attribu		Yes, what is it like?
4.	S	relo: person on-s: person	verbal mental	on-s: person relo: person	My mother told me that you can only depend on our, relatives in Beijing, and not strangers.
5.	T/1	on-s: person	attribu material	relo: person	Not strangers, not to depend on strangers, ern, when you are in great difficulty, when you are in trouble, you have to turn to relatives – you have relatives in Beijing.
	T/2	relo: person	verbal	on-s: person	Now, what did your parents say to you?
6.	S	relo: person on-s: person	verbal identi	on-s: person	My parents said that the only one you can depend on is yourself.

(Continued)

t	sp/m	1st participant	process	2nd participant	text
7.	T/1	on-s: person	mental	on-s: person	Depend on yourself, you can't depend, you know, you can't trust, you can't depend on anybody else, just yourself.
	T/2	on-s: person	attribu / material		But if you were badly in need of help, what would you do, suppose you are badly wounded?
8.	S	on-s: person	material	thing: gener	I'll call, call the police, or call the emergence agency. (laugh)
9.	T/1	on-s: person	attribu		Okay, okay, that's right.
	T/2	relo: person	verbal / mental	on-s: person / relo: person	Now, why do you think they advised you not to trust strangers, why did, did your parents advise you not to trust strangers?
10.	S				Yes, especially in a train.
11.	T	thing: abstract	identi	thing: abstract	especially in a train, why – my question is why?
12.	S	thing: abstract	attribu		... because the society is very complex,
13.	T				umm
14.	S	relo: person	existent		and there are many bad person we don't know.
15.	T/1	relo: person / on-s: person	exi/men / attribu	relo: person	Yes, there are a lot of bad persons, so you can't trust strangers, maybe this is right, maybe this is right.
	T/2	relo: person	existent		But at the same time, well, it seems that there are also good people.
	T/3	generalized	verbal / attribu	thing: abstract	But everywhere in the world, people say that they are losing their faith in the goodness of human nature.
	T/4	thing: abstract	identi	thing: abstract	So whether we can still depend on the help of strangers, this is the question that I think a lot of people have in mind.

No.					
	T/5	textbook	verbal	textbook	And the text today, the text we are going to have today, answers the question whether we can still depend on the kindness of strangers, in other words, whether we can still depend on a kind stranger to help us when we are badly in need.
	T/6	on-s: person	verbal	on-s: person	Well, now, so now let me ask you some questions about the text.
	T/7	on-s: person textbook	mental identi	on-s: person textbook	First, what do you know about the title, what do you know about the title – the title is *The Kindness of Strangers* – what does that mean?
	T/8				Anyone?
	[more than 6 seconds, no response]				
	T/9	relo: person	material	textbook	Now, where did he – em, I think you have read the notes – where did the writer get the title from?
	T/10				Xxx.
16.	S	relo: person	material	textbook	En, where he get the title?
17.	T	relo: person	material	textbook	Yeah, the title *The Kindness of Strangers*, do you know where the writer, you know, got the title from?
18.	S				From a movie,
19.	T				yes
20.	S				en, from a movie called *A Streetcar Named Desire*.
21.	T/1	textbook relo: person	attribu verbal attribu	textbook	Yes, *A Streetcar Named Desire*, that's from a movie, that is, at the end of this play or the movie, yes, a character said. "you can still depend on – I can still depend on the kindness of strangers", and so on, okay, that's right.
	T/2	textbook	mental verbal	textbook	So em, now, the next question is, what did he, what did the writer – what does the writer want to say to the reader through his experience described in the passage, what do you think, the writer wants to tell the reader?
	T/3				Anyone?
	T/4				Yes.

(Continued)

t	sp/m	1st participant	process	2nd participant	text
22.	S	generalized	mental		Now you can still depend on the kindness of stranger.
23.	T/1	textbook	mental verbal		So the writer wants to convince the reader that you can still depend on the kindness of strangers, in spite of the increasing crime.
	T/2	relo: person	mental		Why – well, how did he come to this conclusion, how did he come to this conclusion?
	T/3				Well, maybe I will ask somebody – Xxx.
24.	S	relo: person	material		Because he traveled fourteen states through America with no money, just by the help of strangers.
25.	T/1	relo: person	mental material		Ern yes, okay, he came to the conclusion after traveling across fourteen states of the United States, wholly depending on the kindness of strangers.
	T/2	relo: person	material		OK, so, what kind of journey did he have – did he, er, make the journey by trains, by bus, or by driving his own car, how?
	T/5				Xxx.
26.	S	(relo: person)	(materi)		By hitchhike.
27.	T/1	on-s: person	verbal		By hitchhiking – you said 'by hitchhike'.
	T/2	lang; point	identi		But what is the meaning of the word 'hitchhike'?
28.	S	relo: person	attribu material	thing: gener	Yes, he didn't have a penny and he didn't drive a bike, so he had to, en, on other person's bike, to carry on his journey.
29.	T/1				Not his bike, I think in the United States, people don't ... (laugh).
	T/2	generalized	material		Now, if you want to 'get a ride' – that means to get a ride from somebody, from a driver, from a car or a truck passing by – what do you do"?
	T/3				Anyone – Xxx.
30.	S	generalized	material	thing: gener	I think you wave your hands.

31.	T	generalized	material		you wave your –
32.	S	relo: person	attribu	thing: gener	And in this text, the stranger has his thumb up.
33.	T/1				Un-hun, right.
	T/2	generalized	material identi	thing: gener	And also, sometimes, you also carry a sign, indicating or displaying where you are going.
	T/3	generalized	material		For instance, if you want to go to Chicago, you have this word 'Chicago'.
	T/4	generalized	material identi	thing: gener	So you hold a sign, displaying the destination and then you thumb out, you thumb out.
	T/5	generalized	material	thing: gener	That is to say, you, er, you stretch out your arm and wave your thumb, this way.
	T/6	relo: person	attribut material	thing: gener	OK, now, well, I remember Xxx said he didn't have a penny with him, and, well, of course you can get a ride – he can get a ride by hitchhiking, but what about the food and shelter, what about the food and shelter, where did he get food and shelter?
	T/7				Xxx.
34.	S	relo: person	material	thing: gener	He get [got] food from, strangers.
35.	T/1				Strangers, okay.
	T/2				But what about the shelter?
36.	s				In strangers' house.
37.	T	relo: person	material	thing: gener	In what – in strangers' house – do you think he, he always passed the night in strangers' house?
38.	S				I think that depends.
39.	T				yes

(*Continued*)

t	sp/m	1st participant	process	2nd participant	text
40.	S	relo: person	material	thing: gener	He put up a tent.
41.	T/1	relo: person	attribu / material	thing: gener	Yes, that's right, sometimes he put up a tent – so you can imagine that he had brought with him a tent.
	T/2	thing: abstract	identi		OK, now, next question: what do you think, what do you think, was the biggest problem during the journey?
	T/3				Anyone?
	[more than 6 seconds, no response]				
	T/4	thing: abstract	identi	thing: abstract	Well, you think chiefly the problems were, ern, whether he could get rides, whether the drivers would stop to pick him up, whether he can get food, and whether he can get shelter to pass the night – he can't sleep in the open, especially in some places.
	T/5	thing: abstract	identi		So, what do you think, what do you think was the biggest problem?
	[more than 6 seconds, no response]				
	T/6	textbook on-s: person	verbal BEHAV		Well, if the text does not tell you directly, I think you can infer from what he said.
	T/7	relo: person	material	thing: gener	You remember what kind of journey was he going to make?
42.	Sn				From coast to coast.
43.	T/1	relo: person	material	thing: gener	Yeah, he was going to make a coast to coast journey.
	T/2	thing: special	attribu		Well, it's a large area in United States, from the Pacific to the Atlantic, from coast to coast.
	T/3	thing: abstract	identi		So you can imagine what, what was the biggest problem?
44.	S				[confusion]

			BEHAV		
45.	T	(on-s: person)	(identi)		Yes, speak louder.
46.	S	(thing: abstr)		thing; gener	Rides.
47.	T/1	generalized	verbal	lang; point	You don't say 'rides', but 'getting rides', 'getting rides'.
	T/2	thing; gener	identi	thing; abstract	Now, was it so important – why was it the biggest problem, have you got any idea?
	T/3				Anyone?
	[more than 6 seconds, no response]				
	T/4	on-s: person	mental		Xxx, have you got any idea?
48.	S				No.
49.	T				Erm, yes Xxx.
50.	S	on-s: person	mental	thing; abstract	I didn't hear clearly what she said.
51.	T	thing; abstract	identi		Well, she said getting, getting rides was the biggest problem, during the journey.
52.	S				En, I think so.
53.	T				Why do you think so?
54.	S	relo: person / relo: thing	material / material	thing; gener	Because if he didn't get a ride in time, perhaps some, some dangerous things will happen, like some robbers, some thieves may do some harm to him.
55.	T/1	relo: person	material	relo: person	Yes, they may attack him.
	T/2	thing; abstract	attribu		Now, do you think it is easy to get a ride, is it easy to get a ride from strangers?
56.	Sn				No.
57.	T	thing; abstract	attribu		Why not, do you think? Why isn't it so easy to get a ride?
58.	S	thing; abstract	attribu		I think it isn't easy to make people believe that you are innocent,
59.	T				yes, un-hun

(Continued)

t	sp/m	1st participant	process	2nd participant	text
60.	S	generalized	material		you must, must make them believe that you are just a passerby, you won't do any harm to them, so they will offer you a ride.
61.	T/1				Yes, okay.
	T/2	relo: person generalized	attribu mental material	thing: gener	Now, so we say, well, about food, Americans are always very generous: if you want food, they would like to offer food readily because if not, you know, I think it can be dangerous for them.
	T/3	relo: person	material	thing: gener	Then also about shelter, well, Xxx said that he must have brought a tent with him; he could pitch his tent in any place.
	T/4	textbook relo: person	verbal men/mat	thing: gener	Well, but actually in the text, somewhere I think, the writer mentions that he wanted to pitch a tent, sometimes.
	T/5	relo: person	mental material	thing: gener	OK, now, how come he wanted to make a trip like that – it was a very hard journey, I suppose – how come he came to make, to decide that he should make a trip like that?
	T/6				Xxx.
62.	S	relo: person	material	relo: person	Because he used to pass by a hitch, hitch …
63.	T			relo: person	hitchhiker
64.	S	relo: thing	material	relo: person	hitchhiker, and this made him think a lot,
65.	T				un-hun
66.	S	relo: person	men/mat	relo: person	whether people in the United States would still like to help a stranger.
67.	T/1	relo: person	attribu material mental		That's right, that's right, because he himself once drove past a hitchhiker, well he didn't hesitate at that time, but later on, later on, he felt very bad; that is why he wanted to make a – such a trip, depending totally on the kindness of strangers.

	T/2	relo: person	mental material	thing; gener	OK, so why did he make, why did he decide to make a coast-to-coast journey – why didn't he concentrate, or why didn't he limit his journey in one area, for instance, the eastern part of United States, the central part, or the western part, why?
	T/3				Xxx.
68.	S	relo: person	mental material	thing; abstract	Because different path roads in different parts of America – he wanted to experience the differences between different parts.
69.	T				Different parts, and also?
70.	S				the whole country
71.	T/1				the whole country
	T/2	relo: person	mental material	thing; abstract	So, he wanted to experience, he wanted to know how he would be treated in different parts of United States, whether people everywhere, er, would treat him in the same way.
	T/3	relo: person	material	thing; abstract	This way, he would make his conclusion more convincing, so that is why.
	T/4	relo: person	material	relo: person	Now, the next question: how was he received by the people, in the 14 states, generally speaking, well, how was he received?
	T/5				Anyone?
	T/6				Yes, Xxx.
72.	S	relo: person	material		I think he was warmly received.
73.	T	relo: person	material		He was warmly – do you mean he was always, warmly received?
74.	S	relo: person	material		Not always, but generally speaking he was lucky.
75.	T/1	relo: person	attri/mat		He was lucky, he was warmly received.
	T/2	relo: person on-s: person relo: person	attribu verbal material	on-s: person	Well, were people ready to give him a ride – erm how, if I ask you how he was warmly received, how would you answer the question?

(Continued)

t	sp/m	1st participant	process	2nd participant	text
76.	S	relo: person	attri/mat	thing: gener	En, a lot of people were so kind as to give him ride,
77.	T				yes
78.	S	relo: person	material	thing: gener	some people shared food and shelter with him,
79.	T				yes
80.	S	relo: person	material	thing: gener	and some even gave him gift.
81.	T/1		attribu		Yes, gave him gift, that's right.
	T/2	relo: person	material		OK, so er, well, was he ever rejected – I mean when he wanted to get a ride, was he ever rejected?
82.	Sn				Yes.
83.	T/1				Yes, yes, sometimes, sometimes yes.
	T/2	relo: person	material		He was rejected once, for instance – when?
84.	S	relo: person	material		One day, in the rain, en, he can't get a ride, so he was left stand out in the rain,
85.	T				yeah
86.	S	relo: person	material		until a truck driver arrived.
87.	T/1	relo: person	mat/attri		That's right, yes, until a truck driver arrived.
	T/2	thing: gener relo: person	material material	relo: person	That is to say, well, several cars or trucks passed by and nobody, no driver picked him up, so he had to stand in the rain, for sometime until a truck driver came along.
	T/3	thing: gener	attribu		Well, maybe this was not the first time, this was not the only time he was rejected.

			material	textbook	
	T/4	relo: person			But generally speaking, he was warmly received.
	T/5	on-s: person	verbal daily-mat	textbook	All right, well, I think you can all answer [all answered] the questions very well, and you did a very good job, in previewing the lesson.
	T/6	on-s: person	daily-mat BEH	textbook	Now, let's open our book, and we'll ask someone to read the first paragraph.
	T/7	on-s: person	BEH	textbook	Xxx, would you like to read the first paragraph?
88.	S				OK. "One summer I was driving from my hometown of Ta ..."
89.	T				Well, it's 'Tahoe'.
90.	S				"Tahoe city, Cali ..."
91.	T				California
92.	S				"California, to New ..."
93.	T				New Orleans
94.	S				"New Orleans. In the middle of the desert, I came upon a young man standing by the roadside. He had his thumb out and held a gas can in his other hand. I drove right by him. There was a time in the country when you'd be considered a jerk if you passed by somebody in need. Now you are fool for helping. With gangs, drug addicts, murderers, rapists, and thieves lurking everywhere, 'I don't want to get involved' has become a national motto."
95.	T/1	on-s: person thing: special relo: person	verbal exi/attri verbal		OK, now, here you have this: "I was driving from my hometown of Tahoe city ..." Now I asked someone where Tahoe city is located, and they say it's somewhere in California, it's somewhere, you know [points at a map], in the northern part of the mountains.
	T/2	thing: special	attribu		You see, here are the mountains.

(*Continued*)

t	sp/m	1st participant	process	2nd participant	text
	T/3	thing; special	attribu		It's somewhere here.
	T/4	thing; special	attribu		You have this word, 'California', right below the word California, that is where Tahoe city is located.
	T/5	thing; special	attribu		So that's his hometown.
	T/6	generalized	verbal		And "was driving from my hometown of Tahoe city, California", now, if you mention 'Tahoe', a small town in the United States, you usually also mention where, in which state, this place is located.
	T/7	thing; abstract thing; gener	attribu existen		And I think this is a very good thing, because maybe sometimes, sometimes you know, in different states, they have towns with the same name.
	T/8	thing; special thing; special	existen attribu		For instance, in China, there are more than one 'Linxia', but one is in Henan, the other may be in other places.
	T/9	thing; gener	attribu	thing; gener	So, and "California ..." – each state has a short form – er, so, "... California to New Orleans", well, I think that's a long trip, it's a long trip.
	T/10	textbook	verbal	thing; gener	So, the first paragraph tells us an incident that actually made the writer decide to take this long, cross-country journey.
	T/11	thing; gener	identi		Well, what is it, what is the incident that's talked about?
	T/12	relo: person	material		OK, he did not stop for a hitchhiker.
	T/13	on-s: person	daily-mat		Now, let's come to some of the words.
	T/14	lang; point	identi	lang; point	Er, "I came upon ..." What is the meaning of 'came upon'?
96.	S	lang; point	identi		It means 'to find someone by chance'.

97.	T/1	relo: person	material		Yes, 'to find someone or something by chance', so he happened to find a man standing by the roadside.
	T/2	lang; point generalized	identi material	thing; abstract	Now, "He had his thumb out ..." This means if you want to get a ride – I think we talked about this – if you want to get a ride, then you stretch your arm, and wave your thumb like this.
	T/3	lang; point	identi	thing; abstract	This means that you want to get a ride.
	T/4	lang; point	identi		OK, so this person, ern, "had his thumb out and held a gas can in his other hand", now, why does he hold a gas can – what does that mean?
	T/5	lang; point relo: person	identi attribu	thing; gener	Some people think that this means that he, ern, he ran out of gas, and he couldn't drive on, but I don't think so, I don't think he had a car, en, this person.
	T/6	lang; point	identi		So, what does that mean, 'holding a gas can'?
	T/7	on-s: person	mental		Well, I'm not quite sure but you can guess, you can guess why.
98.	S				Maybe the petrol.
99.	T/1	lang; point lang; point relo: person	identi attribu material	lang: label thing; gener	Yes, yes, so this shows that, probably, he would share the gas – Americans call it 'gas'; 'petrol' is a British word – or he was ready to share, I think, the money the driver would have to pay, for gas.
	T/2	on-s: person relo: person	verbal attribu		But maybe we have to ask some Americans, since maybe in different states, people, you know, have different ways we don't know.
	T/3	thing: abstract	attribu		But this is only a guess.
	T/4	relo: person	material		Then, well, in the next sentence, the writer mentions what – did people usually pass by hitchhikers, well, did people, in the past, usually pass by hitchhikers?

(Continued)

t	sp/m	1st participant	process	2nd participant	text
	T/5	lang; point	identi	thing; abstract	No, so the writer says "there was a time in the country when you'd be considered a jerk" – a very stupid person, well, a very unkind person – "if you did that, in the past." So that means in the past people were ready to picky up hitchhikers, but now, no.
	T/6	lang; point	identi		Now, the writer says "now you are a fool for helping." It means things have changed a great deal.
	T/7	lang; point	identi	lang; point	The writer says "with gangs". That means 'because of gangs'.
	T/8	lang; point	identi	lang; point	"... drug addicts, murderers, rapists, thieves lurking everywhere", what is the meaning of 'lurking everywhere'?
100.	S	(lang; point)	(identi)	lang; point	'Hiding'.
101.	T/1	(lang; point)	(identi)	lang; point	'Hiding somewhere, waiting to do something very bad', so, 'lurking'.
	T/2	lang; point	identi		So, "I don't want to get involved has become a national motto", but, now, what is, er, what is a 'motto'?
	T/3	lang; point	identi		Xxx, do you know what a 'motto' is?
102.	S	lang; point	identi	lang; label	En, it means a short sentence or phrase chosen and used as a guide or rule of behavior, or as an expression of the aims or ideas of a family, a country, an institution.
103.	T/1	lang; point	identi	lang; label	Yeah, that's a very short sentence or phrase, you know, er, in which people express their purpose in life, and maybe it tells us the guiding principle of a certain group, or a certain school.
	T/2	thing; special	existen		So, "... a national motto ..." you know the national motto, of United States, do you know, there is a national motto of the US?

104.	Sn				Yeah.
105.	T/1	thing; special	identi		But what is it?
	T/2	thing; special	identi	lang; point	It's not of course "I don't want to get involved", of course this is not their national motto, but there is one.
	T/3	thing; special	attribu		OK, do you know anything about this?
	T/4	thing; special generalized	identi material	thing; special	Well, *In God We Trust* – this is the national motto of the United States – this, you find this motto, their motto, national motto, in their currency – money, the coins, also paper money – er; *In God We Trust*.
	T/5	thing; special thing; gener	attribu	thing; gener thing; special	Of course, it is taken, I think it is derived, it derives from a song, a battle song, which later became the national anthem of the United States.
	T/6	thing; gener	existen		Well, there is another motto.
	T/7	thing; gener	identi	thing; special	That is called the United States motto.
	T/8	on-s: person	attribu		But I think we don't have time.
	T/9	lang; point	identi	thing; special	Now, do you think, er, "I don't want to get involved" has been made officially the national motto of the United States?
106.	Sn				No.
107	T	textbook	verbal		Now, why do you think does the writer say this, if it is, er, it's not a really a national motto, why does the writer say this?
108.	S				Humorous.

(*Continued*)

t	sp/m	1st participant	process	2nd participant	text
109.	T/1	textbook	attribu		Well, I don't think it's humorous, but it's sarcastic, bitter, sarcastic, the tone's sarcastic.
	T/2	lang; point thing; special	identi material	thing: special	Actually, nobody say this is the national motto, as *In God We Trust* actually was made official, was adopted by Congress in 1956.
	T/3	textbook	attribu verbal		But, well, I think the writer is being very sarcastic, saying that "I don't want to get involved" – that I don't want to help a stranger, for fear – well, I don't want to help a stranger, because I don't want to get attacked, because he or she might be a murderer, and so on.
	T/4	textbook thing; abstract generalized	mental attribu verbal		So this shows, the writer thinks, you know, er, the moral of the nation is declining; instead of helping other people, they say 'I don't want to get involved, I have to protect myself'.
	T/5	lang; point	identi	thing: abstract	Well, about 'mottos', you know, it also embodies the principle.
	T/6	thing: gener	attribu		For instance, now, some schools have mottos, such as Unity, Honor and so on.
	T/7	on-s: person	mental material		So I think you may want to create a motto for your class, maybe you can think about that.
	T/8	on-s: person	daily-mat	(textbook)	Now let's come to the next paragraph, the next paragraph.
	T/9	on-s: person	BEH	(textbook)	Well, let's see, Xxx, would you like to read?
110.	S				"Several states later, I was still thinking about the hitchhiker, leaving him stranded in the desert did not bother me too much. What bothered me was how easily I had reached the decision. I never even lifted my foot off the accelerator …"

Appendix III: Text 5 coded textually

t	sp/m	move type	textual choice	text
1.				Good morning, everybody.
	T/1	orientate	initiative	Er, you probably guess, I think, that I am not going to give you a written check on preview because I have written all the useful expressions I expect you to use when you answer my questions, so let me ask you a few questions.
	T/2	ask	adversative temporal	But before I ask you – the first question is: before you came to Beijing, er, did your parents give you any advice, for instance, you see, when you are badly in need of help, who you can depend on?
	T/3	invite	elli: inter proj	Anyone?
	T/4	ask		Xxx, did your parents give you any advice?
200.	S	answer	elli: polarity	Yes.
3.	T	hint	repetition+	Yes, what is it like?
4.	S	repair		My mother told me that you can only depend on our, relatives in Beijing, and not strangers.
5.	T/1	ackn	paraphrase	Not strangers, not to depend on strangers, erm, when you are in great difficulty, when you are in trouble, you have to turn to relatives – you have relatives in Beijing.
	T/2	ask	boundive repeated Q	Now, what did your parents say to you?
6.	S	answer		My parents said that the only one you can depend on is yourself.
7.	T/1	ackn	paraphrase	Depend on yourself, you can't depend, you know, you can't trust, you can't depend on anybody else, just yourself.
	T/2	ask	adversative	But if you were badly in need of help, what would you do, suppose you are badly wounded?
8.	S	answer		I'll call, call the police, or call the emergence agency. (laugh)

(Continued)

t	sp/m	move type	textual choice	text
9.	T/1	evaluate		Okay, okay, that's right.
	T/2	ask	boundive	Now, why do you think they advised you not to trust strangers, why did, did your parents advise you not to trust strangers?
10.	S	answer	continuative elli: adjunct	Yes, especially in a train.
11.	T/1	hint	repetition+	especially in a train, why – my question is why?
12.	S	repair		... because the society is very complex,
13.	T	backch		umm
14.	S	continue		and there are many bad person we don't know.
15.	T/1	evaluate	continuative repetition+	Yes, there are a lot of bad persons, so you can't trust strangers, maybe this is right, maybe this is right.
	T/2	state	adversative	But at the same time, well, it seems that there are also good people.
	T/3	state	adversative	But everywhere in the world, people say that they are losing their faith in the goodness of human nature.
	T/4	state	causal	So whether we can still depend on the help of strangers, this is the question that I think a lot of people have in mind.
	T/5	state	additive	And the text today, the text we are going to have today, answers the question whether we can still depend on the kindness of strangers, in other words, whether we can still depend on a kind stranger to help us when we are badly in need.
	T/6	orientate	boundive	Well, now, so now let me ask you some questions about the text.
	T/7	ask	temporal	First, what do you know about the title, what do you know about the title – the title is *The Kindness of Strangers* – what does that mean?
	T/8	invite	elli: inter proj	Anyone?

				[more than 6 seconds, no response]
16.	T/9	ask	boundive	Now, where did he – erm, I think you have read the notes – where did the writer get the title from?
	T/10	nominate		Xxx.
17.	S	request	repetition	En, where he get the title?
18.	T	resolve	continuative repetition	Yeah, the title *The Kindness of Strangers*, do you know where the writer, you know, got the title from?
19.	S	answer	elli: wh-resp	From a movie,
	T	backch	continuative	yes
20.	S	continue		en, from a movie called *A Streetcar Named Desire*.
21.	T/1	evaluate	continuative repetition+	Yes, *A Streetcar Named Desire*, that's from a movie, that is, at the end of this play or the movie, yes, a character said: "you can still depend on – I can still depend on the kindness of strangers", and so on, okay, that's right.
	T/2	ask	boundive temporal	So erm, now, the next question is, what did he, what did the writer – what does the writer want to say to the reader through his experience described in the passage, what do you think, the writer wants to tell the reader?
	T/3	invite	elli: inter proj	Anyone?
	T/4	nominate		Yes.
22.	S	answer		Now you can still depend on the kindness of stranger.
23.	T/1	ackn	causal paraphrase	So, the writer wants to convince the reader that you can still depend on the kindness of strangers, in spite of the increasing crime.
	T/2	ask	continuative	Why – well, how did he come to this conclusion, how did he come to this conclusion?
	T/3	nominate		Well, maybe I will ask somebody – Xxx.
24.	S	answer		Because he traveled fourteen states through America with no money, just by the help of strangers.

(Continued)

t	sp/m	move type	textual choice	text
25.	T/1	ackn	continuative paraphrase	Erm yes, okay, he came to the conclusion after traveling across fourteen states of the United States, wholly depending on the kindness of strangers.
	T/2	ask	initiative	OK, so, what kind of journey did he have – did he, er, make the journey by trains, by bus, or by driving his own car, how?
	T/3	nominate		Xxx.
26.	S	answer	elli: adjunct	By hitchhike.
27.	T/1	ackn	repetition+	By hitchhiking – you said 'by hitchhike'.
	T/2	ask	adversative	But what is the meaning of the word 'hitchhike'?
28.	S	answer	continuative	Yes, he didn't have a penny and he didn't drive a bike, so he had to, en, on other person's bike, to carry on his journey.
29.	T/1	evaluate	repetition+	Not his bike, I think in the United States, people don't ... (laugh).
	T/2	ask	boundive	Now, if you want to 'get a ride' – that means to get a ride from somebody, from a driver, from a car or a truck passing by – what do you do"?
	T/3	nominate		Anyone – Xxx.
30.	S	answer		I think you wave your hands.
31.	T	hint	repetition–	you wave your –
32.	S	repair	additive	And in this text, the stranger has his thumb up.
33.	T/1	evaluate		Un-hun, right.
	T/2	state	additive	And also, sometimes, you also carry a sign, indicating or displaying where you are going.
	T/3	state	exemplify	For instance, if you want to go to Chicago, you have this word 'Chicago'.
	T/4	state	causal/paraph	So you hold a sign, displaying the destination and then you thumb out, you thumb out.
	T/5	restate	expository	That is to say, you, er, you stretch out your arm and wave your thumb, this way.

	T/6	ask	boundive	OK, now, well, I remember Xxx said he didn't have a penny with him, and, well, of course you can get a ride – he can get a ride by hitchhiking, but what about the food and shelter, what about the food and shelter, where did he get food and shelter?
34.	T/7	nominate		Xxx.
35.	S	answer		He get [got] food from, strangers.
	T/1	evaluate	repetition	Strangers, okay.
	T/2	ask	adversative elli: complem	But what about the shelter?
36.	S	answer	elli: wh-resp	In strangers' house.
37.	T	request	repetition+	In what – in strangers' house – do you think he, he always passed the night in strangers' house?
38.	S	resolve		I think that depends.
39.	T	backch	continuative	yes
40.	S	continue		He put up a tent.
41.	T/1	evaluate	continuative repetition+	Yes, that's right, sometimes he put up a tent – so you can imagine that he had brought with him a tent.
	T/2	ask	boundive temporal	OK, now, next question: what do you think, what do you think, was the biggest problem during the journey?
	T/3	invite	elli: inter proj	Anyone?
[more than 6 seconds, no response]				
	T/4	state	initiative	Well, you think chiefly the problems were, em, whether he could get rides, whether the drivers would stop to pick him up, whether he can get food, and whether he can get shelter to pass the night – he can't sleep in the open, especially in some places.
	T/5	ask	causal	So what do you think, what do you think was the biggest problem?

(*Continued*)

t	sp/m	move type	textual choice	text
	[more than 6 seconds, no response]			
	T/6	direct	initiative	Well, if the text does not tell you directly, I think you can infer from what he said.
	T/7	ask		You remember what kind of journey was he going to make?
42.	Sn	answer	elli: wh-resp	From coast to coast.
43.	T/1	ackn	continu/rep+	Yeah, he was going to make a coast to coast journey.
	T/2	state	initiative	Well, it's a large area in United States, from the Pacific to the Atlantic, from coast to coast.
	T/3	ask	causal	So you can imagine what, what was the biggest problem?
44.	S	answer		[confusion]
45.	T	request	continuative	Yes, speak louder.
46.	S	resolve	elli: complem	Rides.
47.	T/1	evaluate	repetition+	You don't say 'rides', but 'getting rides', 'getting rides'.
	T/2	ask	boundive	Now, was it so important – why was it the biggest problem, have you got any idea?
	T/3	invite	elli: inter proj	Anyone?
	[more than 6 seconds, no response]			
	T/4	invite	elli: inter proj	Xxx, have you got any idea?
48.	S	answer	elli: polarity	No.
49.	T	nominate		Ern, yes Xxx.
50.	S	request		I didn't hear clearly what she said.
51.	T	resolve	continuative	Well, she said getting, getting rides was the biggest problem, during the journey.
52.	S	answer	elli: inter proj	En, I think so.
53.	T	request	repetition+	Why do you think so?

54.	S	resolve		Because if he didn't get a ride in time, perhaps some, some dangerous things will happen, like some robbers, some thieves may do some harm to him.
55.	T/1	ackn	continu/paraph	Yes, they may attack him.
	T/2	ask	boundive	Now, do you think it is easy to get a ride, is it easy to get a ride from strangers?
56.	Sn	answer	elli: polarity	No.
57.	T	request	repetition+	Why not, do you think? Why isn't it so easy to get a ride?
58.	S	resolve		I think it isn't easy to make people believe that you are innocent,
59.	T	backch	continuative	yes, un-hun
60.	S	continue		you must, must make them believe that you are just a passerby, you won't do any harm to them, so they will offer you a ride.
61.	T/1	evaluate	continuative	Yes, okay.
	T/2	state	boundive	Now, so we say, well, about food. Americans are always very generous: if you want food, they would like to offer food readily because if not, you know, I think it can be dangerous for them.
	T/3	state	additive	Then also about shelter, well, Xxx said that he must have brought a tent with him; he could pitch his tent in any place.
	T/4	state	adversative clarifying	Well, but actually in the text, somewhere I think, the writer mentions that he wanted to pitch a tent, sometimes.
	T/5	ask	boundive	OK, now, how come he wanted to make a trip like that – it was a very hard journey, I suppose – how come he came to make, to decide that he should make a trip like that?
	T/6	nominate		Xxx.
62.	S	answer		Because he used to pass by a hitch, hitch …
63.	T	prompt	repetition+	hitchhiker
64.	S	resume	repetition	hitchhiker, and this made him think a lot,

(Continued)

t	sp/m	move type	textual choice	text
65.	T	backch		un-hun
66.	S	continue		whether people in the United States would still like to help a stranger.
67.	T/1	evaluate	paraphrase	That's right, that's right, because he himself once drove past a hitchhiker, well he didn't hesitate at that time, but later on, later on, he felt very bad; that is why he wanted to make a – such a trip, depending totally on the kindness of strangers.
	T/2	ask	initiative	OK, so why did he make, why did he decide to make a coast-to-coast journey – why didn't he concentrate, or why didn't he limit his journey in one area, for instance, the eastern part of United States, the central part, or the western part, why?
	T/3	nominate		Xxx.
68.	S	answer		Because different path roads in different parts of America – he wanted to experience the differences between different parts.
69.	T	hint	repetition+	Different parts, and also – ?
70.	S	repair		the whole country
71.	T/1	ackn	repetition	the whole country
	T/2	state	causal paraphrase	So, he wanted to experience, he wanted to know how he would be treated in different parts of United States, whether people everywhere, er, would treat him in the same way.
	T/3	state		This way, he would make his conclusion more convincing, so that is why.
	T/4	ask	boundive temporal	Now, the next question: how was he received by the people, in the 14 states, generally speaking, well, how was he received?
	T/5	invite	elli: inter proj	Anyone?
	T/6	nominate		Yes, Xxx.

72.	S	answer		I think he was warmly received.
73.	T	request	repetition+	He was warmly – do you mean he was always, warmly received?
74.	S	resolve		Not always, but generally speaking he was lucky.
75.	T/1	ackn	repetition+	He was lucky, he was warmly received.
	T/2	ask	initiative	Well, were people ready to give him a ride – erm how, if I ask you how he was warmly received, how would you answer the question?
76.	S	answer		En, a lot of people were so kind as to give him ride,
77.	T	backch	continuative	yes
78.	S	continue		some people shared food and shelter with him,
79.	T	backch	continuative	yes
80.	S	continue		and some even gave him gift.
81.	T/1	evaluate	repetition	Yes, gave him gift, that's right.
	T/2	ask	initiative	OK, so er, well, was he ever rejected – I mean when he wanted to get a ride, was he ever rejected?
82.	Sn	answer	elli: polarity	Yes.
83.	T/1	ackn	repetition+	Yes, yes, sometimes, sometimes yes.
	T/2	ask	exemplify	He was rejected once, for instance – when?
84.	S	answer		One day, in the rain, en, he can't get a ride, so he was left stand out in the rain,
85.	T	backch	continuative	yeah
86.	S	continue		until a truck driver arrived.

(*Continued*)

t	sp/m	move type	textual choice	text
87.	T/1	evaluate	repetition	That's right, yes, until a truck driver arrived.
	T/2	state	expository	That is to say, well, several cars or trucks passed by and nobody, no driver picked him up, so he had to stand in the rain, for sometime until a truck driver came along.
	T/3	state	initiative	Well, maybe this was not the first time, this was not the only time he was rejected.
	T/4	state	adversative	But generally speaking, he was warmly received.
	T/5	recap	boundive	All right, well, I think you can all answer [all answered] the questions very well, and you did a very good job, in previewing the lesson.
	T/6	orientate	boundive	Now, let's open our book, and we'll ask someone to read the first paragraph.
	T/7	order		Xxx, would you like to read the first paragraph?
88.	S	comply	continuative	Okay. "One summer I was driving from my hometown of Ta …"
89.	T	prompt	repetition+	Well, it's 'Tahoe'.
90.	S	resume	repetition	"Tahoe city, Cali …"
91.	T	prompt	repetition+	California
92.	S	resume	repetition	"California, to New …"
93.	T	prompt	repetition+	New Orleans
94.	S	resume	repetition	"New Orleans. In the middle of the desert, I came upon a young man standing by the roadside. He had his thumb out and held a gas can in his other hand. I drove right by him. There was a time in the country when you'd be considered a jerk if you passed by somebody in need. Now you are fool for helping. With gangs, drug addicts, murderers, rapists, and thieves lurking everywhere, 'I don't want to get involved' has become a national motto."
95.	T/1	state	boundive locative	OK, now, here you have this: "I was driving from my hometown of Tahoe city …" Now I asked someone where Tahoe city is located, and they say it's somewhere in California, it's somewhere, you know [points at a map], in the northern part of the mountains.
	T/2	state		You see, here are the mountains.

	T/3	state		It's somewhere here.
	T/4	state		You have this word, 'California', right below the word California, that is where Tahoe city is located.
	T/5	state	causal	So, that's his hometown.
	T/6	state	additive locative	And "was driving from my hometown of Tahoe city, California", now, if you mention 'Tahoe', a small town in the United States, you usually also mention where, in which state, this place is located.
	T/7	state	additive	And I think this is a very good thing, because maybe sometimes, sometimes you know, in different states, they have towns with the same name.
	T/8	state	exemplify	For instance, in China, there are more than one 'Linxia', but one is in Henan, the other may be in other places.
	T/9	state	additive locative	So, and "California ..." – each state has a short form – er, so, "... California to New Orleans", well, I think that's a long trip, it's a long trip.
	T/10	state	causal	So, the first paragraph tells us an incident that actually made the writer decide to take this long, cross-country journey.
	T/11	ask[psuedo]		Well, what is it, what is the incident that's talked about?
	T/12	state		OK, he did not stop for a hitchhiker.
	T/13	orientate	boundive	Now, let's come to some of the words
	T/14	ask	initia/locative	Er, "I came upon ..." What is the meaning of 'came upon'?
96.	S	answer		It means 'to find someone by chance'.
97.	T/1	ackn	continuative repetition+	Yes, 'to find someone or something by chance', so he happened to find a man standing by the roadside.
	T/2	state	initiative locative	Now, "He had his thumb out ..." This means if you want to get a ride – I think we talked about this – if you want to get a ride, then you stretch your arm, and wave your thumb like this.
	T/3	state	paraphrase	This means that you want to get a ride.

(Continued)

t	sp/m	move type	textual choice	text
	T/4	ask[psuedo]	initiative locative	OK, so this person, erm, "had his thumb out and held a gas can in his other hand", now, why does he hold a gas can – what does that mean?
	T/5	state		Some people think that this means that he, erm, he ran out of gas, and he couldn't drive on, but I don't think so, I don't think he had a car, en, this person.
	T/6	ask	causal	So what does that mean, 'holding a gas can'?
	T/7	direct	initiative	Well, I'm not quite sure but you can guess, you can guess why.
98.	S	answer	elliptical	Maybe the petrol.
99.	T/1	evaluate	continuative repetition+	Yes, yes, so this shows that, probably, he would share the gas – Americans call it 'gas'; 'petrol' is a British word – or he was ready to share, I think, the money the driver would have to pay, for gas.
	T/2	state	adversative	But maybe we have to ask some Americans, since maybe in different states, people, you know, have different ways we don't know.
	T/3	state	adversative	But this is only a guess.
	T/4	ask[psuedo]	initiative locative	Then, well, in the next sentence, the writer mentions what – did people usually pass by hitchhikers, well, did people, in the past, usually pass by hitchhikers?
	T/5	state	initiative locative	No, so the writer says "there was a time in the country when you'd be considered a jerk" – a very stupid person, well, a very unkind person – "if you did that, in the past." So that means in the past people were ready to picky up hitchhikers, but now, no.
	T/6	state	initiative locative	Now, the writer says "now you are a fool for helping." It means things have changed a great deal.
	T/7	state	locative	The writer says "with gangs". That means 'because of gangs'.
	T/8	ask	locative	" … drug addicts, murderers, rapists, thieves lurking everywhere", what is the meaning of 'lurking everywhere'?
100.	S	answer	elli: wh-resp	'Hiding'.

101.	T/1	ackn	repetition+	'Hiding somewhere, waiting to do something very bad', so, 'lurking'.
	T/2	ask	initiative locative	So, "I don't want to get involved has become a national motto", but, now, what is, er, what is a 'motto'?
	T/3	nominate		Xxx, do you know what a 'motto' is?
102.	S	answer		En, it means a short sentence or phrase chosen and used as a guide or rule of behavior, or as an expression of the aims or ideas of a family, a country, an institution.
103.	T/1	ackn	continuative paraphrase	Yeah, that's a very short sentence or phrase, you know, er, in which people express their purpose in life, and maybe it tells us the guiding principle of a certain group, or a certain school.
	T/2	ask	initiative locative	So, "… a national motto…" you know the national motto, of United States, do you know, there is a national motto of the US?
104.	Sn	answer	elli: polarity	Yeah.
105.	T/1	ask[psuedo]	adversative	But what is it?
	T/2	state		It's not of course "I don't want to get involved", of course this is not their national motto, but there is one.
	T/3	ask[psuedo]	initiative	OK, do you know anything about this?
	T/4	state	initiative	Well, *In God We Trust* – this is the national motto of the United States – this, you find this motto, their motto, national motto, in their currency – money, the coins, also paper money – er, *In God We Trust*.
	T/5	state	clarifying	Of course, it is taken, I think it is derived, it derives from a song, a battle song, which later became the national anthem of the United States.
	T/6	state	initiative	Well, there is another motto, that is called the United States motto.
	T/7	state	adversative	But I think we don't have time.
	T/8	ask	boundive	Now, do you think, er, "I don't want to get involved" has been made officially the national motto of the United States?

(Continued)

t	sp/m	move type	textual choice	text
106.	Sn	answer	elli: polarity	No.
107.	T	ask	boundive	Now, why do you think does the writer say this, if it is, er, it's not a really a national motto, why does the writer say this?
108.	S	answer	elliptical	Humorous.
109.	T/1	evaluate	repetition+	Well, I don't think it's humorous, but it's sarcastic, bitter, sarcastic, the tone's sarcastic.
	T/2	state	clarifying	Actually, nobody say this is the national motto, as *In God We Trust* actually was made official, was adopted by Congress in 1956.
	T/3	state	adversative	But, well, I think the writer is being very sarcastic, saying that "I don't want to get involved" – that I don't want to help a stranger, for fear – well, I don't want to help a stranger, because I don't want to get attacked, because he or she might be a murderer, and so on.
	T/4	state	causal	So this shows, the writer thinks, you know, er, the moral of the nation is declining; instead of helping other people, they say 'I don't want to get involved, I have to protect myself.'
	T/5	state	initiative	Well, about 'mottos', you know, it also embodies the principle.
	T/6	state	exemplify	For instance, now, some schools have mottos, such as Unity, Honor and so on.
	T/7	state	causal	So I think you may want to create a motto for your class, maybe you can think about that.
	T/8	orientate	boundive	Now let's come to the next paragraph, the next paragraph.
	T/9	order	initiative	Well, let's see, Xxx, would you like to read?
110.	S	comply		"Several states later, I was still thinking about the hitchhiker, leaving him stranded in the desert did not bother me too much. What bothered me was how easily I had reached the decision. I never even lifted my foot off the accelerator …"

Appendix IV: interpersonal, ideational and textual logogenetic patterns in Text 5

t	sp/m	text	textual	interpersonal	ideational
1.		Good morning, everybody.			
	T/1	Er, you probably guess, I think, that I am not going to give you a written check on preview because I have written all the useful expressions I expect you to use when you answer my questions, so let me ask you a few questions.	activity boundary	orientation	daily event / verbal event
	T/2	But before I ask you – the first question is: before you came to Beijing, er, did your parents give you any advice, for instance, you see, when you are badly in need of help, who you can depend on?	expansion complex exchange: initiation/ response-dependent	personal story exchange	complex experience
	T/3	Anyone?			
	T/4	Xxx, did your parents give you any advice?			
2.	S	Yes.			
3.	T	Yes, what is it like?			
4.	S	My mother told me that you can only depend on our, relatives in Beijing, and not strangers.			
5.	T/1	Not strangers, not to depend on strangers, ern, when you are in great difficulty, when you are in trouble, you have to turn to relatives, you have relatives in Beijing.			
	T/2	Now, what did your parents say to you?	rotation simple exchange	personal story exchange	
6.	S	My parents said that the only one you can depend on is yourself.			
7.	T/1	Depend on yourself, you can't depend, you know, you can't trust, you can't depend on anybody else, just yourself.			

(*Continued*)

t	sp/m	text	textual	interpersonal	ideational
	T/2	But if you were badly in need of help, what would you do, suppose you are badly wounded?	expansion simple exchange	judgement exchange	
8.	S	I'll call, call the police, or call the emergence agency. (laugh)			
9.	T/1	Okay, okay, that's right.			
	T/2	Now, why do you think they advised you not to trust strangers, why did, did your parents advise you not to trust strangers?	continuation complex exchange: response-dependent	personal story exchange	
10.	S	Yes, especially in a train.			
11.	T	especially in a train, why – my question is why?			
12.	S	... because the society is very complex,			
13.	T	umm			
14.	S	and there are many bad person we don't know.			
15.	T/1	Yes, there are a lot of bad persons, so you can't trust strangers, maybe this is right, maybe this is right.			
	T/2	But at the same time, well, it seems that there are also good people.	expansion chunk: follow-up addition	knowledge statement series: Variant 3	
	T/3	But everywhere in the world, people say that they are losing their faith in the goodness of human nature.			
	T/4	So whether we can still depend on the help of strangers, this is the question that I think a lot of people have in mind.			
	T/5	And the text today, the text we are going to have today, answers the question whether we can still depend on the kindness of strangers, in other words, whether we can still depend on a kind stranger to help us when we are badly in need.			beyond-text

			activity boundary	orientation	verbal event
	T/6	Well, now, so now let me ask you some questions about the text.			
	T/7	First, what do you know about the title, what do you know about the title – the title is *The Kindness of Strangers* – what does that mean?	[serial] exchange failure	knowledge exchange	[unclear]
	T/8	Anyone?			
	[more than 6 seconds, no response]				
	T/9	Now, where did he – ern, I think you have read the notes – where did the writer get the title from?	continuation complex exchange: initiation / response-dependent	story exchange	in-text
	T/10	Xxx.			
16.	S	En, where he get the title?			
17.	T	Yeah, the title *The Kindness of Strangers*, do you know where the writer, you know, got the title from?			
18.	S	From a movie,			
19.	T	yes			
20.	S	en, from a movie called *A Streetcar Named Desire*,			
21.	T/1	Yes, *A Streetcar Named Desire*, that's from a movie, that is, at the end of this play or the movie, yes, a character said: "you can still depend on – I can still depend on the kindness of strangers", and so on, okay, that's right.			

(Continued)

t	sp/m	text	textual	interpersonal	ideational
	T/2	So ern, now, the next question is, what did he, what did the writer – what does the writer want to say to the reader through his experience described in the passage, what do you think, the writer wants to tell the reader?	[serial] continuation complex exchange: initiation-dependent	knowledge exchange	beyond-text
	T/3	Anyone?			
	T/4	Yes.			
22.	S	Now you can still depend on the kindness of stranger.			
23.	T/1	So the writer wants to convince the reader that you can still depend on the kindness of strangers, in spite of the increasing crime.			
	T/2	Why – well, how did he come to this conclusion, how did he come to this conclusion?	continuation complex exchange: initiation-dependent	story exchange	
	T/3	Well, maybe I will ask somebody – Xxx.			
24.	S	Because he traveled fourteen states through America with no money, just by the help of strangers.			
25.	T/1	Ern yes, okay, he came to the conclusion after traveling across fourteen states of the United States, wholly depending on the kindness of strangers.			
	T/2	OK, so, what kind of journey did he have – did he, er, make the journey by trains, by bus, or by driving his own car, how?	continuation complex exchange: initiation-dependent	story exchange	in-text
	T/3	Xxx.			
26.	S	By hitchhike.			
27.	T/1	By hitchhiking – you said 'by hitchhike'.			

				meaning
			knowledge exchange	
			knowledge exchange	
T/2	But what is the meaning of the word 'hitchhike'?	expansion simple exchange		
28.	S	Yes, he didn't have a penny and he didn't drive a bike, so he had to, en, on other person's bike, to carry on his journey.			
29.	T/1	Not his bike, I think in the United States, people don't … (laugh).			
	T/2	Now, if you want to 'get a ride' – that means to get a ride from somebody, from a driver, from a car or a truck passing by – what do you do"?	continuation complex exchange: initiation / response-dependent	knowledge exchange	
30.	S	Anyone – Xxx.			
31.	T	I think you wave your hands.			
32.	S	you wave your –			
33.	T/1	And in this text, the stranger has his thumb up.			
		Un-hun, right.			
	T/2	And also, sometimes, you also carry a sign, indicating or displaying where you are going.	expansion chunk: follow-up addition (exemplification)	knowledge statement series: Variant 3	
	T/3	For instance, if you want to go to Chicago, you have this word 'Chicago'.			
	T/4	So you hold a sign, displaying the destination and then you thumb out, you thumb out.			
	T/5	That is to say, you, er, you stretch out your arm and wave your thumb, this way.			
	T/6	OK, now, well, I remember Xxx said he didn't have a penny with him, and, well, of course you can get a ride – he can get a ride by hitchhiking, but what about the food and shelter, what about the food and shelter; where did he get food and shelter?	continuation complex exchange: initiation-dependent	story exchange	in-text
34.	S	Xxx.			
35.	S	He get [got] food from, strangers.			
	T/1	Strangers, okay.			

(Continued)

t	sp/m	text	textual	interpersonal	ideational
36.	T/2	But what about the shelter?	expansion complex exchange: response-dependent	story exchange	
	S	In strangers' house.			
37.	T/1	In what – in strangers' house – do you think he, he always passed the night in strangers' house?			
38.	S	I think that depends.			
39.	T	yes			
40.	S	He put up a tent.			
41.	T/1	Yes, that's right, sometimes he put up a tent – so you can imagine that he had brought with him a tent.			
	T/2	OK, now, next question: what do you think, what do you think, was the biggest problem during the journey?	[serial] continuation exchange failure	story exchange	above-text
	T/3	Anyone?			
	[more than 6 seconds, no response]				
	T/4	Well, you think chiefly the problems were, erm, whether he could get rides, whether the drivers would stop to pick him up, whether he can get food, and whether he can get shelter to pass the night – he can't sleep in the open, especially in some places.	continuation chunk: presentation	story statement series: Variant 3	
	T/5	So, what do you think, what do you think was the biggest problem?	expansion exchange failure	story exchange	
	[more than 6 seconds, no response]				
	T/6	Well, if the text does not tell you directly, I think you can infer from what he said.		direction	beha event

No.		Utterance			in-text / behind-text
	T/7	You remember what kind of journey was he going to make?	continuation simple exchange	story exchange	in-text
42.	Sn	From coast to coast.			
43.	T/1	Yeah, he was going to make a coast to coast journey.			behind-text
	T/2	Well, it's a large area in United States, from the Pacific to the Atlantic, from coast to coast.	conti-chunk: presentation	knowledge statement	
	T/3	So you can imagine what, what was the biggest problem?	expansion complex exchange: response-dependent	story exchange	
44.	S	[confusion]			
45.	T	Yes, speak louder.			
46.	S	Rides.			
47.	T/1	You don't say 'rides', but 'getting rides', 'getting rides'.			
	T/2	Now, was it so important – why was it the biggest problem, have you got any idea?	continuation exchange failure	story exchange	
	T/3	Anyone?			
		[more than 6 seconds, no response]			
	T/4	Xxx, have you got any idea?	rotation exchange failure	story exchange	
48.	S	No.			
49.	T	Ern, yes Xxx.	rotation complex exchange: initiation/ response-dependent	story exchange	
50.	S	I didn't hear clearly what she said.			
51.	T	Well, she said getting, getting rides was the biggest problem, during the journey.			
52.	S	En, I think so.			

(Continued)

t	sp/m	text	textual	interpersonal	ideational
53.	T	Why do you think so?			
54.	S	Because if he didn't get a ride in time, perhaps some, some dangerous things will happen, like some robbers, some thieves may do some harm to him.			
55.	T/1	Yes, they may attack him.			
	T/2	Now, do you think it is easy to get a ride, is it easy to get a ride from strangers?	continuation complex exchange: response-dependent	knowledge exchange	
56.	Sn	No.			
57.	T	Why not, do you think? Why isn't it so easy to get a ride?			
58.	S	I think it isn't easy to make people believe that you are innocent,			
59.	T	yes, un-hun			
60.	S	you must, must make them believe that you are just a passerby, you won't do any harm to them, so they will offer you a ride.			
61.	T/1	Yes, okay.			
	T/2	Now, so we say; well, about food, Americans are always very generous; if you want food, they would like to offer food readily because if not, you know, I think it can be dangerous for them.	continuation chunk: presentation	knowledge statement series: Variant 3	in-text
	T/3	Then also about shelter, well, Xxx said that he must have brought a tent with him; he could pitch his tent in any place.			
	T/4	Well, but actually in the text, somewhere I think, the writer mentions that he wanted to pitch a tent, sometimes.			

	T/5	OK, now, how come he wanted to make a trip like that – it was was a very hard journey, I suppose – how come he came to make, to decide that he should make a trip like that?	continuation complex exchange: initiation/ response-dependent	story exchange
	T/6	Xxx.		
62.	S	Because he used to pass by a hitch, hitch …		
63.	T	hitchhiker		
64.	S	hitchhiker; and this made him think a lot,		
65.	T	un-hun		
66.	S	whether people in the United States would still like to help a stranger.		
67.	T/1	That's right, that's right, because he himself once drove past a hitchhiker, well he didn't hesitate at that time, but later on, later on, he felt very bad; that is why he wanted to make a – such a trip, depending totally on the kindness of strangers.		
	T/2	OK, so why did he make, why did he decide to make a coast-to-coast journey – why didn't he concentrate, or why didn't he limit his journey in one area, for instance, the eastern part of United States, the central part, or the western part, why?	continuation complex exchange: initiation/ response-dependent	story exchange
	T/3	Xxx.		
68.	S	Because different path roads in different parts of America – he wanted to experience the differences between different parts.		
69.	T	Different parts, and also?		
70.	S	the whole country		
71.	T/1	the whole country		

(Continued)

t	sp/m	text	textual	interpersonal	ideational
	T/2	So, he wanted to experience, he wanted to know how he would be treated in different parts of United States, whether people everywhere, er, would treat him in the same way.	expansion chunk: follow-up conclusion	story statement: Variant 3	
	T/3	This way, he would make his conclusion more convincing, so that is why.			
	T/4	Now, the next question: how was he received by the people, in the 14 states, generally speaking, well, how was he received?	[serial] continuation complex exchange: initiation/ response-dependent	story exchange	
	T/5	Anyone?			
	T/6	Yes, Xxx.			
72.	S	I think he was warmly received.	response-dependent		
73.	T	He was warmly – do you mean he was always, warmly received?			
74.	S	Not always, but generally speaking he was lucky.			
75.	T/1	He was lucky, he was warmly received.			
	T/2	Well, were people ready to give him a ride – em how, if I ask you how he was warmly received, how would you answer the question?	continuation complex exchange: response-dependent	story exchange	
76.	S	En, a lot of people were so kind as to give him ride,			
77.	T	yes			
78.	S	some people shared food and shelter with him,			
79.	T	yes			
80.	S	and some even gave him gift.			
81.	T/1	Yes, gave him gift, that's right.			

82.	T/2	OK, so er, well, was he ever rejected – I mean when he wanted to get a ride, was he ever rejected?	continuation simple exchange	story exchange	
83.	Sn	Yes.			
	T/1	Yes, yes, sometimes, sometimes yes.			
	T/2	He was rejected once, for instance – when?	expansion complex exchange: response-dependent	story exchange	
84.	S	One day, in the rain, en, he can't get a ride, so he was left stand out in the rain,			
85.	T	yeah			
86.	S	until a truck driver arrived.			
87.	T/1	That's right, yes, until a truck driver arrived.			
	T/2	That is to say, well, several cars or trucks passed by and nobody, no driver picked him up, so he had to stand in the rain, for sometime until a truck driver came along.	expansion chunk: follow-up exposition	story statement series: Variant 3	
	T/3	Well, maybe this was not the first time, this was not the only time he was rejected.			
	T/4	But generally speaking, he was warmly received.			
	T/5	All right, well, I think you can all answer [all answered] the questions very well,	activity boundary	recapitulation	verbal event
		and you did a very good job, in previewing the lesson.			daily event
	T/6	Now, let's open our book	activity boundary	orientation	
		and we'll ask someone to read the first paragraph.			beha event

(Continued)

t	sp/m	text	textual	interpersonal	ideational
	T/7	Xxx, would you like to read the first paragraph?	continuation	action exchange	
88.	S	OK. "One summer I was driving from my hometown of Ta ..."	complex exchange: response-dependent		
89.	T	Well, it's 'Tahoe'.			
90.	S	"Tahoe city, Cali ..."			
91.	T	California			
92.	S	"California, to New ..."			
93.	T	New Orleans			
94.	S	"New Orleans. In the middle of the desert, I came upon a young man standing by the roadside. He had his thumb out and held a gas can in his other hand. I drove right by him. There was a time in the country when you'd be considered a jerk if you passed by somebody in need. Now you are fool for helping. With gangs, drug addicts, murderers, rapists, and thieves lurking everywhere, 'I don't want to get involved' has become a national motto."			
95.	T/1	OK, now, here you have this: "I was driving from my hometown of Tahoe city ..." Now I asked someone where Tahoe city is located, and they say it's somewhere in California, it's somewhere, you know [points at a map], in the northern part of the mountains.	continuation chunk: text-bound explanation	knowledge statement series: Variant 2	behind-text
	T/2	You see, here are the mountains.			
	T/3	It's somewhere here.			
	T/4	You have this word, 'California', right below the word 'California', that is where Tahoe city is located.			
	T/5	So that's his hometown.			

#	Turn	Utterance			
	T/6	And "was driving from my hometown of Tahoe city, California", now, if you mention 'Tahoe', a small town in the United States, you usually also mention where, in which state, this place is located.	expansion chunk: text-bound explanation	knowledge statement series: Variant 2	usage
	T/7	And I think this is a very good thing, because maybe sometimes, sometimes you know, in different states, they have towns with the same name.			
	T/8	For instance, in China, there are more than one 'Linxia', but one is in Henan; the other may be in other places.			
	T/9	So, and "California ..." – each state has a short form – er, so, " ... California to New Orleans", well, I think that's a long trip, it's a long trip.	expansion chunk: text-bound expla	knowledge state-series: Variant 2	
	T/10	So, the first paragraph tells us an incident that actually made the writer decide to take this long, cross-country journey.	expansion chunk: follow-up conclusion	knowledge chunk: Variant 3	beyond-text
	T/11	Well, what is it, what is the incident that's talked about?			
	T/12	OK, he did not stop for a hitchhiker.			
	T/13	Now, let's come to some of the words.	activity boundary	orientation	daily event
96.	T/14	Er, "I came upon ..." What is the meaning of 'came upon'?	continuation simple exchange:	knowledge exchange	meaning
	S	It means 'to find someone by chance'.			
97.	T/1	Yes, 'to find someone or something by chance', so he happened to find a man standing by the roadside.	continuation chunk: text-bound		
	T/2	Now, "He had his thumb out ..." This means if you want to get a ride – I think we talked about this – if you want to get a ride, then you stretch your arm, and wave your thumb like this.	continuation chunk: text-bound explanation	knowledge statement series: Variant 2	
	T/3	This means that you want to get a ride.			

(*Continued*)

t	sp/m	text	textual	interpersonal	ideational
	T/4	OK, so this person, erm, "had his thumb out and held a gas can in his other hand", now, why does he hold a gas can – what does that mean?	continuation chunk: text-bound explanation	pseudo knowledge exchange: Variant 2	
	T/5	Some people think that this means that he, erm, he ran out of gas, and he couldn't drive on, but I don't think so, I don't think he had a car, en, this person.			
	T/6	So, what does that mean, 'holding a gas can'?	expansion chunk: simple exchange	knowledge exchange (direction)	
	T/7	Well, I'm not quite sure but you can guess why.			
98.	S	Maybe the petrol.			
99.	T/1	Yes, yes, so this shows that, probably, he would share the gas – Americans call it gas; petrol is a British word – or he was ready to share, I think, the money the driver would have to pay, for gas.			behind-text
	T/2	But maybe we have to ask some Americans, since maybe in different states, people, you know, have different ways we don't know.	expansion chunk: follow-up addition	knowledge statement series: Variant 3	
	T/3	But this is only a guess.			
	T/4	Then, well, in the next sentence, the writer mentions what – did people usually pass by hitchhikers, well, did people, in the past usually pass by hitchhikers?	continuation chunk: text-bound explanation	pseudo knowledge exchange: Variant 2	meaning
	T/5	No, so the writer says "there was a time in the country when you'd be considered a jerk" – a very stupid person, well, a very unkind person – "if you did that, in the past." So that means in the past, people were ready to picky up hitchhikers, but now, no.			
	T/6	Now the writer says "now you are a fool for helping," it means things have changed a great deal.	continuation chunk: text-bound expla	knowledge state-series: Variant 2	

#		Utterance	Exchange	Knowledge	
	T/7	The writer says "with gangs". That means 'because of gangs'.	continuation chunk: text-bound expla	knowledge state-series: Variant 2	
100.	T/8	"…drug addicts, murderers, rapists, thieves lurking everywhere", what is the meaning of 'lurking everywhere'?	continuation simple exchange: text-bound	knowledge exchange	
101.	S	'Hiding'.			
	T/1	'Hiding somewhere, waiting to do something very bad', so, 'lurking'.			
	T/2	So, "I don't want to get involved has become a national motto", but, now, what is, er, what is a 'motto'?	continuation simple exchange: text-bound	knowledge exchange	
	T/3	Xxx, do you know what a 'motto' is?			
102.	S	En, it means a short sentence or phrase chosen and used as a guide or rule of behavior, or as an expression of the aims or ideas of a family, a country, an institution.			
103.	T/1	Yeah, that's a very short sentence or phrase, you know, er; in which people express their purpose in life, and maybe it tells us the guiding principle of a certain group, or a certain school.			
	T/2	So, "… a national motto …" you know the national motto, of United States – do you know, there is a national motto of the United States?	continuation simple exchange: text-bound	knowledge exchange	behind-text
104.	Sn	Yeah.	expansion chunk: follow-up addition		
105.	T/1	But what is it?		pseudo knowledge exchange: Variant 3	
	T/2	It's not, of course, "I don't want to get involved", of course this is not their national motto, but there is one.			

(Continued)

t	sp/m	text	textual	interpersonal	ideational
	T/3	OK, do you know anything about this?	continuation	pseudo knowledge exchange: Variant 3	
	T/4	Well, *In God We Trust* – this is the national motto of the United States – this, you find this motto, their motto, national motto, in their currency – money, the coins, also paper money – er, *In God We Trust.*	chunk: presentation		
	T/5	Of course, it is taken, I think it is derived, it derives from a song, a battle song, which later became the national anthem of the United States.			
	T/6	Well, there is another motto, that's called the United States motto.	continuation	knowledge state-series: Variant 3	
	T/7	But I think we don't have time.	chunk: presentation		
	T/8	Now, do you think, er, "I don't want to get involved" has been made officially the national motto of the United States?	continuation simple exchange	knowledge exchange	
106.	Sn	No.			
107.	T	Now, why do you think does the writer say this, if it is, er, it's not a really a national motto, why does the writer say this?	continuation simple exchange	knowledge exchange	beyond-text
108.	S	Humorous.			
109.	T/1	Well, I don't think it's humorous, but it's sarcastic, bitter, sarcastic, the tone's sarcastic.			

T/2	Actually, nobody say this is the national motto, as *In God We Trust* actually was made official, was adopted by Congress in 1956.	expansion chunk: follow-up clarification	knowledge statement series: Variant 3	
T/3	But, well, I think the writer is being very sarcastic, saying that "I don't want to get involved" – that I don't want to help a stranger, for fear – well, I don't want to help a stranger, because I don't want to get attacked, because he or she might be a murderer, and so on.			
T/4	So this shows, the writer thinks, you know, er, the moral of the nation is declining: instead of helping other people, they say 'I don't want to get involved, I have to protect myself.'			
T/5	Well, about 'mottos', you know, it also embodies the principle.	continuation chunk: presentation (exemplification)	knowledge statement series: Variant 3	meaning
T/6	For instance, now, some schools have mottos, such as Unity, Honor and so on.			
T/7	So I think you may want to create a motto for your class, maybe you can think about that.			
T/8	Now let's come to the next paragraph, the next paragraph.	activity boundary	orientation	daily event
T/9	Well, let's see, Xxx, would you like to read?	continuation simple exchange	action exchange	beha event
110.	"Several states later, I was still thinking about the hitchhiker, leaving him stranded in the desert did not bother me too much. What bothered me was how easily I had reached the decision. I never even lifted my foot off the accelerator ..."			

References

Adger, C. T., 2001. 'Discourse in educational settings'. In D. Schiffrin, D. Tannen and H. E. Hamilton (eds), *The Handbook of Discourse Analysis*. London: Blackwell. 503–17.

Allwright, D., 1984. 'The importance of interaction in classroom language learning'. *Applied Linguistics* 5: 156–71.

Allwright, D. and K. Bailey, 1991. *Focus on the Language Classroom: An Introduction to Classroom Research for Language Teachers*. Cambridge: Cambridge University Press.

Austin, J., 1962. *How to Do Things with Words*. London: Oxford University Press.

de Beaugrande, R., 1996. 'The story of discourse analysis'. In van Dijk, T. A. (ed.), *Introduction to Discourse Analysis*. London: Sage. 35–62. [http://beaugrande. bizland. com/StoryDuscAnal.htm]

—— 1997. *New Foundations for a Science of Text and Discourse: Cognition, Communication and Freedom of Access to Knowledge and Society*. Norwood, NJ: Ablex.

—— 2002. 'Course plan for text linguistics' (last revised 9 November 2002). [http:// beaugrande.bizland.com/Course%20plan%for%20Text%20linguistics.htm]

—— and W. Dressler, 1981. *Introduction to Text Linguistics*. London: Longman. [Digitally reformatted 2002.]

Benson, J. D. and W. S. Greaves (eds), 1985. *Systemic Perspectives on Discourse, Volume 1: Selected Theoretical Papers from the Ninth International Systemic Workshop*. Norwood, NJ: Ablex.

Bernstein, B., 1986. 'On pedagogic discourse'. In J. Richardson (ed.), *Handbook of Theory and Research in the Sociology of Education*. New York: Greenwood Press. 205–39.

—— 1990. *The Structuring of Pedagogic Discourse: Class, Codes and Control, Vol. IV*. London: Routledge.

—— 1996. *Pedagogy, Symbolic Control and Identity: Theory, Research and Critique*. London: Taylor and Francis.

Berry, M., 1981a. 'Systemic linguistics and discourse analysis: a multi-layered approach to exchange structure'. In M. Coulthard and M. Montgomery (eds), *Studies in Discourse Analysis*. London: Routledge. 120–45.

—— 1981b. 'Polarity and propositional development, their relevance to the well-formedness of an exchange'. *Nottingham Linguistic Circular* 10(1): 36–63.

—— 1981c. 'Towards layers of exchange structure for directive exchanges'. *Network* 2: 23–32.

—— 1987. 'Is teacher an unanalyzed concept?'. In M. A. K. Halliday and R. P. Fawcett (eds), *New Developments in Systemic Linguistics, Volume 1: Theory and Description*. London: Pinter. 41–63.

Biber, D. and S. Conrad, 2001. 'Register variation: a corpus approach'. In D. Schiffrin, D. Tannen and H. E. Hamilton (eds), *The Handbook of Discourse Analysis*. London: Blackwell. 175–96.

Boulima, J., 1999. *Negotiated Interaction in Target Language Classroom Discourse*. Amsterdam: Benjamins.

Brown, G. and G. Yule, 1983. *Discourse Analysis*. Cambridge: Cambridge University Press.

Burton, D., 1978. 'Towards an analysis of casual conversation'. *Nottingham Linguistics Circular* 17(2): 131–59.

—— 1980. *Dialogue and Discourse: A Sociolinguistic Approach to Modern Drama Dialogue and Naturally Occurring Conversation*. London: Routledge.

—— 1981. 'Analysing spoken discourse'. In M. Coulthard and M. Montgomery (eds), *Studies in Discourse Analysis*. London: Routledge. 61–81.

Butler, C. S., 1985a. *Systemic Linguistics: Theory and Applications*. London: Batsford.

—— 1985b. 'Discourse systems and structures and their place within an overall systemic model'. In J. D. Benson and W. S. Greaves (eds), *Systemic Perspectives on Discourse, Volume 1: Selected Theoretical Papers from the Ninth International Systemic Workshop*. Norwood, NJ: Ablex. 213–28.

—— 2003. *Structure and Function: A Guide to Three Major Structural-Functional Theories*. Amsterdam: Benjamins.

Chaudron, C., 1988. *Second Language Classrooms: Research on Teaching and Learning*. Cambridge: Cambridge University Press.

Cheng, Y., 1989. *English Stylistics*. Shanghai: Shanghai Foreign Language Education Press. 【程雨民，《英语语体学》，上海：上海外语教育出版社。】

Christie, F., 1997. 'Curriculum macrogenres as forms of initiation into a culture'. In F. Christie and J. R. Martin (eds), *Genre and Institutions: Social Processes in the Workplace and School*. London: Continuum. 134–60.

—— 2002. *Classroom Discourse Analysis: A Functional Perspective*. London: Continuum.

—— and J. R. Martin (eds), 1997. *Genre and Institutions: Social Processes in the Workplace and School*. London: Continuum.

Coulthard, M. and M. Montgomery (eds), 1981. *Studies in Discourse Analysis*. London: Routledge.

—— and D. C. Brazil, 1981. 'Exchange structure'. In R. M. Coulthard and M. M. Montgomery (eds), *Studies in Discourse Analysis*. London: Routledge. 82–106.

Dai, W., 2001. 'The construction of the streamline ELT system in China'. *Foreign Language Teaching and Research* 5: 322–7. 【戴炜栋，构建具有中国特色的英语教学 "一条龙" 体系，《外语教学与研究》第5期，322–7页。】

van Dijk, T. A., 1972. *Some Aspects of Text Grammar*. The Hague: Mouton.

—— 1977. *Text and Context: Explorations in the Semantics and Pragmatics of Discourse*. London: Longman.

—— 1985a. 'Introduction: discourse analysis as a new cross-discipline'. In T. A. van Dijk (ed.), *Handbook of Discourse Analysis, Vol. 1*. New York: Academic Press. 1–10.

—— 1985b. 'Introduction: levels and dimensions of discourse analysis'. In T. A. van Dijk (ed.), *Handbook of Discourse Analysis, Vol. 2*. New York: Academic Press. 1–11.

—— 1990. 'The future of the field: Discourse analysis in the 1990s'. *Text* 10 (1/2): 133–56.

—— (ed.), 1997. *Discourse Studies: A Multidisciplinary Introduction (2 vols)*. London: Sage.

—— 1999. 'Discourse Studies: a new multidisciplinary journal for the study of text and talk'. *Discourse Studies* 1 (1): 5–6.

—— 2004. 'From text grammar to critical discourse analysis: a brief academic autobiography'. [http://www.iue.it/SPS/Research/Seminars20042005/Wkshp PDFfiles/vanDijk.pdf]

Drew, P. and J. Heritage (eds), 1992. *Talk at Work: Interaction in Institutional Settings*. Cambridge: Cambridge University Press.

Du, R. and Y. Jiang, 2001. '"China English" in the past 20 years'. *Foreign Language Teaching and Research* 1: 37–41.【杜瑞清，姜亚军，近二十年"中国英语"研究评述，《外语教学于研究》第1期，37–41 页。】

Eggins, S., 1994. *An Introduction to Systemic Functional Linguistics*. London: Pinter.

—— and D. Slade, 1997. *Analysing Casual Conversation*. London: Cassell.

Ellis, R., 1994. *The Study of Second Language Acquisition*. Oxford: Oxford University Press.

Fairclough, N., 1989. *Language and Power*. London: Longman.

Fang, Y., 1998. 'A tentative study of genre'. *Journal of Foreign Languages* 1: 17–22.【方琰，浅谈语类，《外国语》第 1 期，17–22 页。】

—— 2002. 'A brief introduction to genre studies'. *Journal of Tsinghua University (Supplement)* 1: 15–21.【方琰，语篇语类研究，《清华大学学报(哲学社会科学版)》增 1 期，15–21页。】

Fasold, R., 1990. *Sociolinguistics of Language*. Oxford: Blackwell.

Fawcett, R. P., 1980. *Cognitive Linguistics and Social Interaction: Towards an Integrated Model of a Systemic Functional Grammar and the Other Components of a Communicating Mind*. Heidelberg: Groos.

—— 1987. 'The semantics of clause and verb for relational processes in English'. In M. A. K. Halliday and R. P. Fawcett (eds), *New Developments in Systemic Linguistics, Volume 1: Theory and Description*. London: Pinter. 130–83.

——, A. van der Mije and C. van Wissen, 1988. 'Towards a systemic flowchart model for discourse structure'. In R. P. Fawcett and D. Young (eds), *New Developments in Systemic Linguistics, Vol. 2: Theory and Application*. London: Pinter. 116–43.

—— 1999. *A Theory of Syntax for Systemic Functional Linguistics*. Amsterdam: Benjamins.

Firth, A. and J. Wagner, 1997. 'On discourse, communication, and (some) fundamental concepts in SLA research'. *The Modern Language Journal* 81: 285–300.

Firth, J. R., 1957. *Papers in Linguistics 1934–51*. Oxford: Oxford University Press.

Flanders, N. A., 1960. *Interaction Analysis in the Classroom: A Manual for Observers*. Ann Arbor: University of Michigan Press.

Gao, Y. et al., 2000. 'Chinese EFL teachers' attitudes towards research methods: A survey'. *Journal of Foreign Languages* 1: 65–72.【高一虹等，关于外语教学研究方法的调查，《外国语》第 1 期，65–72 页。】

Ghadessy, M. (ed.), 1993. *Register Analysis: Theory and Practice*. London: Pinter.

—— (ed.), 1999. *Text and Context in Functional Linguistics*. Philadelphia: Benjamins.

Gil, G., 2002. 'Two complementary modes of foreign language classroom interaction'. *ELT Journal* 56/3: 273–9.

Goffman, E., 1974. *Frame Analysis.* New York: Harper and Row.

Gregory, M., 1967. 'Aspects of varieties differentiation'. *Journal of Linguistics* (3): 177–98.

—— and S. Carroll, 1978. *Language and Situation: Language Varieties and Their Social Contexts.* London: Routledge.

Grice, H. P., 1975. 'Logic and conversation'. In P. Cole and J. Morgan (eds), *Syntax and Semantics, Volume III: Speech Acts.* New York: Academic Press. 41–58.

Gu, Y., 1996. 'Doctor–patient interaction as goal-directed discourse'. *Journal of Asian Pacific Communication* 7 (3/4): 146–76.

—— 1997. 'Five ways of handling a bedpan'. *Text* 17 (4): 457–75.

—— 1999. 'Towards a model of situated discourse analysis'. In K. Turner (ed.), *The Semantics / Pragmatics Interface from Different Points of View.* Oxford: Elsevier. 149–78.

Gumperz, J., 1962. 'Types of linguistic communities'. *Anthropological Linguistics* 4: 28–40.

—— 1982. *Discourse Strategies.* Cambridge: Cambridge University Press.

Gunnarsson, B-L., P. Linell and B. Nordberg (eds), 1997. *The Construction of Professional Discourse.* London: Longman.

Halliday, M. A. K., 1961. 'Categories of the theory of grammar'. *Word* 17(3): 241–92.

—— 1966. 'Some notes on "deep" grammar'. *Journal of Linguistics* 2: 110–18.

—— 1973. *Explorations in the Functions of Language.* London: Edward Arnold.

—— 1975. *Learning How to Mean: Explorations in the Development of Language.* London: Edward Arnold.

—— 1978. *Language as Social Semiotic: The Social Interpretation of Language and Meaning.* London: Edward Arnold. [Republished jointly by Foreign Language Teaching and Research Press (Beijing) and Edward Arnold, 2001.]

—— 1985a. 'Systemic background'. In J. D. Benson and W. S. Greaves (eds), *Systemic Perspectives on Discourse, Volume 1: Selected Theoretical Papers from the Ninth International Systemic Workshop.* Norwood, NJ: Ablex. 1–15.

—— 1985b. *Language, Context and Text: Aspects of Language in a Socio-Semiotic Perspective.* Geelong, Victoria: Deakin University Press.

—— 1985/1994. *An Introduction to Functional Grammar (First edition /Second edition).* London: Edward Arnold. [Republished jointly by Foreign Language Teaching and Research Press (Beijing) and Edward Arnold, 2001.]

—— 1991. 'Towards probabilistic interpretations'. In E. Ventola (ed.), *Functional and Systemic Linguistics: Approaches and Use.* New York: Mouton de Gruyter. 39–61.

—— 1995. 'On language in relation to the evolution of human consciousness'. In S. Allén (ed.), *Of Thoughts and Words: Proceedings of Nobel Symposium 92 – The Relation Between Language and Mind.* River Edge, NJ: Imperial College Press. 45–84.

—— 1996. 'On grammar and grammatics'. In R. Hasan, C. Cloran and D. Butt (eds), *Functional Descriptions: Theory in Practice.* Amsterdam: Benjamins. 1–38.

—— 1998. 'Things and relations: regrammaticising experience as technical knowledge'. In J. R. Martin and R. Veel (eds), *Reading Science: Critical and Functional Perspectives on Discourse of Science.* London: Routledge. 185–235.

—— 1999. 'The notion of "context" in language education'. In M. Ghadessy (ed.), *Text and Context in Functional Linguistics*. Philadelphia: Benjamins. 1–24.

—— 2002a. *Linguistic Studies of Text and Discourse* (Vol. 2 in *The Selected Works of M. A. K. Halliday*, ed. Jonathan J. Webster). London: Continuum.

—— 2002b. *Studies in Chinese Language* (Vol. 8 in *The Selected Works of M. A. K. Halliday*, ed. Jonathan J. Webster). London: Continuum.

—— (revised by C. M. I. M. Matthiessen), 2004. *An Introduction to Functional Grammar* (Third edition). New York: Edward Arnold.

—— 2007. *On Language and Linguistics* (Vol. 3 in *The Selected Works of M. A. K. Halliday*, ed. Jonathan J. Webster). Beijing: Peking University Press. [First published by Continuum, 2003.]

—— and A. McIntosh, 1966. *Patterns of Language: Papers in General, Descriptive and Applied Linguistics*. London: Longman.

—— and R. Hasan, 1976. *Cohesion in English*. London: Longman.

—— and R. P. Fawcett (eds), 1987. *New Developments in Systemic Linguistics, Volume 1: Theory and Description*. London: Pinter.

—— and Z. L. James, 1993. 'A quantitative study of polarity and primary tense in the English finite clause'. In J. M. Sinclair, M. Hoey and G. Fox (eds), *Techniques of Description: Spoken and Written Discourse*. London: Routledge. 32–66.

—— and C. M. I. M. Matthiessen, 1999. *Construing Experience through Meaning: A Language-based Approach to Cognition*. London: Cassell.

Harré, R., 2001. 'The discursive turn in social psychology'. In D. Schiffrin, D. Tannen and H. E. Hamilton (eds), *The Handbook of Discourse Analysis*. London: Blackwell. 688–706.

Harris, S., 1987. 'Court discussion as genre: some problems and issues'. *Occasional Papers in Systemic Linguistics* (Department of English, University of Nottingham) 2: 35–74.

Harris, Z., 1952. 'Discourse analysis'. *Language* 28: 1–30.

Hasan, R., 1977. 'Text in the systemic-functional model'. In W. Dressler (ed.), *Current Trends in Textlinguistics*. Berlin: Walter de Gruyter. 228–46.

—— 1984. 'The nursery tale as a genre'. *Nottingham Linguistic Circular (Special Issue on Systemic Linguistics)* 13: 71–102. [Republished in R. Hasan, 1996: 51–92.]

—— 1985. *Language, Context and Text: Aspects of Language in a Socio-Semiotic Perspective*. Geelong, Victoria: Deakin University Press.

—— 1995. 'The conception of context in text'. In P. Fries and M. Gregory (eds), *Discourse in Society: Systemic Functional Perspectives*. Norwood, NJ: Ablex. 183–283.

—— 1996. *Ways of Saying: Ways of Meaning: Selected Papers of Ruqaiya Hasan* (ed. C. Cloran, B. Butt and G. Williams). London: Cassell.

Hjelmslev, L., 1961. *Prolegomena to a Theory of Language* (translated by F. J. Whitfield). Madison WI: University of Wisconsin Press.

Hoey, M., 1986. 'Overlapping patterns of discourse organization and their implication for a clause relational analysis of problem–solution texts'. In C. Cooper and S. Greenbaum (eds), *Studying Writing : Linguistic Approaches*. London: Sage. 187–214.

—— 2001. *Textual Interaction: An Introduction to Written Discourse Analysis*. London: Routledge.

Hou, W., 1988. *Varieties of English*. Shanghai: Shanghai Foreign Language Education Press. 【侯维瑞，《英语语体》，上海：上海外语教育出版社。】

Hu, Z., 1994. *Discourse Cohesion and Coherence*. Shanghai: Shanghai Foreign Language Education Press. 【胡壮麟，《语篇的衔接与连贯》，上海：上海外语教育出版社。】

—— 2005. 'Probability theory in systemic functional linguistics'. *Educational Research on Foreign Languages and Arts* 3: 7–15. 【胡壮麟，系统功能语言学的概率理论，《外语艺术教育研究》，第 3 期，7–15 页。】

Huang, G., 2001. *Theory and Practice of Discourse Analysis: A Study in Advertising Discourse*. Shanghai: Shanghai Foreign Language Education Press. 【黄国文，《语篇分析的理论与实践——广告语篇研究》，上海：上海外语教育出版社。】

Hymes, D., 1972. 'Models of the interaction of language and social life'. In J. Gumperz and D. Hymes (eds), *Directions in Sociolinguistics: The Ethnography of Communication*. New York: Holt, Rinehart and Winston. 35–71.

—— 1974. *Foundations in Sociolinguistics: An Ethnographic Approach*. Philadelphia: University of Pennsylvania Press.

Iedema, R., 1997. 'The language of administration: organizing human activity in formal institutions'. In F. Christie and J. R. Martin (eds), *Genre and Institutions: Social Processes in the Workplace and School*. London: Continuum. 73–100.

Jaworski, A. and N. Coupland (eds), 1999. *The Discourse Reader*. London: Routledge.

Jiang, Y. and R. Du, 2003. 'More about "China English" – a response to "Addressing Queries on China English"'. *Foreign Language Education* 1: 27–35. 【姜亚军，杜瑞清，有关 '中国英语' 的问题——对 "中国英语质疑" 一文的回应，《外语教学》第 1 期，27–35 页。】

Kachru, B. B., 2006. *The Handbook of World Englishes*. Malden, MA: Blackwell.

Krashen, S. D., 1981. *Second language Acquisition and Second Language Learning*. Oxford: Pergamon.

—— 1985. *The Input Hypothesis: Issues and Implications*. London: Longman.

Labov, W., 1972. 'The study of language in its social context'. In *Sociolinguistic Patterns*. Philadelphia: University of Pennsylvania Press. 183–259.

—— and J. Waletzky, 1967. 'Narrative analysis'. In J. Helm (ed.), *Essays on the Verbal and Visual Arts*. Seattle: University of Washington Press. 12–44.

—— and D. Fanshel, 1977. *Therapeutic Discourse: Psychotherapy as Conversation*. New York: Academic Press.

Lemke, J. L., 1990. *Talking Science: Language, Learning, and Values*. Norwood, NJ: Ablex.

—— 1993. 'Discourse, dynamics, and social change'. *Cultural Dynamics* 6/1–2: 243–76.

—— 1995. *Textual Politics: Discourse and Social Dynamics*. Bristol, PA: Taylor and Francis.

Long, M., 1983. 'Native speaker / non-native speaker conversation and the negotiation of comprehensible input'. *Applied Linguistics* 4: 126–41.

Martin, J. R., 1984. 'Language, register and genre'. In F. Christie (ed.), *Children Writing: Reader*. Geelong: Deaking University Press. 21–30.

—— 1985. 'Process and text: two aspects of human semiosis'. In J. D. Benson and W. S. Greaves (eds), *Systemic Perspectives on Discourse, Volume 1: Selected Theoretical Papers from the Ninth International Systemic Workshop*. Norwood, NJ: Ablex. 248–74.

—— 1992. *English Text: System and Structure*. Philadelphia: Benjamins.

—— 1997. 'Analysing genre: functional parameters'. In F. Christie and J. R. Martin (eds), *Genre and Institutions: Social Processes in the Workplace and School*. London: Continuum. 3–39.

—— 1999. 'Modeling context: a crooked path of progress in contextual linguistics'. In M. Ghadessy (ed.), *Text and Context in Functional Linguistics*. Philadelphia: Benjamins. 25–61.

—— 2000. 'Beyond exchange: APPRAISAL systems in English'. In S. Hunston and G. Thompson (eds), *Evaluation in Text: Authorial Stance and the Construction of Discourse*. Oxford: Oxford University Press. 142–75.

—— 2001. 'Cohesion and texture'. In D. Schiffrin, D. Tannen and H. E. Hamilton (eds), *The Handbook of Discourse Analysis*. London: Blackwell. 35–53.

—— and R. Veel (eds), 1998. *Reading Science: Critical and Functional Perspectives on Discourses of Science*. London: Routledge.

—— and D. Rose, 2003. *Working with Discourse: Meaning beyond the Clause*. London: Continuum.

—— and P. White, 2005. *The Language of Evaluation: Appraisal in English*. Hampshire: Palgrave Macmillan.

Matthiessen, C. M. I. M., 1993. 'Register in the round: diversity in a unified theory of register analysis'. In M. Ghadessy (ed.), *Register Analysis: Theory and Practice*. London: Pinter. 221–91.

—— 2002a. 'Lexicogrammar in discourse development: logogenetic patterns of wording'. In G. Huang and Z. Wang (eds), *Discourse and Language Functions*. Beijing: Foreign Language Teaching and Research Press. 91–125.

—— 2002b. 'Combining clauses into clause complexes: a multi-faceted view'. In J. Bybee and M. Noonan (eds), *Complex Sentences in Grammar and Discourse: Essays in Honor of Sandra A. Thompson*. Amsterdam: Benjamins. 237–322.

McCarthy, M., 1991. *Discourse Analysis for Language Teachers*. Cambridge: Cambridge University Press.

—— and R. Carter, 1994. *Language as Discourse: Perspectives for Language Teaching*. London: Longman.

Mehan, H., 1979. *Learning Lessons: Social Organization in the Classroom*. Cambridge, MA: Harvard University Press.

Miao, X., 2005. 'Discourse analysis in an age of discursive turn'. In G. Huang et al. (eds), *Functional Linguistics: Theory and Application*. Beijing: Higher Education Press. 17–25. 【苗兴伟，"话语转向"时代的语篇分析，载黄国文等编，《功能语言学的理论与应用》，17–25 页，北京：高等教育出版社。】

O'Halloran, K. (ed.), 2004. *Multimodal Discourse Analysis: Systemic Functional Perspectives*. London: Continuum.

Olshtain, E. and M. Celce-Murcia, 2001. 'Discourse analysis and language teaching'. In D. Schiffrin, D. Tannen and H. E. Hamilton (eds), *The Handbook of Discourse Analysis*. London: Blackwell. 707–24.

Östman, J-O. and T. Virtanen, 2001. *Understanding Text and Discourse*. London: Edward Arnold.

Palmer, F. (ed.), 1968. *Selected Papers of J. R. Firth 1952–1959*. London: Longman.

Parker, I. (ed.), 1999. *Critical Textwork: An Introduction to Varieties of Discourse and Analysis*. Buckingham: Open University Press.

Peng, X., 2002. *Language Process and Dimension*. Beijing: Tsinghua University Press. 【彭宣维，《语言过程与维度》，北京：清华大学出版社。】

—— 2005. 'A process-dimension model of language from a socio-cognitive perspective'. In G. Huang et al. (eds), *Functional Linguistics: Theory and Application*. Beijing: Higher Education Press. 85–100.【彭宣维，以社会·认知为基础的 "过程—维度" 语言模式概说，载黄国文等编，《功能语言学的理论与应用》，85–100 页，北京：高等教育出版社。】

Pica, T., 1988. 'Interlanguage adjustments as an outcome of NS-NNS negotiated interaction'. *Language Learning* 38: 45–73.

——, R. Young and C. Doughty, 1987. 'The impact of interaction on comprehension'. *TESOL Quarterly* 21: 737–58.

——, L. Halliday, N. Lewis and L. Morgenthaler, 1989. 'Comprehensible output as an outcome of linguistic demand on the learner'. *Studies in Second Language Acquisition* 11: 63–90.

Pike, K. L., 1982. *Linguistic Concepts: An Introduction to Tagmemics*. Lincoln: University of Nebraska Press.

Qin, X., 1997. 'A survey of genre analysis'. *Journal of Foreign Languages* 6: 8–15. 【秦秀白，体裁分析"概说，《外国语》第 6 期，8–15 页。】

—— 2002. 'A review of genre-based teaching approaches'. *Foreign Language Teaching and Research* 1: 43–7.【秦秀白，体裁教学法述评，《外语教学与研究》第 1 期，43–7 页。】

Renkema, J., 1993. *Discourse Studies: An Introductory Textbook*. Amsterdam: Benjamins.

Riggenbach, H., 1999. *Discourse Analysis in the Language Classroom: Volume 1. The Spoken Language*. Ann Arbor: The University of Michigan Press.

Sacks, H., E. Schegloff and G. Jefferson, 1974. 'A simplest systematics for the organization of turn-taking for conversation'. *Language* 50(4): 696–735.

Sarangi, S. and M. Coulthard (eds), 2000. *Discourse and Social Life*. London: Longman.

de Saussure, F., 1960. *Course in General Linguistics (translated from French by Wade Badkin)*. London: Owen.

Schegloff, E. and H. Sacks, 1973. 'Opening up closings'. *Semiotica* 7(3/4): 289–327.

Schiffrin, D., 1987. *Discourse Markers*. Cambridge: Cambridge University Press.

—— 1994. *Approaches to Discourse*. Oxford: Blackwell.

——, D. Tannen and H. E. Hamilton (eds), 2001. *The Handbook of Discourse Analysis*. London: Blackwell.

Scott, M. and G. Thompson (eds), 2001. *Patterns of Text: In Honour of Michael Hoey*. Amsterdam: Benjamins.

Searle, J. R., 1969. *Speech Acts: An Essay in the Philosophy of Language*. Cambridge: Cambridge University Press.

Semino, E. and J. Culpeper (eds), 2002. *Cognitive Stylistics: Language and Cognition in Text Analysis*. Amsterdam: Benjamins.

Sinclair, J. M. and M. Coulthard, 1975. *Towards an Analysis of Discourse*. London: Oxford University Press.

—— and M. Coulthard, 1992. 'Towards an analysis of discourse'. In M. Coulthard (ed.), *Advances in Spoken Discourse Analysis*. London: Routledge. 1–34.

Stubbs, M., 1983. *Discourse Analysis: The Sociolinguistic Analysis of Natural Language*. Oxford: Blackwell.

Swain, M., 1985. 'Communicative competence: some roles of comprehensible input and comprehensible output in its development'. In S. M. Gass and C. G. Madden (eds), *Input in Second Language Acquisition.* Rowley, MA: Newbury House. 235–53.

Swales, J. M., 1990. *Genre Analysis – English in Academic and Research Settings.* Cambridge: Cambridge University Press. [Republished by Shanghai Foreign Language Education Press, 2001.]

Taylor, T. and D. Cameron, 1987. *Analysing Conversation: Rules and Units in the Structure of Talk.* Oxford: Pergamon.

Thompson, G. and H. Collins, 2001. 'Interview with M. A. K. Halliday, Cardiff, July 1998'. *DELTA* [online] 17/1:131–53. [http://www.scielo.br/scielo.php?script=sci_arttext&pid=S0102–44502001000100006&lng=en&nrm=iso] ISSN102–4450.

Toolan, M. (ed.), 2002. *Critical Discourse Analysis: Critical Concepts in Linguistics* (4 vols). London: Routledge.

Trimble, M., L. Trimble and K. Drobnic (eds), 1978. *English for Specific Purposes: Science and Technology.* Corvallis: Oregon State University.

Turner, G. J., 1987. 'Sociosemantic networks and discourse structure'. In M. A. K. Halliday and R. P. Fawcett (eds), *New Developments in Systemic Linguistics, Volume 1: Theory and Description.* London: Pinter. 64–93.

Unsworth, L. (ed.), 2000. *Researching Language in Schools and Communities: Functional Linguistic Perspectives.* London: Cassell.

Ure, J. and J. Ellis, 1977. 'Register in descriptive linguistics and linguistic sociology'. In O. Uribe-Villas (eds), *Issues in Sociolinguistics.* The Hague: Mouton. 197–243.

Ventola, E., 1984. 'The dynamics of genre'. *Nottingham Linguistic Circular 13 (Special Issue on Systemic Linguistics):* 103–23.

—— 1987. *The Structure of Social Interaction: A Systemic Approach to the Semiotics of Service Encounter.* London: Pinter.

—— 1988. 'The logical relations in exchanges'. In J. D. Benson and W. S. Greaves (eds), *Systemic Functional Approaches to Discourse.* Norwood, NJ: Ablex. 51–72.

—— 1989. 'Problems of modeling and applied issues within the framework of genre'. *Word* 40 (1–2): 129–61.

Virtanen, T., 2004. *Approaches to Cognition through Text and Discourse.* Berlin: Walter de Gruyter.

Weatherall, A., 2002. *Gender, Language and Discourse.* New York: Routledge.

White, P., 1997. 'Death, disruption and the moral order: the narrative impulse in mass-media "hard news" reporting'. In F. Christie and J. R. Martin (eds), *Genre and Institutions: Social Processes in the Workplace and School.* London: Continuum. 101–33.

Wood, L. A. and R. O. Kroger, 2000. *Doing Discourse Analysis: Methods for Studying Action in Talk and Text.* Thousand Oaks: Sage.

Xia, J., 2002. 'A report on investigating the college English teachers' knowledge of and beliefs in foreign language education and their roles in teaching, researching and professional development'. *Foreign Language World* 5: 36–42. 【夏纪梅，大学英语教师的外语教育观念、知识、能力、科研现状与进修情况调查结果报告，《外语届》第 5 期，36–42 页。】

Xu, J., 1995. 'Discourse analysis in the past two decades'. *Foreign Language Teaching and Research* 1:20–24.【徐赳赳，话语分析二十年，《外语教学与研究》第 1 期，20–24 页。】

Xu, Y., 1992. *Modern English Stylistics*. Kaifeng: Henan University Press.【徐有志，《现代英语文体学》，开封：河南大学出版社。】

Yang, X., 2003. 'On the study of foreign language teachers' classroom strategies'. *Foreign Language Teaching and Research* 1: 40–46.【杨雪燕，外语教师课堂策略研究：状况与意义，《外语教学与研究》第1期，40–46页。】

—— 2006. 'Understanding Halliday's "architecture of language"'. *Linguistic Research* 4: 58–68.【杨雪燕，认识韩礼德的"语言建筑"，《语言学研究》第 4 辑，58–68 页。】

—— 2007a. 'A discourse analysis of EFL teachers' questioning strategies'. *Foreign Languages in China* 1: 50–56.【杨雪燕，外语教师课堂提问策略的话语分析，《中国外语》第 1 期，50–56 页。】

—— 2007b. 'Genre as multi-stratal: seen from the perspective of different genre theories'. *Foreign Language Education* 1: 27–31.【杨雪燕，篇类研究的理论视角及其层次性，《外语教学》第 1 期，27–31 页。】

Zhang, D., 1998. 'On multi-stratality of text structure and its relationship with the clause'. *Journal of Sichuan Foreign Languages Institute* 3: 53–7.【张德禄，语篇结构的多层次性及其与小句的关系，《四川外语学院学报》第 3 期，53–7 页。】

—— 2002a. 'A general survey of genre studies'. *Journal of Foreign Languages* 4: 13–22.【张德禄，语类研究概览，《外国语》第 4 期，13–22 页。】

—— 2002b. 'Exploring the theoretical framework of genre'. *Foreign Language Teaching and Research* 5: 339–44.【张德禄，语类研究理论框架探索，《外语教学与研究》第 5 期，339–44 页。】

Zhou, Y., 2005. 'Needs analysis of EFL teacher development in Chinese universities'. *Foreign Language Teaching and Research* 3: 48–52.【周燕，高校英语教师发展需求调查与研究，《外语教学与研究》第 3 期，48–52 页。】

Index

Lightning Source UK Ltd.
Milton Keynes UK
UKOW032120291111

182827UK00001B/77/P